WEST ACADEMIC PUBLISHING'S EMERITUS ADVISORY BOARD

PRINCIPLES OF CYBERSECURITY LAW

SECOND EDITION

Michael S. Mireles
Professor of Law
University of the Pacific, McGeorge School of Law

Jack L. Hobaugh Jr.
Adjunct Professor for Cybersecurity Law and Privacy Law
University of the Pacific, McGeorge School of Law
Certified Information Systems Security Professional (CISSP)
Fellow of Information Privacy (FIP)
Certified Information Privacy Professional—U.S. Private Sector (CIPP/US)
Certified Information Privacy Professional—Europe (CIPP/E)
Certified Information Privacy Technologist (CIPT)

CONCISE HORNBOOK SERIES™

WEST ACADEMIC

860 Blue Gentian Road, Suite 350
Eagan, MN 55121
1-877-888-1330

Published in the United States of America

ISBN: 978-1-68561-543-7

ACKNOWLEDGEMENTS

Jack Hobaugh wishes to thank his wife Diana for her support, his parents, Violet and Jack, who sent their son on the path to education, and everyone who has mentored him over the years – too many to mention – but you know who you are.

Michael Mireles wishes to thank his family, SS, EM, DM and GM; his parents and in-laws; and his colleagues at University of the Pacific, McGeorge School of Law, in particular Associate Dean for Academic Affairs Mary-Beth Moylan, Associate Deans for Scholarship Frank Gevurtz, and Michael Vitiello, and Dean Michael Hunter Schwartz, for support.

The authors wish to thank Madeline Orlando, Lauren Hirota, Tatum Kennedy, Mark Cayaba, Anastasia Leach, Elena Lucero and Charles Raub for their research and editing assistance. The authors are thankful for their Fall 2020 Cybersecurity Law and Policy class at the University of the Pacific.

Table of Contents

Cases

PRINCIPLES OF CYBERSECURITY LAW

SECOND EDITION

CHAPTER ONE. Introduction

1.1 Overview of This Casebook

The goal of this book is to provide law students, practicing attorneys, and in-house counsel an general overview of cybersecurity and cybersecurity law. The expansive and everchanging area of cybersecurity law requires an understanding of the intersection and interaction of cybersecurity, cybersecurity law, and privacy law. These three areas often overlap but never fully converge. To fully understand cybersecurity law, one must understand the relationships between cybersecurity, cybersecurity law, and privacy law. Throughout this book, the authors will identify and discuss those relationships. Moreover, we will delve into the various substantive areas of cybersecurity, cybersecurity law, and privacy law where those areas are coextensive, but sometimes where they are not.

Cybersecurity law is one of the most important developing legal fields in the world raising issues concerning legal, business and technical risk for companies. In 2023, the cybersecurity company SonicWall released its Cybersecurity Threat Report.[1] The Cybersecurity Threat Report described many of the types of cyber attacks on companies and governments. To understand the scope of the cybersecurity problem facing companies and governments, the report notes that in 2022, there were "493.3 million ransomware attacks," "5.5 billion malware attacks," "6.3 trillion intrusion attempts," and "112 million [Internet of Things] malware."

The question arises as to why there are so many problems with cybersecurity. The answer to that question is relatively complicated and here are some of the reasons. First, software developers tend to focus on speed to market in developing products and services instead of security. Software developers will often integrate open-source software into their products and services which may include vulnerabilities. Second, the attack surface for cyberattacks has increased. Companies and the government have moved their services to the cloud. Additionally, the Internet of Things has resulted in new ways to attack and access systems. Individuals are also using their own devices to access company and

[1] https://www.sonicwall.com/medialibrary/en/white-paper/2023-cyber-threat-report.pdf.

government systems. Third, human beings are fallible. They make mistakes and can unintentionally download malware, for example. Fourth, technological tools are available to undertake and exploit vulnerabilities, including artificial intelligence and hacking tools. Fifth, there are an insufficient number of qualified cybersecurity professionals available to companies and the government. Sixth, there is a significant amount of money available for successful hackers and attribution of attacks is difficult. Finally, there are benefits for rival governments to hack each other's systems.

The relevant substantive law covered by this book includes a patchwork of state, common law and federal laws. This book will analyze the regulations applied by cybersecurity regulators, such as the Federal Trade Commission and the Securities Exchange Commission. The substantive law reviewed also includes various statutory and common law causes of action brought by private parties for data breaches and other related cybersecurity issues. Notably, the book also covers the National Institute of Standards and Technology (NIST) Cybersecurity Frameworks, cybersecurity issues related to the Internet of Things, and data breach and other cybersecurity state laws. Finally, anti-hacking laws and international issues will be discussed. But first, a little computing history.

1.1[A] Brief History of Computing in the Cybersecurity Context

The first computers were standalone, non-connected machines. Hacking would have required physical access to the machine or the medium upon which the code was written before it was submitted to the machine. In those early days, programming code was written by punching holes in tape or punch card (keycards). Then the tape and cards were submitted to the computer operator for submission to the computer. Then came the connectivity between mainframe computers in an effort to connect military computers. Next, was the coming of age of standalone personal computers with hard drives and floppy disk drives. The internet was born, and dial-up modems were used to access the internet through internet service providers. Companies maintained mainframe computers connected to dumb terminals. Eventually, the dumb terminals were replaced with Personal Computers (PCs) in a client-server distributed configuration, where some of the processing could be moved off of the mainframe computer and onto the PC client.

With the success of the internet, companies needed to provide internet access to the public to remain competitive. Thus, companies had to figure out how to have a public facing computer presence while at the same time protecting their internal computing systems that contain sensitive non-public information. A protection zone between the public facing systems and the internal system (intranet) was created using gateways,[2] proxy servers,[3] and firewalls.[4] That zone is referred to as a DMZ. The security team spent a lot of time and effort making sure that the DMZ was not breached. This architecture today is referred to as a legacy system because companies are and have been moving away from that architecture by moving into the cloud.

The cloud provides a cost-effective way for a company to grow its computing resources. In the legacy system, if a company wanted to expand its computing power, it meant buying new systems, a costly endeavor. It was also hard for the information technology ("IT") team to size the systems for projected growth, and if the business had a slow period, it meant systems being underutilized. In contrast, cloud providers can provide extra computing resources on an ad hoc basis and cheaper than purchasing new equipment. With these cost-saving changes come additional challenges for companies to protect ever-increasingly valuable data. The term cloud conjures up a vision of a black box where computing power lives, but how it functions is not immediately visible to the user or company. Legacy systems gave the company control over their systems. Now in the cloud, companies have to rely on the cloud vendor to take over some of the responsibilities that the company had with the legacy systems. So, the company has traded efficiency for control by moving to the cloud.

---

[2] A "gateway" is a node such as router that data passes through in a network.
[3] "A proxy server acts as a gateway between you and the internet. It's an intermediary server separating end users from the websites they browse. Proxy servers provide varying levels of functionality, security, and privacy depending on your use case, needs, or company policy." Jeff Peters, *What is a Proxy Server and How Does it Work?*, VARONIS, https:///www.varonis.com/blog/what-is-a-proxy-server/ (last updated June 10, 2020).
[4] There are several different types of firewalls. Firewalls essentially operate to keep unwanted data or persons from accessing a computer. *See* ZACH CODINGS, COMPUTER PROGRAMMING AND CYBER SECURITY FOR BEGINNERS 268–269 (2019) (discussing packet filters firewall, application firewall, packet firewall and hybrid firewall).

Cloud vendors provide many different services to include:

- Software-as-a-Service ("SaaS");
- Platform-as-a-Service ("PaaS");
- Infrastructure-as-a-Service ("IaaS");
- Database-as-a-Service ("DBaaS");
- Container-as-a-Service ("CaaS");
- Function-as-a-Service ("FaaS");
- Ransomware-as-a-Service ("RaaS") and
- just about anything that can be offered as an outsourced software, hardware, and/or networking service.

If you own or use a personal computer, you likely are also using SaaS. SaaS is a service, normally offered as a subscription, and that service is located in the cloud. One example is Microsoft Office 365. Instead of purchasing the software and keeping the software on your personal computer, one can just purchase a subscription to the software through the SaaS model. One advantage of having the software in the cloud is that the subscription can cover many devices, such as PC, smart pad, smart phone, etc. Another advantage is that as a company adds employees, those employees can be easily added to the service through a subscription process. Cloud vendors take on the task of managing multiple customers in the same SaaS product.

There is nothing really mysterious about cloud computing architecture. Cloud vendors can offer services cheaper than the cost of legacy systems because of virtual machines. When a customer is accessing a virtual machine in the cloud, the customer does not see a difference between a dedicated machine and a virtual machine. But the machine is not dedicated to just one customer. The virtual machine is supporting many customers/clients through the use of a hypervisor. The hypervisor can be either hardware or software that divides the resources of the underlying machine among multiple customers. The vendor can bring down costs with a virtual machine model because the machine can be fully utilized.

PaaS is similar to SaaS, but instead of offering a service such as Microsoft Office 365, PaaS offers a platform for creating applications and other software. So, PaaS is a cloud offering that will likely be used by companies, and not individuals.

IaaS is an offering of infrastructure. DBaaS is an offering of a database service. Basically, a cloud provider has the technology to offer any type of service that is marketable.

CaaS is a cloud-based way of providing containers as a service. Operating System (OS) "virtualization techniques are primarily focused on providing a portable, reusable, and automatable way to package and run applications (apps). The terms application container or simply container are frequently used to refer to these technologies."[5]

FaaS "is a category of cloud computing services that provides a platform allowing customers to develop, run, and manage application functionalities without the complexity of building and maintaining the infrastructure typically associated with developing and launching an app."[6]

Most companies understand that they must invest in protecting digital assets whether they be legacy or cloud through targeted cybersecurity efforts. Thus, it is not surprising that the estimate for global cybersecurity spending will reach $10 billion by 2027.[7] Other interesting statistics include:

1) Small businesses are the target of half of cyber attacks;

2) Damages from cybersecurity attacks could reach $6 trillion by 2021;

3) 90% of cyber crimes go unreported every year in the US;

4) By 2024, the cybersecurity market is expected to be a $300 billion industry;

---

[5] https://csrc.nist.gov/csrc/media/publications/sp/800-190/draft/documents/sp800-190-draft2.pdf.

[6] https://en.wikipedia.org/wiki/Function_as_a_service.

[7] Matt Powell, *11 Eye Opening Cyber Security Statistics for 2019*, CPO MAGAZINE (June 25, 2019), https://www.cpomagazine.com/cyber-security/11-eye-opening-cyber-security-statistics-for-2019/.

5) Ransomeware attacks likely occur every 14 seconds;

6) An Internet of Things (IoT) device may be attacked within 5 minutes of connecting to the Internet.[8]

1.1[B] Introduction to the Relationship Between Cybersecurity, Cybersecurity Law and Privacy Law and "Reasonable Security Measures"

This is a text on cybersecurity law; it is not a book on privacy. Actually, the origin of privacy law had nothing to do with cyberspace. A well-known lawyer and socialite Samuel D. Warren living in the Boston area in the late 1800s became alarmed when another invention the Kodak camera became available to the public. That meant Mr. Warren could not socialize in public without the threat of his activities being photographed by anyone who had purchased a Kodak camera. Future Supreme Court Justice Louis Brandeis joined the fight for privacy, and in doing so created a privacy movement. Thus, in the beginning, computers and the internet were not even on the privacy law radar. Even today, one can violate privacy laws with just paper records. Yes, there can be a data breach with just paper records. Because privacy law predates cybersecurity law, it has been well covered in many texts.

With that said, it would be impossible to ignore privacy law because of its intersection and interaction with cybersecurity law. For example, the Health Insurance Portability and Accountability Act (HIPAA), Children's Online Privacy Protection Act (COPPA), and Gramm-Leach-Bliley Act (GLBA) are federal privacy laws that require the implementation of cybersecurity in some form or fashion. Most privacy books do not delve into the cybersecurity ramifications of these laws. This text does.

Often, cybersecurity and cybersecurity law deficiencies do not become apparent until a privacy law enforcement action has been triggered. For example, a data breach that negatively affects persons can trigger tort negligence actions, federal agency cybersecurity enforcement, state data breach notification (privacy) laws, and state AG cybersecurity investigation and enforcement actions. These events often disclose underlying cybersecurity deficiencies and cybersecurity law infractions that would have gone unnoticed without the breach, such as lack of encryption or

---

[8] *Id.*

"reasonable security measures" to safeguard data. It is often only after the discovery of the privacy infraction, that the underlying and arguably, more important cybersecurity law infractions surface.

This text will look at cybersecurity law through four different perspectives: the courts, the law, the enforcing party, and the defense. The defense will likely win or lose based on whether the cybersecurity measures were determined to be reasonable security measures. Some may argue that a security breach is evidence of negligence just as a plane crash has been argued to be negligence via *res ipsa loquitor*, because planes do not crash without some form of negligence. But, in our opinion, security (data) breaches are not automatically negligence because if a company has on-line systems, it is only a matter of time before those systems are breached, even without an act of negligence. A company can be diligent and implement reasonable security measures but still have a breach. Why? Because testing of software and hardware does not always find every bug.[9] How often do you update your smartphone operating system to fix newly discovered bugs and security flaws? Testing software is hard because it is hard to foresee every use (and an attempted hack) of a software product. Yet, not imagining a test case does not equate to negligence.

---

[9] Professors Jay P. Kesan and Carol M. Hayes note that, "Battles against security flaws are plagued by externality problems." *See* JAY P. KESAN & CAROL M. HAYES, CYBERSECURITY AND PRIVACY LAW IN A NUTSHELL 35 (West Academic 2019). Essentially, the overall harm from a security flaw is greater than any one user bears and each individual user may rely on others to address the harm. *Id.* "So, the social harm of cybersecurity is an externality not borne by the individual users, who have a more limited experience of harm." *Id.* Thus, creators of software are more focused on software functionality instead of security because that is what consumers demand. *Id.* at 35-36. Moreover, the authors note that one study states that, "the average software developed in the United States has 6,000 software flaws per million lines of code, and between one and five percent of software flaws are security vulnerabilities." *Id.* at 16 (citing Carol Woody & Nancy Mead, *Using Quality Metrics and Security Methods to Predict Software Assurance*, SEI BLOG (June 20, 2016), https://insights.sei.cmu.edu/sei_blog/2016/06/using-quality-metrics-and-security-methods-to-predict-software-assurance.html).

There will be companies that have implemented reasonable security measures and companies that have not implemented reasonable security measures. Both will have breaches over time. The difference is that the company that implements reasonable security measures will have a valid argument for not breaching the reasonable security measures standard.

So, who will have the final say as to whether a company implemented reasonable security measures? Ultimately, it will be the courts. Because technology is ever-changing, what are reasonable security measures today, may not be tomorrow. As the technology progresses and threats from bad actors adapt, what are reasonable cybersecurity measures will also necessarily evolve over time. Each case will likely bring a new set of facts and nuances that will need to be processed by the court. It is unlikely that the judge or his/her clerks on the case will be versed in cybersecurity technology, similar to patent law cases that often address complex technology questions. Accordingly, cybersecurity cases will likely become a battle of the experts because the courts will not be equipped to determine whether cybersecurity measures were or were not reasonable on their own. Experts may opine on the content of the actions of a reasonable cybersecurity professional and this introduction provides some guidance as to the job duties of a cybersecurity professional. Reasonable measures to safeguard data will not be a static concept. Moreover, the question of what may be a reasonable measure may be informed by statutes, regulations, agency guidance and matters, court decisions and industry standards.

Many laws will not be pure cybersecurity laws but instead laws that contain cybersecurity law aspects. We will dissect the relevant laws and discuss the cybersecurity portions and how they are being applied. Enforcing parties may be individuals given rights of action, agencies through the law and regulations, and states' attorney generals through state law. We will discuss cases to determine what has not been successful, what was successful, and what actions are likely to be successful in the future.

1.2 What is Cybersecurity Law?

To better understand how to define cybersecurity law and how cybersecurity law fits into the legal landscape, we must first take a look at two closely related subjects: cybersecurity and privacy law. Cybersecurity is the protection of machines, digital data, and networks. The foundation of providing cybersecurity protection is based on maintaining the security triad of confidentiality, integrity, and availability, commonly referred to as CIA. Confidentiality is the protection of data, objects, and resources. Some authors focus mainly on data because privacy law focuses on sensitive data known as personally identifiable information (PII). Integrity is the protection of reliability and correctness of data. Availability is providing uninterrupted and timely access for those appropriately authenticated and authorized for data, objects, and resources. The European Union General Data Protection Regulation (GDPR) added a fourth category of Resilience to CIA that applies to the resilience "of processing systems and services." Thus, we may start to see CIAR instead of the normal CIA.

In contrast to cybersecurity, privacy law is about protecting the privacy of humans. The International Association of Privacy Professionals (IAPP) identifies four main areas of privacy: information privacy, bodily privacy, territorial privacy, and communications privacy. Information privacy is the "claim of individuals, groups or institutions to determine for themselves when, how and to what extent information about them is communicated to others."[10] Bodily privacy "focuses on a person's physical being and any invasion thereof. Such an invasion can take the form of genetic testing, drug testing or body cavity searches."[11] Territorial privacy is "concerned with placing limitations on the ability of one to intrude into another individual's environment. Environment is not limited to the home; it may be defined as the workplace or public space and environmental considerations can be extended to an international level. Invasion into an individual's territorial privacy typically comes in the form of video surveillance, ID checks and use of similar technology and procedures."[12] There is an obvious friction here between the implementation of cybersecurity in the form of video surveillance, ID checks, etc., and territorial privacy. Communications privacy "encompasses protection of the means of correspondence, including postal mail,

[10] IAPP Glossary of Privacy Terms, https://iapp.org/resources/glossary/#identifiability.

[11] IAPP Glossary of Privacy Terms, https://iapp.org/resources/glossary/#background-screening-checks.

[12] IAPP Glossary of Privacy Terms, https://iapp.org/resources/glossary/#t-closeness.

telephone conversations, electronic e-mail and other forms of communicative behavior and apparatus."[13]

So, what is cybersecurity law and how does it relate to cybersecurity and privacy law? Although the term has been quickly adopted as an oft-used legal buzz word and big law is quickly adding cybersecurity law as a practice area, a well-adopted definition does not yet exist. As Professor Jeff Kosseff noted in his 2018 law review article, "Defining Cybersecurity Law", "the U.S. legal system lacks a consistent definition of the term 'cybersecurity law'."[14]

We expect the definition of cybersecurity law to morph over time as regulatory bodies continue to struggle with the term as they attempt to promulgate cybersecurity laws to protect their citizens. For the purposes of this book we define **cybersecurity law** as *any law that is promulgated towards the protection of machines, digital data, and networks*. In essence, cybersecurity law is any law that applies to cybersecurity. There is no protection of humans in our definition of cybersecurity law because that is the role of privacy law. But there is a relationship between privacy law and cybersecurity law. Moreover, this book will also cover some aspects of the protection of humans, but is not an exhaustive coverage of those issues.[15]

And that relationship is easily seen in most of the laws that can be categorized as covering both privacy laws and cybersecurity laws. Upon closer examination, most of these laws are neither pure privacy laws nor pure cybersecurity laws, but instead, a combination of both. We will cover laws in the following chapters that contain separate sections for cybersecurity and privacy. All fifty states now have data breach notification laws. Data breach notification laws can be categorized as privacy laws because they set out requirements to notify people affected by the data breach, also known as customers, so that the people can take appropriate steps to protect their identity. States have also started

---

[13] IAPP Glossary of Privacy Terms, https://iapp.org/resources/glossary/#caching.

[14] Jeff Kosseff, *Defining Cybersecurity Law*, 103 IOWA L. REV. 985, 985 (2018).

[15] A computer virus called Stuxnet was used to disable the Iranian nuclear program by infecting computer systems controlling centrifuges. This is an example of a cyberattack impacting the operation of physical devices. For more information on Stuxnet, please see Kim Zetter, *An Unprecedented Look at Stuxnet, the World's First Digital Weapon*, WIRED, (November 3, 2014), https://www.wired.com/2014/11/countdown-to-zero-day-stuxnet/ (last updated October 9, 2020).

promulgating data protection laws that go beyond just notification of a breach and towards the protection of the companies' digital assets. These laws can be categorized as cybersecurity laws because they address and enforce reasonable security measures for protecting digital assets. Some states keep these two laws separate, but there is at least one state, Alabama, a late comer to mandating notification, that has combined privacy and cybersecurity into one overarching law. The same is true for at least some of the federal laws, such as HIPAA, which obviously attempts to protect people's privacy but also requires technical safeguards that would fall into the cybersecurity category. We will look at these relationships in detail as we step through the federal and state laws.

1.3 Responsibilities of a Cybersecurity Professional

The core responsibility of the cybersecurity professional is the protection of machines, digital data, and networks through the application of the cybersecurity triad—CIA. Confidentiality, Integrity, and Availability (CIA) is the mantra of the cybersecurity professional. The cybersecurity professional strives to protect the confidentiality, integrity, and availability of machines, data, and networks. Although protecting the machines, digital data, and networks is important, that protection should never be at the risk of the loss of human life.

The cybersecurity professional applies CIA across many layers of an organization starting with security governance through the implementation of principles, polices, and procedures. If a security incident or event occurs, the cybersecurity professional is a key member of the incident response team (IRT). The first step in achieving and maintaining CIA begins with identifying cybersecurity risks across all business processes and assets by using a risk management framework. The risk management framework is discussed in more detail in Chapter Ten. Next, each identified risk is either mitigated, avoided or accepted. Risks are specifically addressed through continuity of operations plans, business continuity plans, incident response plans and disaster recovery plans.

Quantifying and qualifying cybersecurity risk is a team effort that requires C-suite buy-in and multiple departments input. Risk is measured by threat * vulnerability. Input from the cybersecurity professional will be essential for determining what threats are out there that could affect the company's computing resources. Likewise, the cybersecurity professional's input will be essential for determining the company's computing resources vulnerabilities. The business departments and legal team will also be invaluable in determining how the risk could affect the company's business and how much resources should be applied to mitigating the risk.

1.3[A] VULNERABILITY ANALYSIS

The threats that a company faces are dynamic because the sources of the threats are dynamic and the cyber landscape of the company is dynamic. The cybersecurity professional must stay informed of the threats. Also, the cybersecurity professional must routinely perform vulnerability analysis of the machines, data and networks. A vulnerability is any type flaw that can be exploited.[16] Vulnerability analysis can be performed through scanning for flaws. Such scanning includes:

- Network Discovery Scanning that identifies open communication ports on a particular network. Open communication ports present the potential for bad actors to access a system through the open port.

- Web Vulnerability Scanning that looks for known vulnerabilities on Web-site applications.

If vulnerabilities are found, a next step can be penetration testing to see if the vulnerability can be exploited. The cybersecurity professional will be careful when using penetration testing because penetration testing can be disruptive to systems. Because of the potential for penetration testing to be disruptive, penetration testing should never be carried out without approval from company management.

Managing vulnerabilities is a complicated task for the cybersecurity professional, because the vulnerabilities can be found in many of the company's computing and networking assets. To name a few, vulnerabilities can be found in:

---

[16] A "zero day vulnerability" is a vulnerability that is unknown to the creator of the software and not addressed. A "zero day exploit" is a the use of the zero day vulnerability before it is addressed. Cybersecurity experts Yuri Diogenes and Erdal Ozkaya discuss past zero day exploits, including vulnerabilities in WhatsApp, Chrome, and Windows. *See* YURI DIOGENES & ERDAL OZKAYA, CYBERSECURITY – ATTACK AND DEFENSE STRATEGIES 180–182 (Packt 2018).

- Hardware such as microchips
- Firmware[17]
- Operating Systems
- Database Systems
- Every software application that the company has.
- Network nodes such as routers
- Firewalls
- Proxy Servers
- Gateways
- Human end users
- WiFi

Vulnerabilities are also found in personal computing devices such as laptops and smart phones. These devices can present a challenge for the cybersecurity professional in a bring-your-own-device (BYOD) architecture because these devices may not be managed by the company and the company may not be able to control the applications that are downloaded onto the device. Thus, the company may not have a good view of the vulnerabilities that are on the device and connected to the company's network. Counsel can be very helpful in advising companies before they decide to go to a BYOD architecture by making sure the employee agreement in such cases addresses giving the company rights to the necessary insight into the device to address vulnerabilities. Counsel should also limit the use of the device on the network, especially when an employee is accessing company data in the cloud. Users have been known to bypass secured applications in favor of using unapproved applications because the user prefers an unapproved application over the approved application.

Following is a discussion of cybersecurity risk by the U.S. Department of Homeland Security (DHS) Cybersecurity and Infrastructure Security Agency (CISA):

---

[17] "Firmware" is "permanent" software programmed on hardware.

Cyberspace and its underlying infrastructure are vulnerable to a wide range of risks stemming from both physical and cyber threats and hazards. Sophisticated cyber actors and nation-states exploit vulnerabilities to steal information and money and are developing capabilities to disrupt, destroy, or threaten the delivery of essential services. Cyberspace is particularly difficult to secure due to a number of factors: the ability of malicious actors to operate from anywhere in the world, the linkages between cyberspace and physical systems, and the difficulty of reducing vulnerabilities and consequences in complex cyber networks. Of growing concern is the cyber threat to critical infrastructure, which is increasingly subject to sophisticated cyber intrusions that pose new risks. As information technology becomes increasingly integrated with physical infrastructure operations, there is increased risk for wide scale or high-consequence events that could cause harm or disrupt services upon which our economy and the daily lives of millions of Americans depend. In light of the risk and potential consequences of cyber events, strengthening the security and resilience of cyberspace has become an important homeland security mission.[18]

On March 31, 2021, "[DHS] Secretary Mayorkas outlined a bold vision for the Department's cybersecurity efforts to confront the growing threat of cyber-attacks, including a series of 60-day sprints to operationalize his vision, to drive action in the coming year, and to raise public awareness about key cybersecurity priorities."[19] Those sprints included:

- Ransomware
- Cybersecurity Workforce
- Industrial Control Systems (ICS)
- Elections Security
- International Cybersecurity

In addition to the series of 60-day springs, the Secretary will focus on four ongoing priorities: (1) cementing the resilience of democratic institutions, including the integrity of elections and

---

[18] *Cybersecurity*, CYBERSECURITY & INFRASTRUCTURE SECURITY AGENCY, https://www.cisa.gov/cybersecurity (last visited Aug. 28, 2020).
[19] https://www.dhs.gov/topic/cybersecurity (last visited Aug. 7, 2021).

institutions outside the executive branch, (2) building back better to strengthen the protection of civilian government networks, (3) advancing a risk-based approach to supply-chain security and exploiting new technologies to increase resilience, and (4) preparing for strategic, on-the-horizon challenges and emerging technology such as the transition to post-quantum encryption algorithms.[20]

The sharing of knowledge greatly helps the cybersecurity professional stay abreast of the ever-increasing list of vulnerabilities. The DHS maintains an online form and email address for disclosing vulnerabilities.[21] A list of common vulnerabilities is maintained by the MITRE Corporation and sponsored by CISA:

Common Vulnerabilities and Exposures (CVE®) is a list of common identifiers for publicly known cybersecurity vulnerabilities.

Use of CVE Entries, which are assigned by CVE Numbering Authorities (CNAs) from around the world, ensures confidence among parties when used to discuss or share information about a unique software or firmware vulnerability, provides a baseline for tool evaluation, and enables automated data exchange.

CVE is:

- One identifier for one vulnerability or exposure
- One standardized description for each vulnerability or exposure
- A dictionary rather than a database
- How disparate databases and tools can "speak" the same language
- The way to interoperability and better security coverage
- A basis for evaluation among services, tools, and databases
- Free for public download and use

[20] *Id.*

[21] https://www.dhs.gov/vulnerability-disclosure-form (last visited Aug. 7, 2021).

- Industry-endorsed via the CVE Numbering Authorities, CVE Board, and numerous products and services that include CVE[22]

Various DHS departments provide information on cybersecurity.[23] Of special interest is the National Cybersecurity and Communications Integration Center (NCCIC):

NCCIC offers no-cost, subscription-based information products to stakeholders through the www.us-cert.gov and www.ics-cert.gov websites. CISA Central designed these products—part of the National Cyber Awareness System (NCAS)—to improve situational awareness among technical and non-technical audiences by providing timely information about cybersecurity threats and issues and general security topics. Products include technical alerts, control systems advisories and reports, weekly vulnerability bulletins, and tips on cyber hygiene best practices. Subscribers can select to be notified when products of their choosing are published.

Service benefits include:

- Current Activity provides up-to-date information about high-impact security activity affecting the community at-large.

- Alerts provide timely information about current security issues, vulnerabilities, and exploits.

- Advisories provide timely information about current ICS security issues, vulnerabilities, and exploits.

- Bulletins provide weekly summaries of new vulnerabilities. Patch information is provided when available.

- Tips provide guidance on common security issues.

For more information on available information products, visit www.us-cert.gov/ncas and www.ics-cert.us-cert.gov/. To subscribe to select products,

---

[22] *About CVE*, COMMON VULNERABILITIES AND EXPOSURES, https://cve.mitre.org/about/index.html (last updated Nov. 6, 2019).

[23] https://uscert.cisa.gov/nccic?__hstc=245485531.267f74747c9821ec26a48120809aad7e.1486339200049.1486339200051.1486339200052.2&__hssc=245485531.1.1486339200052&__hsfp=528229161

visit public.govdelivery.com/accounts/USDHSUSCERT/subscriber/new.[24]

In October of 2009, DHS opened the National Cybersecurity and Communications Integration Center (NCCIC), "a 24 hour, DHS-led coordinated watch and warning center that will improve national efforts to address threats and incidents affecting the nation's critical information technology and cyber infrastructure."[25] NCCIC is now known as "CISA Central." The DHS has placed an emphasis on sharing cybersecurity information by creating the Cyber Information Sharing and Collaboration Program (CISCP):

> Cyber Information Sharing and Collaboration Program (CISCP) enables information exchange and the establishment of a community of trust between the Federal Government and critical infrastructure owners and operators. CISCP and its members can share cyber threat, incident, and vulnerability information in near real-time to collaborate and better understand cyber threats. By leveraging CISA Central, formerly known as the National Cybersecurity and Communications Integration Center (NCCIC), members can receive guidance on cyber-related threats to prevent, mitigate or recover from cyber incidents.
>
> CISCP membership provides access to the full suite of CISA Central products and services to support information exchange. Upon receiving indicators of observed cyber threat activity from its members, CISCP analysts redact proprietary information and collaborate with both government and industry partners to produce accurate, timely, actionable data and analytical products.[26]

CISA also maintains a webpage for tracking current activity.[27] Included on this webpage:

- Access to the National Cyber Awareness System
    - Current Activity

---

[24] *Information Sharing and Awareness*, CYBERSECURITY & INFRASTRUCTURE SECURITY AGENCY, https://www.cisa.gov/information-sharing-and-awareness (last revised June 3, 2020).

[25] https://www.dhs.gov/news/2009/10/30/new-national-cybersecurity-center-opened (last visited Aug. 7, 2021).

[26] https://www.cisa.gov/information-sharing-and-awareness (last Updated Date: June 29, 2021).

[27] https://us-cert.cisa.gov (last visited August 7, 2021).

    - Alerts
    - Bulletins
    - Analysis Reports
- Recent Vulnerabilities
- Link to the National Vulnerability Database
- View of Vulnerability Notes
- Announcements
- Sections on:
    - reporting:
        - incidents
        - phishing
        - malware
        - vulnerabilities
- email signup to subscribe to alerts from US-CERT.

So, just how frequent are alerts and communications? The communications are very frequent. A one-week summary included around 18 separate issues with source and patch information for just the "High Vulnerabilities."

In another proactive cybersecurity step, CISA on July 30, 2021, announced the Vulnerability Disclosure Policy (VDP) Platform:

CISA has announced the establishment of its Vulnerability Disclosure Policy (VDP) Platform for the federal civilian enterprise, which will allow the Federal Civilian Executive Branch to coordinate with the civilian security research community in a streamlined fashion. The VDP Platform provides a single, centrally managed website that agencies can leverage as the primary point of entry for intaking, triaging, and routing vulnerabilities disclosed by researchers. It enables researchers and members of the general public to find vulnerabilities in agency websites and submit reports for analysis.

This new platform allows agencies to gain greater insights into potential vulnerabilities, which will improve their cybersecurity posture. This approach also means agencies no longer need to develop separate systems to enable vulnerability reporting and triage of identified vulnerabilities, providing government-wide cost savings that CISA estimates at over $10 million.

For more details, see the blog post by CISA's Executive Assistant Director for Cybersecurity, Eric Goldstein.[28]

When a vulnerability is discovered, the proper patch or other solution, such as an adjustment to the configuration will be applied after proper testing of the patch or configuration. A patch is just a portion of new code that can be implemented into an existing operational system to fix a bug or vulnerability. Configuration is also known as settings on some devices. Most devices come with a default configuration recommended by the manufacturer. For example, users can then set the settings on their smart phone manually to meet their personal preferences. Hackers understand configuration settings and if a vulnerability is known for a particular setting, that setting can become a target for the hackers. For a major system, such as a server, there will be configuration files that can be tweaked by the IT department.

Testing is crucial because a company does not want to apply a patch or configuration that would break the company's system(s). The vendor should have thoroughly tested the patch or recommended configuration, but it is impossible to test for every environment that the patch may be placed into. There may be times when the risk and vulnerability are so grave that in-house testing may be passed over for expediency of a fix. Otherwise, the company will likely set up a testing sandbox to test the new patch or configuration. A sandbox is a secure area where code, patches, and configurations can be tested without the risk of contaminating any company systems already in operation. After successful sandbox

[28] https://us-cert.cisa.gov/ncas/current-activity/2021/07/30/cisa-announces-vulnerability-disclosure-policy-vdp-platform (last visited Aug. 7, 2021).

testing, review, and management approval, the patch or configuration can be implemented into operational systems.

After adding the patch or adjusting the configuration, a new system baseline should be captured and backed up for future use. In the event of a system crash, the baseline can be used to restore the system to the proper setup. The baseline can also be used to set up a new system to ensure that all systems are equally configured and patched.

So, what if the software code was developed in-house? The first step is to investigate the source of the vulnerability. It could come from in-house, an ethical hacker (a good hacker, also sometimes known as a "white hat" (someone who works for the company) or "gray hat" (an independent or affiliated with another company) as opposed to a "black hat" (someone with nefarious purposes)), a blog entry, a complaint, or even a breach. Then it is up to the company's IT department to build a patch or a new configuration. The operational testing requirement remains the same.

Vulnerability tracking and responding with the implementation of new patches and configuration is a never-ending task and probably keeps the security professional awake at night because the security professional can never know for sure if all vulnerabilities have been discovered. It is a best effort task.

But vulnerability analysis is only part of the risk = vulnerability * threat analysis. Vulnerabilities are not an issue if there is no threat of attacking the vulnerability. The threat can come from many places. The threat can be external and originate from a hacker sitting in Russia or China or the United States.[29] The threat can be internal and originate from a disgruntled employee. Internal or external, the cybersecurity professional must understand and be aware of the threats, and where possible, take action to protect the company's resources from attack. The cybersecurity professional may not know the actual threat but instead understand the type of threat that may attack in the future. Or the cybersecurity professional may be informed of a known threat. For example, the cybersecurity professional may receive an

[29] An "advanced persistent threat" is usually a prolonged attack that accesses a system repeatedly. It may be instigated by a nation-state.

alert, that identifies the vulnerability along with the threat, such as:

Alert (AA20-206A)

Threat Actor Exploitation of F5 BIG-IP CVE-2020-5902

Summary

The Cybersecurity and Infrastructure Security Agency (CISA) is issuing this alert in response to recently disclosed exploits that target F5 BIG-IP devices that are vulnerable to CVE-2020-5902. F5 Networks, Inc. (F5) released a patch for CVE-2020-5902 on June 30, 2020.[1]

Unpatched F5 BIG-IP devices are an attractive target for malicious actors. Affected organizations that have not applied the patch to fix this critical remote code execution (RCE) vulnerability risk an attacker exploiting CVE-2020-5902 to take control of their system. **Note:** F5's security advisory for CVE-2020-5902 states that there is a high probability that any remaining unpatched devices are likely already compromised.

CISA expects to see continued attacks exploiting unpatched F5 BIG-IP devices and strongly urges users and administrators to upgrade their software to the fixed versions. CISA also advises that administrators deploy the signature included in this Alert to help them determine whether their systems have been compromised.

This Alert also provides additional detection measures and mitigations for victim organizations to help recover from attacks resulting from CVE-2020-5902. CISA encourages administrators to remain aware of the ramifications of exploitation and to use the recommendations in this alert to help secure their organization's systems against attack.

Background

CISA has conducted incident response engagements at U.S. Government and commercial entities where malicious cyber threat actors have exploited CVE-2020-5902—an RCE vulnerability in the BIG-IP Traffic Management User Interface (TMUI)—to take control of victim systems. On June 30, F5 disclosed CVE-2020-5902, stating that it allows attackers to, "execute arbitrary system commands, create or delete files, disable services, and/or execute arbitrary Java code."

On July 4, open-source reporting indicated a proof-of-concept code was available and threat actors were exploiting the vulnerability by attempting to steal credentials. On July 5, security researchers posted exploits that would allow threat actors to exfiltrate data or execute commands on vulnerable devices. The risk posed by the vulnerability is critical.

Technical Details

CISA has observed scanning and reconnaissance, as well as confirmed compromises, within a few days of F5's patch release for this vulnerability. As early as July 6, 2020, CISA has seen broad scanning activity for the presence of this vulnerability across federal departments and agencies—this activity is currently occurring as of the publication of this Alert.

CISA has been working with several entities across multiple sectors to investigate potential compromises relating to this vulnerability. CISA has confirmed two compromises and is continuing to investigate. CISA will update this Alert with any additional actionable information.

Detection Methods

CISA recommends administrators see the F5 Security Advisory K52145254 for indicators of compromise and F5's CVE-2020-5902 IoC Detection Tool.[2]

CISA also recommends organizations complete the following actions in conducting their hunt for this exploit:

- Quarantine or take offline potentially affected systems
- Collect and review artifacts such as running processes/services, unusual authentications, and recent network connections
- Deploy the following CISA-created Snort signature to detect malicious activity:

    alert tcp any any -> any $HTTP_PORTS (msg:"BIG-IP:HTTP URI GET contains '/tmui/login.jsp/..|3b|/tmui/':CVE-2020-5902"; sid:1; rev:1; flow:established,to_server; content:"/tmui/login.jsp/..|3b|/tmui/"; http_uri; fast_pattern:only; content:"GET"; nocase; http_method;

priority:2; reference:url,github.com/yassineaboukir/CVE-2020-5902; reference:cve,2020-5902; metadata:service http;)

Mitigations

CISA strongly urges organizations that have not yet done so to upgrade their BIG-IP software to the corresponding patches for CVE-2020-5902. If organizations detect evidence of CVE-2020-5902 exploitation after patching and applying the detection measures in this alert, CISA recommends taking immediate action to reconstitute affected systems.

Should an organization's IT security personnel discover system compromise, CISA recommends they:

- Reimage compromised hosts
- Provision new account credentials
- Limit access to the management interface to the fullest extent possible
- Implement network segmentation
    - **Note:** network segmentation is a very effective security mechanism to help prevent an intruder from propagating exploits or laterally moving within an internal network. Segregation separates network segments based on role and functionality. A securely segregated network can limit the spread of malicious occurrences, reducing the impact from intruders that gain a foothold somewhere inside the network.[30]

1.3[B] CYBERSECURITY TOOLS

These threat alerts and known vulnerability databases are extremely helpful to the cybersecurity professional. But the cybersecurity professional must also be proactive by using technology tools to protect the company's computing and network assets from harm because not every vulnerability will be discovered and placed in the database or every threat result in an email or

[30] *Alert (AA20-206A)*, CYBERSECURITY & INFRASTRUCTURE SECURITY AGENCY (July 24, 2020), https://us-cert.cisa.gov/ncas/alerts/aa20-206a.

SMS alert. For example, maybe the threat is internal, such as an employee sending confidential data over the company's network to an outside party. Or maybe the data meant for investor A is sent to Investor B without any nefarious intent, it was just a mistake. Or maybe an employee clicks on a link that the employee incorrectly thinks is valid and from the IT department, and that causes a cybersecurity breach. There are many communication channels, hosts, and endpoints that need to be monitored.

Some of the tools that are available to cybersecurity professional include:

- Intrusion Protection Systems (IPS)
- Intrusion Detection Systems (IDS)
- Data Loss Prevention (DLP)
- Security Information and Event Management systems (SIEM).

An IPS "is software that has all the capabilities of an intrusion detection system and can also attempt to stop possible incidents."[31]

An IDS "is software that automates the intrusion detection process."[32]

IPS technologies are differentiated from IDS technologies by one characteristic: IPS technologies can respond to a detected threat by attempting to prevent it from succeeding. They use several response techniques, which can be divided into the following groups:

- The IPS stops the attack itself. Examples of how this could be done are as follows:

---

[31] Peter Mell & Karen Scarfone, *Guide to Intrusion Detection and Prevention Systems (IDPS) (Draft)*, NATIONAL INSTITUTE OF STANDARDS AND TECHNOLOGY 3 (July 2012), *available at* https://csrc.nist.gov/CSRC/media/Publications/sp/800-94/rev-1/draft/documents/draft_sp800-94-rev1.pdf.

[32] *Id.*

– Terminate the network connection or user session that is being used for the attack

– Block access to the target (or possibly other likely targets) from the offending user account, IP address, or other attacker attribute

– Block all access to the targeted host, service, application, or other resource.

- The IPS changes the security environment. The IPS could change the configuration of other security controls to disrupt an attack. Common examples are reconfiguring a network device (e.g., firewall, router, switch) to block access from the attacker or to the target, and altering a host-based firewall on a target to block incoming attacks. Some IPSs can even cause patches to be applied to a host if the IPS detects that the host has vulnerabilities.

- The IPS changes the attack's content. Some IPS technologies can remove or replace malicious portions of an attack to make it benign. A simple example is an IPS removing an infected file attachment from an email and then permitting the cleaned email to reach its recipient. A more complex example is an IPS that acts as a proxy and normalizes incoming requests, which means that the proxy repackages the payloads of the requests, discarding header information. This might cause certain attacks to be discarded as part of the normalization process.[33]

For brevity, NIST uses the combined term of "intrusion detection and prevention systems (IDPS):[34]

There are many types of IDPS technologies. For the purposes of this document, they are divided into the following four groups based on the type of events that they monitor and the ways in which they are deployed:

- Network-Based, which monitors network traffic for particular network segments or devices and analyzes the

[33] *Id.* at 5.

[34] *Id.* at 3.

network and application protocol activity to identify suspicious activity. It can identify many different types of events of interest. It is most commonly deployed at a boundary between networks, such as in proximity to border firewalls or routers, virtual private network (VPN) servers, remote access servers, and wireless networks. Section 4 contains extensive information on network- based IDPS technologies.

- Wireless, which monitors wireless network traffic and analyzes its wireless networking protocols to identify suspicious activity involving the protocols themselves. It cannot identify suspicious activity in the application or higher-layer network protocols (e.g., TCP, UDP) that the wireless network traffic is transferring. It is most commonly deployed within range of an organization's wireless network to monitor it, but can also be deployed to locations where unauthorized wireless networking could be occurring. More information on wireless IDPSs is presented in Section 5.

- Network Behavior Analysis (NBA), which examines network traffic to identify threats that generate unusual traffic flows, such as distributed denial of service (DDoS) attacks, certain forms of malware (e.g., worms, backdoors), and policy violations (e.g., a client system providing network services to other systems). NBA systems are most often deployed to monitor flows on an organization's internal networks, and are also sometimes deployed where they can monitor flows between an organization's networks and external networks (e.g., the Internet, business partners' networks). NBA products are discussed in more detail in Section 6.

- Host-Based, which monitors the characteristics of a single host and the events occurring within that host for suspicious activity. Examples of the types of characteristics a host-based IDPS might monitor are network traffic (only for that host), system logs, running processes, application activity, file access and modification, and system and application configuration changes. Host-based IDPSs are most commonly deployed on critical hosts such as publicly accessible servers and servers containing sensitive information. Section 7 contains additional information on host-based IDPSs.[35]

Most IDPSs use multiple detection methodologies, either separately or integrated, to provide more broad and accurate detection. The primary classes of detection methodologies are as follows:

- Signature-based, which compares known threat signatures to observed events to identify incidents. This is very effective at detecting known threats but largely ineffective at detecting unknown threats and many variants on known threats. Signature-based detection cannot track and understand the state of complex communications, so it cannot detect most attacks that comprise multiple events.

- Anomaly-based detection, which compares definitions of what activity is considered normal against observed events to identify significant deviations. This method uses profiles that are developed by monitoring the characteristics of typical activity over a period of time. The IDPS then compares the characteristics of current activity to thresholds related to the profile. Anomaly-based detection methods can be very effective at detecting previously unknown threats. Common problems with anomaly-based detection are inadvertently including malicious activity within a profile, establishing profiles that are not sufficiently complex to reflect real-world computing activity, and generating many false positives.

- Stateful protocol analysis, which compares predetermined profiles of generally accepted definitions of benign protocol activity for each protocol state against observed events to identify deviations. Unlike anomaly-based detection, which uses host or network-specific profiles, stateful protocol analysis relies on vendor-developed universal profiles that specify how particular protocols should and should not be used. It is capable of understanding and tracking the state of protocols that have a notion of state, which allows it to detect many attacks that other methods cannot. Problems with stateful protocol analysis include that it is often very difficult or impossible to develop completely accurate models of protocols, it is very resource-intensive, and it

---

[35] *Id.* at 9.

> cannot detect attacks that do not violate the characteristics of generally acceptable protocol behavior.[36]

A data loss prevention (DLP) system looks to recognize and block attempts at data exfiltration. A DLP can look at data classification or do pattern matching on data being removed from the system. Pattern matching can concentrate of such sensitive data as social security numbers or credit card numbers. DLP systems are normally focused on networks and endpoint-based computing assets. Key detection areas are emails and USB drives. Some operating systems can capture the attachment of a USB drive and record forensic information for further analysis. Upon detection, the DLP can take action to block. Encryption will defeat DLP systems.

A security information and event system (SIEM) is a system that collects data from many systems across the enterprise. The data is normally captured in a log file at an end point such as a personal work computer or from hosts such as servers or other points of interest with logging capability within the enterprise network. The SIEM can be configured to collect and review the data from all of these log files to look for trends or events of interest to determine if an incident has occurred.

All of these tools require constant fine-tuning for threats through proper configuration and follow-up analysis of captured events and incidents. The cybersecurity professional is to the daily operation of machines, data and networks as a doctor is to the ongoing diagnosis of a patient.

Some companies will also set up what is known as a honeypot, which is a decoy system that looks like it contains sensitive and important data but does not. The honeypot is a trap where information about the hacker can be collected while the hacker is probing the honeypot. And as long as the perpetrator is spending time in the honeypot, the perpetrator is ignoring the other valid and valuable systems.

Companies should remove all systems, applications, and services from the network when they are no longer needed. Leaving

[36] *Id.* at 10.

active but retired assets on the company's network allows unnecessary access ports and opportunity of entry.[37]

1.3[C] INHOUSE DEVELOPMENT OF PRODUCTS AND SERVICES

Many companies develop their own software in-house when it is cheaper than buying software or when software is not available commercially off the shelf with the feature set the company desires. Having an in-house development team is costly but it gives the company the flexibility to pursue the features they want in the software on their priority timetable. The application of reasonable security measures should start with the design and development of the software.

Privacy by Design is a phrase often used by privacy professionals. Privacy by Design is the concept whereby the designing stage for software incorporates privacy considerations. As already noted, privacy considerations apply to the protection of data that could adversely affect a person if the data is compromised. Thus, Privacy by Design is data-centric and could be referred to as security by design. Just as important if not more so, would be the application of cybersecurity testing during the design and development phases of software.

Software has a Software Development Life Cycle (SDLC) that includes many phases from conception through the retirement of the software. Secure SDLC adds a focus on maintaining security through the SDLC. Security of the application should be addressed and monitored throughout the SDLC starting with the conception and design phase. Design teams along with development teams are often under a lot of pressure to produce code that works and is done on-time and on-budget to meet a particular market cycle. For example, a smartphone that goes to market after Christmas will miss market share. Sometimes, in that process, testing for security in addition to functionality can be overlooked. To remedy that situation, the cybersecurity team should establish a good relationship with the design and development teams.

---

[37] A black hat hacker may access a computer or multiple computers to use them to attack another system. The utilized computers are sometimes called "bad bots" or "zombies." Cyber Blog Team, *Bots and Cybersecurity*, LIFARS (2020), www.lifars.com/2020/06/bots-and-cybersecurity/amp/. The group of bad bots or zombies may be called a "bot net." *Id.* A "bot net" can be used for a Distributed Denial of Service (DDoS) attack, which can overload a system. *Id.* A "bot net" attack can be used to steal personal information. *Id.*

Cybersecurity counsel can also be helpful in being part of that relationship. The design and development teams may not fully understand the consequences of not incorporating security measures early on. Education of the development and design teams on the challenges faced by both counsel and the cybersecurity team can go a long way in providing a working partnership across all teams on addressing cybersecurity for the good of all.

The disconnect often stems from each team not understanding why something has to be done or how it affects the company as a whole. Because each team uses different terminology for communicating about their performance goals, communication can be difficult. Engineers will not understand the legal world and vice versa. Engineers may not understand the daily challenges of the cybersecurity team and vice versa. For example, one of the authors was brought into a case before the FTC. It became apparent early on that the engineers and the attorneys were very dedicated to solving issues that affected the company's bottom line but that neither side understood the challenges of the other's task. The engineers were designing communication devices that had a short shelf live and a new product pipeline had to be maintained to keep adding new product features and have new products delivered on time for seasonal markets. The legal department was focused on protecting the company against the enforcement powers of the FTC. The author was able to explain the issue to each side in their terms. The engineers were more than happy to cooperate after the issue was put into their language and after they understood the risk of cybersecurity was equivalent, if not greater than missing a product deadline.

A good relationship and partnership with operations is also crucial in maintaining good cybersecurity practices. This goal has led to the development and implementation of a DevOps solution.

The DevOps approach is a team effort between operations, development, and cybersecurity. Some may use the term Quality Assurance (QA) instead of cybersecurity. QA is fine as long as that team also has a focus on cybersecurity.

1.3[D] Incident Response Responsibilities

The cybersecurity professional responsibilities that we have discussed so far in this chapter are proactive protection and detection responsibilities. The cybersecurity professional also has incident response responsibilities. An incident response plan is crucial for a proper response to an incident. Events and incidents are distinguishable:

> An event is any observable occurrence in a system or network. Events include a user connecting to a file share, a server receiving a request for a web page, a user sending email, and a firewall blocking a connection attempt. Adverse events are events with a negative consequence, such as system crashes, packet floods, unauthorized use of system privileges, unauthorized access to sensitive data, and execution of malware that destroys data. This guide addresses only adverse events that are computer security-related, not those caused by natural disasters, power failures, etc.
>
> A computer security incident is a violation or imminent threat of violation of computer security policies, acceptable use policies, or standard security practices. Examples of incidents are:
>
> - An attacker commands a botnet to send high volumes of connection requests to a web server, causing it to crash.
> - Users are tricked into opening a "quarterly report" sent via email that is actually malware; running the tool has infected their computers and established connections with an external host.
> - An attacker obtains sensitive data and threatens that the details will be released publicly if the organization does not pay a designated sum of money.
> - A user provides or exposes sensitive information to others through peer-to-peer file sharing services.[38]

A good incident response plan will include personnel and associated responsibilities, communication information, steps to be taken in the event of an incident, and chain of command. The cybersecurity professional will likely be a member of the computer incident response team (CIRT), also known as computer security incident response team (CSIRT). NIST has developed an incident response life cycle that includes preparation, detection and

---

[38] Paul Cichonski, et. al., *Computer Security Incident Handling Guide*, NATIONAL INSTITUTE STANDARDS AND TECHNOLOGY 6 (Aug. 2012), *available at* https://nvlpubs.nist.gov/nistpubs/SpecialPublications/NIST.SP.800-61r2.pdf.

analysis, containment eradication and recovery, and post-incident activity:[39]

NIST provides a checklist for the action to take for a suspected incident:[40]

	Action	Completed
	Detection and Analysis	
1.	Determine whether an incident has occurred	
1.1	Analyze the precursors and indicators	
1.2	Look for correlating information	
1.3	Perform research (e.g., search engines, knowledge base)	
1.4	As soon as the handler believes an incident has occurred, begin documenting the investigation and gathering evidence	
2.	Prioritize handling the incident based on the relevant factors (functional impact, information impact, recoverability effort, etc.)	
3.	Report the incident to the appropriate internal personnel and external organizations	
	Containment, Eradication, and Recovery	
4.	Acquire, preserve, secure, and document evidence	
5.	Contain the incident	
6.	Eradicate the incident	
6.1	Identify and mitigate all vulnerabilities that were exploited	
6.2	Remove malware, inappropriate materials, and other components	
6.3	If more affected hosts are discovered (e.g., new malware infections), repeat the Detection and Analysis steps (1.1, 1.2) to identify all other affected hosts, then contain (5) and eradicate (6) the incident for them	
7.	Recover from the incident	
7.1	Return affected systems to an operationally ready state	
7.2	Confirm that the affected systems are functioning normally	
7.3	If necessary, implement additional monitoring to look for future related activity	
	Post-Incident Activity	
8.	Create a follow-up report	
9.	Hold a lessons learned meeting (mandatory for major incidents, optional otherwise)	

Even with a thorough IRP and checklist, do not expect the response to an incident to go smoothly. Expect the incident to happen on a Friday evening after everyone has left and are

[39] *Id.* at 21.
[40] *Id.* at 42.

pursuing their weekend plans. Expect that responding to a verifiable incident will be stressful. Companies should conduct table-top exercises to give participants practice and to identify gaps in the plan or checklist. Companies should also provide training to potential participants. And it is a good idea to get the legal department involved at the beginning of the incident.

1.4 Responsibilities of a Cybersecurity Counselor

We chose the term Cybersecurity Counselor over Cybersecurity Attorney because a counselor is a broader term that designates providing advice beyond just cybersecurity legalities. A cybersecurity counselor will have the opportunity to advise clients across a broad swath of cybersecurity-related issues. The cybersecurity counselor may be involved in all aspects of a company's cybersecurity lifecycle, including but not limited to the creation of initial cybersecurity policies, controls, guidance and procedure, risk analysis under a risk analysis framework, business continuity planning, disaster recovery planning, training, and incident response. A competent cybersecurity counselor can become a liaison or bridge between the C-suite or General Counsel's office and the cybersecurity professional.

As a cybersecurity counsel just joining the legal department of a company, you will need to understand the business models of your company. After understanding the business models, you will need to determine which regulators and agencies regulate your industry and/or business models. Once the regulators and agencies are identified, research must be done to establish which cybersecurity and privacy laws apply to your company along with the legal risk for each. Next, counsel should acquire an inventory of the company's data and cyber assets. With this information in hand, counsel must make a determination as to whether the company is in compliance and whether "reasonable security measures" are in place for the data and cyber assets. The chapter on the NIST Cybersecurity Framework provides a methodology for assessing what may be reasonable security measures under the specific circumstances involved. If the company is not in compliance with reasonable security measures, counsel must drive efforts to get into compliance and maintain reasonable security measures by ensuring the proper cybersecurity policies and procedures are developed and then maintained. Counsel must also determine whether the policies and procedures are being followed by all employees and provide proper training as needed on the policies and procedures. Indeed, one common source of cybersecurity issues involve employees who are not properly trained in recognizing attempts to breach a particular system. Efforts to breach systems by relying on humans is generally known as social engineering and may include phishing or even just searching through trash for passwords.

The cybersecurity in-house counsel will ideally be a liaison between General Counsel and the company person responsible for maintaining cybersecurity and responding to incidents. Cybersecurity counsel will maintain communication channels with cyber-related departments and business departments, whose business requirements are driving cyber-related efforts. By doing so, cybersecurity counsel should not be surprised when a new product is placed in the network. Also, when needed, cybersecurity counsel will manage outside cybersecurity legal-related efforts.

Counsel should also establish and maintain contacts and relationships with the FBI and Secret Service departments that pursue data breach incidents. Counsel should be prepared to advise on when to contact law enforcement, the FBI, or the Secret Service.

The cybersecurity landscape is dynamic. Counsel will also need to stay on top of changing and new laws at the federal and state levels. Companies are also dynamic. Counsel will need to be aware of any upcoming mergers and then participate in the merger to make sure the company maintains it cybersecurity posture across the merger. In a smaller company, counsel may also be asked to take on privacy duties. Notably, cybersecurity counsel may be litigators and transactional attorneys. As we explore future chapters, cybersecurity litigation as well as transactions are important areas of cybersecurity legal work. Moreover, cybersecurity legal issues cross the public and private spheres as well as cut across all industries in the private arena.

Most companies are transactional in nature. There are contracts for outsourcing, providing services to customers, and receiving services from vendors. In today's connected world, a majority of these contracts will have the need for a watchful cybersecurity eye and a cybersecurity legal eye. As mentioned *supra*, the move of company services to the cloud have presented good economic opportunities to save money, but there are also opportunities for security gaps. For example, who is responsible for every aspect of security, the cloud provider, the customer, or both? Counsel will need to understand whether the company is a controller or processor of data. Counsel will also need to verify that the vendor will handle sensitive data properly. Does the vendor meet compliance standards? Is the vendor ISO 27001 certified?[41] Has the vendor gone through SOC audits?[42] Were those SOC audits made available for review, and did they pass?

As we have noted, the United States has a patchwork of regulations that cover privacy and cybersecurity law enforced by a number of agencies. In the following chapters, we will provide detail for those regulations and who is covered. The first step is determining the character and make-up of the client or company. Are they a pure investment firm covered by the SEC or do they dabble in many areas, covered by cybersecurity laws and regulations written for various agencies and enforced by many agencies?

As we have noted, the United States has a patchwork of regulations that cover privacy and cybersecurity law enforced by a number of agencies. In the following chapters, we will provide detail for those regulations and who is covered.

---

[41] The Independent Standards Organization [ISO]:

> ISO is an independent, non-governmental international organization with a membership of 167 national standards bodies.
> Through its members, it brings together experts to share knowledge and develop voluntary, consensus-based, market relevant International Standards that support innovation and provide solutions to global challenges. ISO - About us

ISO 27001:

> ISO/IEC 27001 is widely known, providing requirements for an information security management system (ISMS), though there are more than a dozen standards in the ISO/IEC 27000 family. Using them enables organizations of any kind to manage the security of assets such as financial information, intellectual property, employee details or information entrusted by third parties. ISO - ISO/IEC 27001 — Information security management

[42] "SOC is an acronym that now stands for System and Organization Controls (previously Service Organization Controls) and is an audit of a companies controls that are in place to help ensure the Security, Availability, Processing Integrity, Confidentiality and Privacy of their customers data. The SOC control standards were created and overseen by the American Institute of Certified Public Accountants (AICPA)." Adsero Security, *Security 101, SOC Audit, What is a SOC Audit*, available at What is a SOC Audit? - Adsero Security (last visited May 23, 2022).

CHAPTER TWO. Federal Trade Commission Enforcement and Cybersecurity Law

2.1 Introduction

This Chapter reviews the Federal Trade Commission (FTC) enforcement actions concerning cybersecurity. The FTC is a federal agency tasked with protecting consumers and promoting competition.[43] In recent years the FTC has taken enforcement action against many companies, small and large, under "unfair or deceptive acts or practices in or affecting commerce" that have been clear-cut privacy enforcement actions. The "unfair or deceptive acts or practices in or affecting commerce" enforcement powers of the FTC come from Section 5 of the 1914 FTC Act. The FTC has been particularly successful in enforcing consumer privacy through the deceptive acts prong by pursuing companies that collect personal data beyond that which is disclosed in the companies' privacy notices. Of course, in 1914 cybersecurity was not envisioned as something that would be covered by the Act. But with the proliferation of computers and the connection of computers with the internet, cybersecurity has become a hot topic, and the FTC has found a way to add cybersecurity to its enforcement regiment.

In 2002, the FTC started asserting claims based on "unfair" cybersecurity practices. For the next 10 years, all actions brought by the FTC resulted in negotiated consent agreements, with no company testing the FTC's statutory authority to regulate cybersecurity. While some companies questioned the FTC's authority, they all settled rather than engage in an embarrassing legal battle. That changed when the FTC sued Wyndham Worldwide Corp. in 2012.[44]

In the Matter of HTC America Inc., the FTC brought a complaint with one count of unfair security practices and two counts of deception. The FTC claimed that HTC failed to "employ reasonable security in the customization of its mobile devices." In paragraph 7 of the complaint the FTC asserted:

---

[43] *What We Do*, FEDERAL TRADE COMMISSION, https://www.ftc.gov/about-ftc/what-we-do (last visited May 12, 2021).

[44] *Id.*

> Until at least November 2011, respondent engaged in a number of practices that, taken together, failed to employ reasonable and appropriate security in the design and customization of the software on its mobile devices. Among other things, respondent: (a) failed to implement an adequate program to assess the security of products it shipped to consumers; (b) failed to implement adequate privacy and security guidance or training for its engineering staff; (c) failed to conduct assessments, audits, reviews, or tests to identify potential security vulnerabilities in its mobile devices; (d) failed to follow well- known and commonly-accepted secure programming practices, including secure practices that were expressly described in the operating system's guides for manufacturers and developers, which would have ensured that applications only had access to users' information with their consent; and (e) failed to implement a process for receiving and addressing security vulnerability reports from third-party researchers, academics or other members of the public, thereby delaying its opportunity to correct discovered vulnerabilities or respond to reported incidents.[45]

Two points are noteworthy about this case and many other cases brought by the FTC. First, the FTC does not enumerate what comprises "reasonable and appropriate security." Such a road map could potentially box the FTC into a corner and allow an entity to escape the grasp of the FTC because the entity followed the enumerated factors but still failed to have adequate security based on other factors that the FTC may have not considered at the time it would have enumerated the factors. By not enumerating "reasonable and appropriate security" factors, the FTC can remain flexible in its complaints. Also, "reasonable and appropriate security" factors today may not be the same in the future after hackers evolve to circumvent today's reasonable and appropriate security" measures. The FTC methodology is somewhat similar to the Supreme Court's statement that the Court knows obscenity when it sees it.[46] Same for the FTC, it knows bad security practices

[45] Complaint at 2, HTC America Inc., F.T.C. No. C-4406 (July 2, 2013).

[46] *See* Jacobellis v. State of Ohio, 84 S. Ct. 1676, 1683 (1964) (Stewart, J., concurring) ("I shall not today attempt to further define the kinds of material I understand to be embraced within that shorthand description; and perhaps I

when it sees it and may rely on industry standards to help define it. However, those standards evolve over time to react to some of the afore-mentioned changes.

Second, the FTC must rely on other sources to provide the evidence or at least point the FTC to the evidence of unreasonable or inappropriate security practices that lead to a potential finding of unfair security practices. In the HTC matter, it was security researchers who first notified HTC of the vulnerabilities and then went public after HTC failed to respond to the researchers input.[47] After the evidence is revealed to the FTC, it can be an aggressive bulldog in seeking enforcement, but the FTC does not have the resources to monitor inappropriate security practices. An entity that expects an FTC enforcement action because of negative publicity should immediately remedy the publicized cybersecurity shortcomings and any others that might surface during an FTC matter, and prepare to receive interrogatories from the FTC. In or about the time of the HTC matter, the FTC's string of cybersecurity consent agreements without a court challenge came to an end when the FTC went after Wyndham Worldwide Corp.

2.2 Wyndham and Subsequent Enforcement Actions

The Wyndham case was the first court test of the FTC's unfair practices application of the "reasonable and appropriate security" standard.

In *Federal Trade Commission v. Wyndham*,[48] the Third Circuit decided that the FTC has authority to regulate cybersecurity based on the unfairness prong of the FTC Act and that Wyndham had sufficient notice that its deficient cybersecurity practices could violate the FTC Act. The court noted that the unfairness prong of the FTC Act was designed to be flexible and cover evolving content. The court pointed to the legal rule involved: "whether 'the act or practice causes or is likely to cause substantial injury to consumers which is not reasonably avoidable by consumers themselves and not outweighed by countervailing benefits to consumers or to competition.'" The Court noted that the

---

could never succeed in intelligibly doing so. But I know it when I see it, and the motion picture involved in this case is not that.").

[47] John P. Mello Jr., *'Massive Security Vulnerability' in HTC Android Phones Claimed*, PCWORLD (Oct. 2, 2011), https://www.pcworld.com/article/240958/massive_security_vulnerability_in_htc_android_phones_claimed.html.

[48] 799 F.3d 236 (3rd Cir. 2015).

thrust of the standard is a cost benefit analysis, including "factors [such as] the probability and expected size of reasonably unavoidable harms to consumers given a certain level of cybersecurity and the costs to consumers that would arise from investment in stronger cybersecurity." Moreover, the court pointed to numerous FTC documents, including complaints and consent decrees, which set forth deficient cybersecurity practices which would serve as notice of problematic cybersecurity measures.

With the Wyndham decision, the FTC no longer needed to add deception to its compliant to have an iron-clad case. Unfair security practices could now stand on their own as an action in the complaint under the unfairness prong.

Post *Wyndham* FTC Actions

After Wyndham, the FTC began positioning some of its enforcement actions as data security actions. Numerous actions have been so designated by the FTC since 2016. The FTC maintains a list of the enforcement actions on its website. Here is a list of some of those actions:

- SkyMed International, Inc., In the Matter of (December 16, 2020)
- Ascension Data & Analytics, LLC, In the Matter of (December 15, 2020)
- Zoom Video Communications, Inc., In the Matter of (November 9, 2020)
- NTT Global Data Centers Americas, Inc., In the Matter of (July 9, 2020)
- Tapplock, Inc., In the Matter of (May 20, 2020)
- InfoTrax Systems, L.C. (November 12, 2019)
- LightYear Dealer Technologies, LLC, In the Matter of (September 6, 2019)
- LabMD, Inc. v. Federal Trade Commission (August 30, 2019)
- Equifax, Inc. (July 31, 2019)
- James V. Grago, Jr. doing business as ClixSense.com, In the Matter of (July 2, 2019)
- D-Link (July 2, 2019)
- Office Depot, Inc. (March 29, 2019)
- mResource LLC (Loop Works LLC), In the Matter of (November 19, 2018)
- VenPath, Inc., In the Matter of (November 19, 2018)

- SmartStart Employment Screening, Inc., In the Matter of (November 19, 2018)
- Uber Technologies, Inc., In the Matter of (October 29, 2018)
- IDmission LLC, In the Matter of (October 11, 2018)
- BLU Products and Samuel Ohev-Zion, In the Matter of (September 11, 2018)
- PayPal, Inc., In the Matter of (May 24, 2018)
- VTech Electronics Limited (January 8, 2018)
- TaxSlayer, In the Matter of (November 8, 2017)
- Ashley Madison (September 27, 2017)[49]

The FTC complaint counts fall into the following basic areas:

1) Deception including deception regarding cybersecurity practices;
2) Misrepresentations including misrepresentations regarding cybersecurity practices;
3) Unfair security practices;
4) Violations of the Privacy Rule and Reg. P (FTC enforcement under the GLBA);
5) Violations of the Safeguards Rule (FTC enforcement under the GLBA); and
6) COPPA enforcement.

To understand how the FTC approaches claims of unfair security practices, we take a closer look at three cases that include claims of unfair security practices:

1) ASUSTeK Computer LLC;
2) James V. Grago, Jr. doing business as ClixSense.com; and
3) LightYear Dealer Technologies, LLC.

In the *ASUSTek Computer LLC* ("ASUSTek") complaint, count 5 set forth the cause of action for unfair security practices alleging the respondent "failed to take reasonable steps to secure the software for its routers, which respondent offered to consumers for the purpose of protecting their local networks and accessing sensitive personal information. Respondent's actions caused or are

---

[49] *Data Security*, FEDERAL TRADE COMMISSION, https://www.ftc.gov/datasecurity (last visited May 12, 2021).

likely to cause substantial injury to consumers in the United States that is not outweighed by countervailing benefits to consumers or competition and is not reasonably avoidable by consumers themselves . . . in violation of Section 5(a) of the Federal Trade Commission Act, 15 U.S.C. § 45(a)."[50]

It is likely that the FTC did not gather all of the needed information for the complaint on day one. The FTC likely became interested either through consumer complaints as detailed in the complaint or through following scientific or watchdog blogs, or bulletins. The FTC would have also likely followed up the leads with specific interrogatories to the company. At the end of this process, the FTC has compiled a long list of cybersecurity mistakes, missteps, and failures that it can list and compare against known industry cybersecurity practices to point out gaps in "reasonable security." Basically, here is what a reasonable company does regarding cybersecurity practices and here is what you did. In the end, the company is left with no choice but to agree to a consent agreement with the FTC.

In the *James V. Grago, Jr.* ("ClixSense") complaint, count 3, Unfairness: Failure to Employ Reasonable Security Practices, set forth the cause of action for unfair security practices including "[r]espondent's failure to employ reasonable security practices caused or is likely to cause substantial injury to consumers that is not outweighed by countervailing benefits to consumers or competition and is not reasonably avoidable by consumers themselves. This practice is an unfair act or practice [and] [t]he acts and practices of Respondent as alleged in this complaint constitute unfair or deceptive acts or practices in or affecting commerce in violation of Section 5(a) of the FTC Act, 15 U.S.C § 45(a)."[51] Some of the cybersecurity issues highlighted by the FTC included failing to limit access, storing plain text user credentials, failure to change default login and password credentials for third-party company network resources, and storing sensitive information in clear text. Eventually, in 2016, hackers took advantage of these security failures and "downloaded a copy of the ClixSense user table, which contained clear text information regarding 6.6 million consumers—including some 500,000 U.S. consumers."[52]

---

[50] Complaint, ASUSTeK Computer Inc., F.T.C. No. C-4587 (July 18, 2016).

[51] Complaint at 6, James V. Grago, Jr., doing business as ClixSense.com, F.T.C. No. C-4678 (July 2, 2019).

[52] Complaint at 3–5, James V. Grago, Jr., doing business as ClixSense.com, F.T.C. No. C-4678 (July 2, 2019).

In *LightYear Dealer Technologies, LLC* ("LightYear") complaint, count 1, Unfair Data Security Practices, set forth the cause of action for unfair security practices alleging "[r]espondent's failure to employ reasonable measures to protect personal information caused or is likely to cause substantial injury to consumers that is not outweighed by countervailing benefits to consumers or competition and is not reasonably avoidable by consumers themselves."[53] Some of the cybersecurity problems identified by the FTC for LightYear included failure "to develop, implement, or maintain a written organizational information security policy", failure to "implement reasonable guidance or training for employees or third-party contractors, regarding data security and safeguarding consumers' personal information", failure "to assess the risks to the personal information stored on its network, such as by conducting periodic risk assessments or performing vulnerability and penetration testing of the network", failure "to use readily available security measures to monitor its systems and assets at discrete intervals to identify data security events", failure "to impose reasonable data access controls, such as restricting inbound connections to known IP addresses, and requiring authentication to access backup databases", storing "consumers' personal information on Respondent's computer network in clear text", and failure "to have a reasonable process to select, install, secure, and inventory devices with access to personal information."[54]

The FTC's complaint for each of the above three cases was tailored to cover specific cybersecurity failures for each company. The FTC listed failures but did not give the public guidance on an all-inclusive specific list of what would be reasonable security measures in the complaints themselves. Even without a specific list, a couple of best security practices are evident such as:

1) Use readily available measures especially if they are low cost;
2) Do some vulnerability and penetration testing to identify weak areas;
3) Use encryption instead of clear text.

---

[53] Complaint, LightYear Dealer Technologies, LLC., F.T.C. No. C-4687 (Sept. 6, 2019).

[54] Complaint at 3, LightYear Dealer Technologies, LLC., F.T.C. No. C-4687 (Sept. 6, 2019).

Each of the above would easily fit into a list of cybersecurity best practices. And the FTC has taken its guidance one step further by providing the business community with a "Start with Security – A Guide for Business – Lessons Learned from FTC Cases."[55]

The guidance covered in this short document include:

1) Start with security;
2) Control access to data sensibly;
3) Require secure passwords and authentication;
4) Store sensitive personal information securely and protect it during transmission;
5) Segment your network and monitor who's trying to get in and out;
6) Secure remote access to your network;
7) Apply sound security practices when developing new products;
8) Make sure you service providers implement reasonable security measures;
9) Put procedures in place to keep your security current and address vulnerabilities that may arise;
10) Secure paper, physical media, and devices.[56]

As with the FTC cases, the above guidance is part of the normal best practices landscape practiced by cybersecurity professionals. It is also a clear signal that the FTC is and will be taking an active and proactive role in cybersecurity.

In 2023, the FTC issued an Order in In re Matter of Drizly. FTC adds data minimization to reasonable information security practices.[57] In that matter, the FTC found respondents "failed to use reasonable information security practices to protect consumers' personal information."[58] The FTC enumerated the failed practices

[55] *Start with Security—A Guide for Business—Lessons Learned from FTC Cases*, FEDERAL TRADE COMMISSION, *available at* https://www.ftc.gov/system/files/documents/plain-language/pdf0205-startwithsecurity.pdf.

[56] *See id* (listing and describing the various steps businesses should take to ensure security).

[57] In re Matter of Drizly, FTC Complaint C-4780, available at https://www.ftc.gov/system/files/ftc_gov/pdf/2023185-drizly-combined-consent.pdf.

[58] *Id.* at 3.

as written information security standards, policies, procedures, or practices; secure storage of login credentials; reasonable data access controls; data loss prevention; and testing and auditing of security controls. These focus on recommended reasonable security controls. The FTC also added data minimization as a security measure by stating that respondents failed to "[h]ave a policy, procedure, or practice for inventorying and deleting consumers' personal information stored on its network that was no longer necessary."[59]

Data minimization is normally considered a privacy principle. By adding data minimization to the complaint, the FTC broadened its unfair information security practices authority to include a privacy principle. Such a broadening is interesting because it can be argued that reasonable security measures do not change based on whether the data should have been minimized or deleted. Reasonable security measures are normally applied across all data sources. From a risk perspective, it appears that the FTC is taking a stand that keeping unnecessary data increases the risks to more individuals should there be a breach of the data.

Companies are now well advised that the FTC may use their unfair information security practices to include the privacy concept of data minimization as a reasonable security measure. Companies likely will not be able to argue that all data is adequately protected by reasonable security measures regardless of whether the data is stale. Under this complaint it is clear that companies can no longer add security controls to its data without understanding the data. This isn't necessarily a new task for the CISO but may be for the Chief Privacy Officer (CPO) for companies that have not taken a data inventory, also known as a data map. The CPO will likely take on the task of obtaining a data inventory, creating a more specific data minimization policy, and ensuring that the policy is properly communicated both to the public and internally.

The following provision is from the 2023185 order:

II. Mandated Deletion and Data Minimization

[59] *Id.* at 4.

IT IS FURTHER ORDERED that Corporate Respondent must:

A. Within 60 days after the issuance date of this Order, Delete or destroy all Covered Information that is not being used or retained in connection with providing products or services to Corporate Respondent's customers, and provide a written statement to the Commission, pursuant to the Provision entitled Compliance Report and Notices, confirming that all such data has been Deleted or destroyed specifically enumerating which types of information were Deleted or destroyed; and

B. Refrain from collecting or maintaining any Covered Information not necessary for the specific purpose(s) provided in the retention schedule required under Provision III entitled Data Retention Limits.

Provided, however, that any data that Corporate Respondent is required to Delete or destroy pursuant to this Provision may be retained if required by law, regulation, court order, contractual obligations requiring Corporate Respondent to maintain records on behalf of retailers to document the retailers' compliance with state or local liquor regulations, or legal process, including as required by rules applicable to the safeguarding of evidence in pending litigation.

III. Data Retention Limits

IT IS FURTHER ORDERED that Corporate Respondent, in connection with the collection, maintenance, use, or disclosure of, or provision of access to, Covered Information, must:

A. Within 60 days of issuance of this Order, document, adhere to, and make publicly available on its website(s) or app(s), a retention schedule for Covered Information, setting forth: (1) the purpose or purposes for which each type of Covered Information is collected; (2) the specific business

> needs for retaining each type of Covered Information; and (3) a set timeframe for Deletion of each type of Covered Information that precludes indefinite retention of any Covered Information . . . .[60]

2.3 The Sufficiency of FTC Complaints: D-Link Systems

In D-Link Systems, the FTC challenged the security practices of router and IP camera products made by D-Link Systems. In its complaint, the FTC alleged that D-Link Systems engaged "in unfair or deceptive acts or practices in violation of Section 5(a) of the FTC Act, 15 U.S.C. § 45(a)" and failed "to take reasonable steps to secure the routers and Internet-protocol cameras they designed for, marketed, and sold to United States consumers." FTC v. D-Link Systems Complaint for Permanent Injunctive and Other Equitable Relief in Federal District Court (March 20, 2017).

In Federal Trade Commission v. D-Link Systems,**[61]** D-Link Systems challenged the complaint under Federal Rules of Civil Procedure 12(b)(6), 8(a), and 9(b).[62] "To meet the pleading requirements of Rule 8(a) and to survive a Rule 12(b)(6) motion to dismiss, a claim must provide "a short and plain statement ... showing that the pleader is entitled to relief," Fed. R. Civ. P. 8(a)(2), including "enough facts to state a claim ... that is plausible on its face." *Bell Atl. Corp. v. Twombly*, 550 U.S. 544, 570 (2007). A claim is plausible on its face if, accepting all factual allegations as true and construing them in the light most favorable to the plaintiff, the Court can reasonably infer that the defendant is liable for the misconduct alleged. *Ashcroft v. Iqbal*, 556 U.S. 662, 678 (2009). The plausibility analysis is "context-specific" and not only invites but "requires the reviewing court to draw on its judicial experience and common sense." *Id.*" Because the court dismissed the unfairness

---

[60] In re Matter of Drizly, FTC Decision and Order C-4780, 3-4, available at https://www.ftc.gov/system/files/ftc_gov/pdf/2023185-drizly-combined-consent.pdf.

[61] 2017 WL 4150873 (N.D. Cal. 2017).

[62] Editors: Federal Rule of Civil Procedure 9(b) states: "**(b) Fraud or Mistake; Conditions of Mind.** In alleging fraud or mistake, a party must state with particularity the circumstances constituting fraud or mistake. Malice, intent, knowledge, and other conditions of a person's mind may be alleged generally." Fed. R. Civ. P. 9(b) (emphasis is original).

claim under Rule 8, the court did not have to make a decision under Rule 9(b) on the unfairness claim.

With regard to the unfairness claim, the court found that the FTC did "not allege any actual consumer injury in the form of a monetary loss or an actual incident where sensitive personal data was accessed or exposed. Instead, the FTC relies solely on the likelihood that DLS put consumers at "risk" because "remote attackers could take simple steps, using widely available tools, to locate and exploit Defendants' devices, which were widely known to be vulnerable." Dkt. No. 1 ¶ 17; see also id. ¶ 18 (attacker "could compromise" a router and thereby "could obtain" tax returns or other sensitive files).

> That is effectively the sum total of the harm allegations, and they make out a mere possibility of injury at best. The FTC does not identify a single incident where a consumer's financial, medical or other sensitive personal information has been accessed, exposed or misused in any way, or whose IP camera has been compromised by unauthorized parties, or who has suffered any harm or even simple annoyance and inconvenience from the alleged security flaws in the DLS devices. The absence of any concrete facts makes it just as possible that DLS's devices are not likely to substantially harm consumers, and the FTC cannot rely on wholly conclusory allegations about potential injury to tilt the balance in its favor. The lack of facts indicating a likelihood of harm is all the more striking in that the FTC says that it undertook a thorough investigation before filing the complaint, . . . and that the DLS devices have had the challenged security flaws since 2011. This complaint stands in sharp contrast to complaints that have survived motions to dismiss in other cases involving data security issues. See, e.g., FTC v. Wyndham Worldwide, 799 F.3d 236, 242 (3d. Cir. 2015) (sustaining complaint that alleged data theft of personal information of hundreds of thousands of consumers with over $10.6 million in fraudulent charges).

2.4 The LabMD Matter

The following two LabMD cases concern inadequate data security programs by a medical company. The first case is an opinion and order from the Federal Trade Commission. The second opinion is from a federal appellate court overturning the Federal Trade Commission's opinion and order.

In the Matter of LabMD,[63] the FTC alleged that LabMD failed to implement "reasonable security measures" in order "to protect the sensitive personal information, including medical information, of consumers whose physicians had entrusted that information to the company." The FTC alleged that LabMD "data security practices were unfair under Section 5 of the Federal Trade Commission Act." The FTC complaint was dismissed by an Administrative Law Judge who held that "Complaint Counsel had not shown that LabMD's data security practices either caused or were likely to cause substantial injury." The FTC concluded that "the ALJ applied the wrong legal standard for unfairness" and reversed the ALJ's decision in finding the data security practices to be unfair in violation of Section 5(n) because "the exposure of sensitive medical and personal information via a peer-to-peer file-sharing application was likely to cause substantial injury and that the disclosure of sensitive medical information did cause substantial injury." The FTC also found that the injuries could not be reasonably avoided by consumers and that the consumers' injuries "were not outweighed by countervailing benefits to consumers or to competition." As an appropriate remedy required to prevent further consumer injury, the FTC ordered LabMD to "notify affected consumers, establish a comprehensive information security program reasonably designed to protect the security and confidentiality of the personal consumer information in its possession, and obtain independent assessments regarding its implementation of the program." LabMD appealed to the Eleventh Circuit to vacate the FTC order and won.

In *LabMD v. Federal Trade Commission*,[64] LabMD contended that "the order is unenforceable because it does not direct LabMD to cease committing an unfair act or practice within the meaning of Section 5(a)." The first question for the court was whether "LabMD's failure to implement and maintain a reasonably designed data-security program constituted an unfair act or practice within the ambit of Section 5(a)." The court "assume[d] arguendo that the Commission is correct and that LabMD's

---

[63] 2016 WL 4128215 (FTC 2016).

[64] 894 F.3d 1221 (11th Cir. 2018).

negligent failure to design and maintain a reasonable data-security program invaded consumers' right of privacy and thus constituted an unfair act or practice." The second question for the court was "whether the Commission's cease and desist order, founded upon LabMD's general negligent failure to act, is enforceable." The court found the order unenforceable.

> In sum, assuming arguendo that LabMD's negligent failure to implement and maintain a reasonable data-security program constituted an unfair act or practice under Section 5(a), the Commission's cease and desist order is nonetheless unenforceable. It does not enjoin a specific act or practice. Instead, it mandates a complete overhaul of LabMD's data-security program and says precious little about how this is to be accomplished. Moreover, it effectually charges the district court with managing the overhaul. This is a scheme Congress could not have envisioned. We therefore grant LabMD's petition for review and vacate the Commission's order.

2.5 Negligence Actions Related to FTC Act Violations

At least one Federal Appellate Court in *In re SuperValu*, 925 F.3d 955 (8th Cir. 2019), has held that Illinois courts likely will not recognize a duty on behalf of retailers to safeguard customer data in a negligence claim concerning a data security breach. Moreover, that Court determined that the Federal Trade Commission Act does not create a duty on behalf of retailers. The Court stated, in relevant part:

> To state a claim for negligence under Illinois law, a complaint must allege "facts that establish the existence of a duty of care owed by the defendant to the plaintiff, a breach of that duty, and an injury proximately caused by that breach." Marshall v. Burger King Corp., 222 Ill.2d 422, 305 Ill.Dec. 897, 856 N.E.2d 1048, 1053 (2006). Holmes's claim is primarily premised on the view that SuperValu, as a retailer, had a duty to safeguard his credit-card information from cyberattacks. Whether a defendant owes a legal duty to the plaintiff is a question of state law. See Iseberg v. Gross, 227 Ill.2d 78, 316 Ill.Dec. 211, 879 N.E.2d 278, 284 (2007). In Illinois, generally there is no affirmative duty to

protect another from a criminal attack unless one of four historically recognized "special relationships" exists between the parties. See id., 316 Ill.Dec. 211, 879 N.E.2d at 284–85.

The parties agree that the Illinois Supreme Court has not yet addressed whether a retailer has a qualifying special relationship with its customers such that it is obligated to protect their financial information from hackers. In these circumstances, our role is to predict how that court would rule if faced with the issue. Blankenship v. USA Truck, Inc., 601 F.3d 852, 856 (8th Cir. 2010). The Seventh Circuit recently addressed the same question and predicted that Illinois would not impose such a duty on retailers like SuperValu. See Cmty. Bank of Trenton v. Schnuck Mkts., Inc., 887 F.3d 803, 816 (7th Cir. 2018). The Seventh Circuit based its ruling on Cooney v. Chicago Public Schools, an Illinois Appellate Court decision that appears to hold that the state does not recognize a duty in tort to safeguard sensitive personal information. See 407 Ill.App.3d 358, 347 Ill.Dec. 733, 943 N.E.2d 23, 28–29 (2010). Holmes has not drawn our attention to any Illinois authority contrary to Cooney. We agree with the Seventh Circuit's reading of Cooney and accordingly adopt its conclusion. The failure of Illinois law to impose this type of common-law duty on merchants mandates dismissal of Holmes's negligence claim.

In the alternative, Holmes argues that his negligence claim is premised on a duty imposed by federal statute, specifically the Federal Trade Commission Act (FTCA). The FTCA gives the Federal Trade Commission the authority to, among other things, enforce against "unfair or deceptive acts or practices in or affecting commerce." 15 U.S.C. § 45(a). The Commission has used this authority to bring a number of enforcement actions against companies that have purportedly failed to protect consumer financial data against hackers. See FTC v. Wyndham Worldwide Corp., 799 F.3d 236, 240 (3d Cir. 2015). The FTCA creates no private right of action. FTC v. Johnson, 800 F.3d 448, 452 (8th Cir. 2015).

Illinois courts have held that statutes "designed to protect human life or property" can establish the "standard of conduct required of a reasonable person" and therefore "fix the measure of legal duty" in a negligence action. Noyola v. Bd. of Educ., 179 Ill.2d 121, 227 Ill.Dec. 744, 688 N.E.2d 81, 84–85 (Ill. 1997). If a defendant violates such a statute, a right of action may be implied in tort if four conditions are met: (1) the plaintiff is a member of the class for whose benefit the statute was enacted, (2) the right of action is consistent with the underlying purpose of the statute, (3) the plaintiff's injury is one the statute was designed to prevent, and (4) the right of action is necessary to provide an adequate remedy for violations of the statute. Id., 227 Ill.Dec. 744, 688 N.E.2d at 85.

Several of these conditions are absent here. Congress empowered the Commission—and the Commission alone—to enforce the FTCA. Implying a cause of action would be inconsistent with Congress's anticipated enforcement scheme. Holmes points to nothing suggesting that the Commission's enforcement efforts have been inadequate to redress violations of the statute in this area. At least one court has expressly rejected the proposition that § 45(a) creates a duty enforceable through an Illinois negligence action. See Cmty. Bank of Trenton v. Schnuck Mkts., Inc., 210 F. Supp. 3d 1022, 1041 (S.D. Ill. 2016). Holmes cites no authority to the contrary. We conclude that Illinois is unlikely to recognize a legal duty enforceable through a negligence action arising from the FTCA. The district court's dismissal of this claim was proper." *Id. See also In re Sonic Customer Data Security Breach Litigation*, 2020 WL 3577341 (N.D. Ohio 2020) ("The Court finds that because the FTC Act Section 5 does not lay out objective standards, it does not support a claim for negligence per se under Oklahoma law. By its terms, the statute only prohibits unfair competition or unfair or deceptive acts. While the FTC and other courts have interpreted Section 5's terms to apply to data security requirements, the statute's actual terms do not lay out positive, objective standards that, if

> violated, could give the standard for a negligence per se claim under Oklahoma law.").

Another court has found that the FTC Act can serve as the basis of a negligence per se claim in the data security breach context under Georgia law. See *In re Marriott International Customer Data Security Breach Litigation*, 2020 WL 869241 (D. Md. 2020). Moreover, the FTC Act can be used as evidence of foreseeable risk to demonstrate that a duty exists. See *In re Brinker Data Incident Litigation*, 2020 WL 691848, 9 (M.D. Fla. 2020).

CHAPTER THREE. The Gramm-Leach-Bliley Act and FTC Safeguards Rule

3.1 Introduction

The United States relies on a patch work of federal and state cybersecurity and privacy laws. The Gramm-Leach-Bliley Act (GLBA) is one of those laws. One might normally think of the GLBA as primarily a financial privacy law. However, there is also an important cybersecurity requirement called the Safeguards Rule that is enforced by the FTC.

This chapter primarily reviews the regulations implementing the GLBA as well as FTC enforcement. This chapter also examines case law concerning the GLBA and the Safeguards Rule in private litigation as well as standards regarding credit cards. Additionally, the chapter examines the New York Department of Financial cybersecurity rules and a case involving those rules. Finally, additional regulations and enforcement by other regulators concerning the GLBA is reviewed.

3.2 FTC's Jurisdiction under GLBA

The purpose and scope of sections 501 and 505(b)(2) of the GLBA are implemented by the regulations in Title 16, Chapter I, Subchapter C Part 314. The Purpose identifies "standards for developing, implementing, and maintaining reasonable administrative, technical, and physical safeguards to protect the security, confidentiality, and integrity of customer information." The Scope gives the FTC jurisdiction for "the handling of customer information by all financial institutions over which the Federal Trade Commission ("FTC" or "Commission") has jurisdiction."[65]

The first question is which entities are included in the phrase: "financial institutions over which the [FTC] has jurisdiction." The FTC provides advice concerning who may be covered by the GBLA:

> The definition of 'financial institution' includes many businesses that may not normally describe

[65] 16 C.F.R. §314.1(a)-(b) (2002).

themselves that way. In fact, the Rule applies to all businesses, regardless of size, that are 'significantly engaged' in providing financial products or services. This includes, for example, check-cashing businesses, payday lenders, mortgage brokers, nonbank lenders, personal property or real estate appraisers, professional tax preparers, and courier services. The Safeguards Rule also applies to companies like credit reporting agencies and ATM operators that receive information about the customers of other financial institutions. In addition to developing their own safeguards, companies covered by the Rule are responsible for taking steps to ensure that their affiliates and service providers safeguard customer information in their care.[66]

3.3 GLBA and FTC Safeguards Rule

In late October 2021, the FTC published new regulations implementing the GLBA which are more detailed than prior regulations. The new regulations implementing the GLBA provide specific cybersecurity standards for safeguarding customer information by requiring a "comprehensive information security program." Important definitions can be found in §314.2. There are definitions for such terms as Information Security Program, Encryption, Financial Institutions, Multi-Factor Authentication, Nonpublic Personal Information, Penetration Testing, Security Event and Personally Identifiable Financial Information.[67]

The Safeguards Rule requires an information security program. Information Security Program is defined as "the administrative, technical or physical safeguards you use to access, collect, distribute, process, protect, store, use, transmit, dispose of, or otherwise handle customer information." The Safeguards Rule contains extensive definitions concerning the customer information subject to the rule. Customer information is defined as, "any record containing nonpublic personal information about a customer [in any] form that is handled or maintained by or on behalf of you or your affiliates." Non-public information is defined as "Personally identifiable financial information" and "[a]ny list, description or other grouping of consumers (and publicly available information

---

[66] FEDERAL TRADE COMMISSION, 16 CFR Part 314, RIN 3084-AB35, *Standards for Safeguarding Customer Information* (October 27, 2021), available at Standards for Safeguarding Customer Information (ftc.gov).

[67] 16 C.F.R. §314.2 (2021).

pertaining to them) that is derived using any personally identifiable financial information that is not publicly available." Importantly, the regulation clarifies what nonpublic information does not include such as publicly available information or "list, description or other grouping" that was not created from using "personally identifiable financial information that is not publicly available." Personally identifiable financial information includes any information that a consumer provides to the institution in a financial transaction. Personally identifiable financial information does not include, in part, "[i]nformation that does not identify a consumer, such as aggregate information or blind data that does not contain personal identifiers such as account numbers, names or addresses." Publicly available information is defined as "any information that you have a reasonable basis to believe is lawfully made available to the general public from: (i) Federal, State, or local government records; (ii) Widely distributed media; (iii) or Disclosures to the general public that are required to be made by Federal, State, or local law." Publicly available information further includes information that "[y]ou have a reasonable basis to believe that information is lawfully made available to the general public if you have taken steps to determine: (i) That the information is of the type that is available to the general public; and (ii) Whether an individual can direct that the information not be made available to the general public and, if so, that your consumer has not done so." Examples are provides such as government records including "real estate records and security interest filings." Reasonable basis is defined with examples that include mortgage information that is included in a public record where the mortgage is recorded.

Penetration Testing is "a test methodology in which assessors attempt to circumvent or defeat the security features of an information system by attempting penetration of databases or controls from outside or inside your information systems." Security Event is "an event resulting in unauthorized access to, or disruption or misuse of, an information system, information stored on such information system, or customer information held in physical form."

Section 314.3 provides the standards for the safeguarding of customer information. The standards include an information security program and objectives. The information security program mandates a written comprehensive information security program based on administrative, technical, and physical safeguards appropriate for the size and complexity of the organization, "the nature and scope" of the organization's activities, and the customer information sensitivity level. The information security program must be designed to meet the stated objectives of (1) Insure the security and confidentiality of customer information; (2) Protect against any anticipated threats or hazards to the security or integrity of such information; and (3) Protect against unauthorized access to or use of such information that could result in substantial harm or inconvenience to any customer.[68] The designated elements can be found in §314.4.[69] Some of the elements include, designating an employee to be responsible for the information security program; utilizing a risk assessment process to identify reasonably foreseeable internal and external risks; safeguards to protect against risks such authentication; utilize measures to dispose of unneeded data; testing security measures; have procedures for change management; provide security training; and oversee service providers. Financial institutions with less than five thousand customers are exempt from certain elements such as a written risk assessment, certain testing requirements and incident planning.[70]

3.4 FTC GBLA/FTC Safeguards Rule Cases

Per the FTC's enforcement data base, the following cases are at least partially categorized as GLBA cases since 2011.[71] Of course, that does not mean that every case covers the Safeguard Rule because there are other causes of action under the GBLA such as the Privacy Rule and our focus is on the Safeguard Rule.

Updated	Title	FTC Matter/File No.
December 15, 2020	Ascension Data & Analytics, LLC, in the Matter of (Administrative)	192 3126

[68] 16 C.F.R. §314.3 (2021).
[69] 16 C.F.R. §314.4 (2021).
[70] 16 C.F.R. §314.6 (2021).
[71] *See Cases and Proceedings: Advanced Search*, FEDERAL TRADE COMMISSION, https://www.ftc.gov/enforcement/cases-proceedings/advanced-search?combine=&date_filter%5Bmax%5D%5Bdate%5D=&date_filter%5Bmin%5D%5Bdate%5D=&field_case_action_type_value=All&field_competition_topics_tid=All&field_consumer_protection_topics_tid=250&field_enforcement_type_tid=All&field_federal_court_tid=All&field_industry_tid=All&field_matter_number_value=&field_mission_tid_1=All&field_release_date_value%5Bmax%5D%5Bdate%5D=&field_release_date_value%5Bmin%5D%5Bdate%5D=&items_per_page=20 (last visited May 16, 2021) (listing the different case names from most recent to least recent with an advanced search option).

January 7, 2020	Mortgage Solutions FCS, Inc. (Federal)	182 3199
September 6, 2019	LightYear Dealer Technologies, LLC, In the Matter of (Administrative)	172 3051
July 31 2019	Equifax, Inc. (Federal)	172 3203
May 24, 2018	PayPal, Inc., In the Matter of (Administrative)	162 3102
November 8, 2017	TaxSlayer, In the Matter of (Administrative)	1023172
November 7, 2012	PLS Financial Services, Inc., et al. (Federal)	1023172
August 19, 2011	ACRAnet, Inc., In the Matter of (Administrative)	092 3088
August 19, 2011	SettlementOne Credit Corporation (Administrative)	082 3208
August 19, 2011	Fajilan and Associates, Inc., also d/b/a Statewide Credit Services, In the Matter of (Administrative)	092 3089

In *United States v. Mortgage Solutions FCS, Inc.*[72], the Plaintiff brought the action under several causes of action including "the rule regarding the Standards for Safeguarding Customer Information ('Safeguards Rule'), 16 C.F.R. Part 314, issued pursuant to Title V, Subtitle A, of the Gramm-Leach-Bliley Act ('GLB Act'), 15 U.S.C. §§ 6801(b), 6805(b)(2)."[73] The court found that Mortgage Solution qualified as a "financial institution" under Section 509(3)(A) of the GLB Act, 15 U.S.C. § 6809(3)(A), and thus, was "subject to FTC enforcement of the Safeguards Rule pursuant to Section 505 of the GLB Act, 15 U.S.C. § 6805(a)(7), 16 C.F.R. § 314.1, 16 C.F.R. § 314.2, and 12 C.F.R. § 1016.3(l)(3)."[74] In that matter, one of defendant's employees publicly disclosed customer information, including "consumers' sources of income, debt-to-income ratios, credit history, taxes, family relationships, and health [data]."

[72] *United States v. Mortgage Solutions FCS, Inc.* (January 7, 2020) Complaint.

[73] Complaint at 1–2, United States v. Mortgage Solutions FCS, Inc., No. 4:20-cv-110 (2020).

[74] Complaint at 9, United States v. Mortgage Solutions FCS, Inc., No. 4:20-cv-110 (2020).

The complaint notes that Mortgage Solutions implemented an information security program around September 2017 but made "no provision for regularly testing or assessing its own effectiveness, and in fact Defendants have failed to engage in any regular testing or assessment of the effectiveness of the Information Security Plan's key controls, systems, and procedures." Additionally, Mortgage Solutions did not have an information security program during a time period required by the Safeguards Rule until September 2017. The Defendants settled the case with the FTC and a stipulated order was entered.

In the order the term "Information Security Program" was defined as "means a comprehensive policy that is written in one or more readily accessible parts and contains administrative, technical, and physical safeguards that are appropriate to Defendants' size and complexity, the nature and scope of Defendants' activities, and the sensitivity of any customer information at issue."[75] The order addressed the security concerns by mandating minimums for an information security program.

The court also ordered third-party information security assessments for "each 2-year period thereafter for ten (10) years after issuance of the Order for the biennial Assessments." The court also required an annual certification by management that " (1) each Covered Business has established, implemented, and maintained the requirements of this Order; (2) each Covered Business is not aware of any material noncompliance that has not been (a) corrected or (b) disclosed to the Commission; and (3) includes a brief description of any Covered Incident."

3.5 Private Cause of Action Using GLBA and Safeguards Rule

In the following case, a motion to dismiss under FRCP 12(b)(6) and 9(b), a district court held that the GLBA and Safeguards Rule did not provide a private cause of action.

In *Thymes v. Gillman Companies*,[76] the plaintiff brought a total of five causes of action including violations of the Federal Trade Commission ("FTC") Safeguard Rule and the Gramm–Leach–Bliley Act ("GLBA"), and disclosure of private consumer financial information in violation of the GLBA. The defendant

---

[75] United States v. Mortgage Solutions FCS, Inc. Stipulated Order for Permanent Injunction, Civil Penalties and Other Relief.

[76] 2018 WL 1281852 (S.D. Tex. 2018).

moved to dismiss all causes of action. The court concluded that the plaintiff had no cause of action "under the GLBA, 15 U.S.C. § 68 01 et seq or under the FTC Safeguard Rule, 16 C.F.R. § 314.1 et seq." because neither authorized a private cause of action. In its ruling the court relied on "Hall v. Phenix Investigations, Inc., Civil Action No. 3:14–0665–D, 2014 WL 5697856, at *9 (N.D. Tex. Nov. 5, 2014). The court in Hall explained that "[c]onsidering that Congress expressly provided for administrative and criminal enforcement of GLBA, 'it is highly improbable that Congress absentmindedly forgot to mention an intended private action.'" Hall, 2014 WL 5697856 at *9. Based on the plain readings of the statute and the regulation, the court agrees with the holding[] of Hall . . . that the GLBA does not provide a private right of action." The court further reasoned that "[b]ecause the FTC Safeguards Rule implements the enforcement provision of the GLBA, and because the GLBA does not provide a private cause of action, the court concludes that the FTC Safeguards Rule does not provide a private cause of action."

In the following data breach case, *In re Equifax Customer Data Security Breach Litigation*,[77] the district court held that although the GLBA could not serve as the basis of a negligence per se claim, the Safeguards Rule could serve as the basis of such a claim in the data breach context.

The Equifax data breach received a lot of media exposure. It was on September 7, 2017 that Equifax announced the data breach that was one of the largest data breaches in history. "From mid-May through the end of July 2017, hackers stole the personal information of nearly 150 million Americans." The data, classified as personally identifiable information ("PII") included but was not limited to names, Social Security numbers, birth dates, addresses, driver's license numbers, images of taxpayer ID cards and passports, photographs associated with government-issued identification, payment card information. The plaintiffs tied the data breach to "the direct result of Equifax's disregard for cybersecurity." Per the plaintiffs, Equifax had been repeatedly warned "that its cybersecurity was dangerously deficient, and that it was vulnerable to data theft and security breaches." And to make matters worse, "Equifax had suffered multiple security breaches in the past, showing that the Data Breach was not an isolated incident." "However, despite these warnings, Equifax did not take

[77] 371 F.Supp.3d 1150 (N.D. Ga. 2019).

the necessary steps to improve its data security or prepare for the known cybersecurity risks."

The plaintiffs' negligence per se claim alleged that "Equifax violated the Gramm-Leach-Bliley Act, Section 5 of the FTC Act, and similar state statutes, by maintaining security programs and safeguards that 'were not appropriate to Equifax's size and complexity' and by 'mishandling consumer data and not using reasonable measures to protect PII and by not complying with applicable industry standards.'" In order to succeed on this claim, "the plaintiff must show that it is within the class of persons intended to be protected by the statute and that the statute was meant to protect against the harm suffered." The court dismissed the negligence per se claims under the GLBA because "the GLBA does not provide a specific standard of conduct that is sufficient to give rise to a legal duty under Georgia law."

The plaintiffs also argued that Equifax "breached a statutory duty owed under the regulations implementing the GLBA" because Equifax failed to maintain reasonable data security measures to protect consumer information violates the Safeguards Rule, which constitutes a violation of the GLBA." Equifax argued that "the Safeguards Rule, like the GLBA itself, cannot serve as the basis for a statutory duty because it merely provides general requirements for data security, and does not provide an ascertainable standard of conduct." The court responded that "that the Safeguards Rule provides an ascertainable standard of conduct permitting it to serve as the basis for a negligence per se claim." The court reasoned that "[i]n contrast to the GLBA, the Safeguards Rule provides for certain duties that financial institutions must perform, and provides an ascertainable standard of conduct." Accordingly, the court found that the plaintiffs' allegations were "sufficient to avoid dismissal."

3.6 Other Legal Regulation Concerning Financial Institutions[78]

As one might expect, the focus of the FTC's GLBA enforcement is on protecting consumers, which is the normal jurisdiction of the FTC. But there are other federal agencies that have jurisdiction and oversight responsibilities over financial institutions and thus, are also empowered under the GLBA to promulgate and enforce cyber security guidelines within the

[78] This section is not intended to be comprehensive.

direction of the GLBA. These federal agencies are known as federal banking agencies. Title 12 U.S. Code Section 1462 defines Federal Banking Agencies as:

- Office of the Comptroller of the Currency (OCC)
- Board of Governors of the Federal Reserve System and
- Federal Deposit Insurance Corporation

These federal banking agencies enforce cybersecurity standards for financial institutions within their jurisdiction through the Interagency Guidelines Establishing Information Security Standards, known as the "Security Guidelines." The Security Guidelines apply to the following types of financial institutions:

> National banks, Federal branches and Federal agencies of foreign banks and any subsidiaries of these entities (except brokers, dealers, persons providing insurance, investment companies, and investment advisers) (OCC); member banks (other than national banks), branches and agencies of foreign banks (other than Federal branches, Federal agencies, and insured State branches of foreign banks), commercial lending companies owned or controlled by foreign banks, Edge and Agreement Act Corporations, bank holding companies and their nonbank subsidiaries or affiliates (except brokers, dealers, persons providing insurance, investment companies, and investment advisers) (Board); state non-member banks, insured state branches of foreign banks, and any subsidiaries of such entities (except brokers, dealers, persons providing insurance, investment companies, and investment advisers) (FDIC); and insured savings associations and any subsidiaries of such savings associations (except brokers, dealers, persons providing

insurance, investment companies, and investment advisers) (OTS).[79]

Another Federal agency involved in financial institution cybersecurity standards is the Federal Financial Institutions Examination Council (FFIEC). The FFIEC provides a nice summary[80] of the Federal agency enforcement actions by agency and type of financial institution:

Enforcement actions and orders against institutions or their affiliated parties can be found at the website of the institution's regulator:

Board of Governors of the Federal Reserve System (FRB)	▸ State member banks ▸ Bank holding companies ▸ Nonbank subsidiaries of bank holding companies ▸ Savings and loan holding companies ▸ Edge and agreement corporations ▸ Branches and agencies of foreign banking organizations operating in the United States and their parent banks ▸ Officers, directors, employees, and certain other categories of individuals associated with the above banks, companies, and organizations (referred to as "institution-affiliated parties")
Federal Deposit Insurance Corporation (FDIC)	▸ Insured State chartered banks that are not members of the Federal Reserve System (State nonmember banks) ▸ Insured branches of foreign banks ▸ Officers, directors, employees, controlling shareholders, agents, and certain other categories of individuals

[79] *Interagency Guidelines Establishing Information Security Standards*, BOARD OF GOVERNORS OF THE FED. RES. SYS., https://www.federalreserve.gov/supervisionreg/interagencyguidelines.htm (last visited May 16, 2021) (referring to FN 2).

[80] *Enforcement Actions and Orders*, FED. FIN. INST. EXAMINATION COUNCIL, https://www.ffiec.gov/enforcement.htm (last modified Apr. 15, 2020, 11:10 AM).

	(institution-affiliated parties) associated with such institutions
National Credit Union Administration (NCUA)	▸ Credit unions
Office of the Comptroller of the Currency (OCC)	▸ National banks and their subsidiaries ▸ Federally chartered savings associations and their subsidiaries ▸ Federal Branches and agencies of foreign banks ▸ Institution-affiliated parties (IAPs), including (a) Officers, directors, and employees, and (b) A bank's controlling stockholders, agents, and certain other individuals

The Financial Services Information Sharing and Analysis Center (FS-ISAC) is also worth noting. "FS-ISAC, or the Financial Services Information Sharing and Analysis Center, is the global financial industry's go to resource for cyber and physical threat intelligence analysis and sharing."[81] Additional information on FS-ISAC can be found at www.fsisac.com.

The following sections will first discuss security guidelines and then will address enforcement actions.

3.6[A] SECURITY GUIDELINES

The following material concerns the Security Guidelines.

"Background and Overview of Security Guidelines

---

[81] *Applications for Deposit Insurance Additional Resources*, FED. DEPOSIT INS. CORP., https://www.fdic.gov/regulations/applications/depositinsurance/contact.html (last visited May 16, 2021).

The Security Guidelines implement section 501(b) of the Gramm-Leach-Bliley Act (GLB Act) and section 216 of the Fair and Accurate Credit Transactions Act of 2003 (FACT Act). The Security Guidelines establish standards relating to administrative, technical, and physical safeguards to ensure the security, confidentiality, integrity and the proper disposal of customer information.

Each of the requirements in the Security Guidelines regarding the proper disposal of customer information also apply to personal information a financial institution obtains about individuals regardless of whether they are the institution's customers ("consumer information"). Consumer information includes, for example, a credit report about: (1) an individual who applies for but does not obtain a loan; (2) an individual who guarantees a loan; (3) an employee; or (4) a prospective employee. A financial institution must require, by contract, its service providers that have access to consumer information to develop appropriate measures for the proper disposal of the information.

Under the Security Guidelines, each financial institution must:

- Develop and maintain an effective information security program tailored to the complexity of its operations, and
- Require, by contract, service providers that have access to its customer information to take appropriate steps to protect the security and confidentiality of this information.

  The standards set forth in the Security Guidelines are consistent with the principles the Agencies follow when examining the security programs of financial institutions.[6] Each financial institution must identify and evaluate risks to its customer information, develop a plan to mitigate the risks, implement the plan, test the plan, and update the plan when necessary. If an Agency finds that a financial institution's performance is deficient under the Security Guidelines, the Agency may take action, such as requiring that the institution file a compliance plan."[82]

Each of the federal banking agencies has adopted amendments to their rules and regulations to address the Security Guidelines: 12 CFR part 30 for the Office of the Comptroller of the Currency; 12 CFR part 263 for the Board of Governors of the Federal Reserve System; and, 12 CFR part 308, subpart R and 12 CFR part 391, subpart B for the Federal Deposit Insurance Corporation.

3.6[B] ENFORCEMENT

The Federal bank agencies and the NCUA can instigate enforcement actions in this field. Next, a look at OCC enforcement.

3.6[B][I] OCC ENFORCEMENT

The OCC supervises the following entities and has the statutory authority to take enforcement actions against them:

National banks and their subsidiaries
Federally chartered savings associations and their subsidiaries
Federal branches and agencies of foreign banks
Institution-affiliated parties (IAPs), including:

Officers, directors, and employees

A bank's controlling stockholders, agents, and certain other individuals.[83]

The OCC maintains an enforcement group that:

---

[82] *Interagency Guidelines Establishing Information Security Standards*, BOARD OF GOVERNORS OF THE FED. RES. SYS., https://www.federalreserve.gov/supervisionreg/interagencyguidelines.htm (last visited May 16, 2021).

[83] *Enforcement Actions Search Tool*, OFF. OF THE COMPTROLLER OF THE CURRENCY, https://apps.occ.gov/EASearch/?Search=capital+one&Category=&ItemsPerPage=10&Sort=&AutoCompleteSelection= (last visited May 16, 2021).

Serves as the OCC's counsel on matters related to investigations, enforcement actions, and administrative litigation;

Conducts formal and informal investigations;

Advises on whether OCC-supervised institutions and institution affiliated parties (IAPs) have engaged in unsafe or unsound banking practices, violations of laws and regulations, or breaches of fiduciary duty;

Handles matters involving Bank Secrecy Act/Anti-Money Laundering law violations, consumer law violations, and fraud related actions, among other areas;

Advises the OCC's supervisory, compliance, and licensing units on the legal requirements for enforcement actions and on enforcement-related policies and procedures;

Litigates all OCC enforcement actions before the Office of Financial Institution Adjudication (OFIA), including civil money penalties, prohibitions and removals, and cease-and-desist orders;

Refers criminal acts involving OCC-supervised institutions or IAPs to the U.S. Department of Justice; and

Coordinates with the federal banking agencies; and other regulatory agencies, including the Financial Crimes Enforcement Network, the U.S. Securities and Exchange Commission, and the Consumer Financial Protection Bureau on matters involving OCC-supervised institutions.[84]

---

[84] *Chief Counsel's Office*, OFF. OF THE COMPTROLLER OF THE CURRENCY, https://www.occ.gov/about/who-we-are/organizations/chief-counsels-office/index-chief-counsels-office.html (Expand Enforcement under Sub-Organizations; last visited May 16, 2021).

3.6[B][II] FDIC ENFORCEMENT

The FDIC can also enforce the Security Guidelines:

> **SAFETY AND SOUNDNESS ORDERS**
> Section 39 of the FDI Act requires the federal banking authorities to establish various safety and soundness standards. The Act allows the FDIC to request corrective plans from financial institutions that do not meet the standards, which are set forth in Part 364 and the interagency guidelines in Appendix A and Appendix B to Part 364.
> If the FDIC requests an informal compliance plan to correct identified deficiencies and the institution fails to submit an acceptable plan, or fails to adhere to a submitted plan, the FDIC will pursue an enforceable order under Section 8 of the FDI Act. In addition, the FDIC may require by order, other corrective measures, such as restricted asset growth, higher capital levels, limits on deposit interest rates, or any other measure deemed necessary to effect corrective action.[85]

Also, as one of the federal bank agencies, the Federal Reserve System can also enforce the Security Guidelines as part of unsafe or unsound practices.

The Federal Reserve supervises the following entities and has the statutory authority to take formal enforcement actions against them:

- State member banks
- Bank holding companies
- Savings and loan holding companies
- Nonbank subsidiaries of bank holding companies and of savings and loan holding companies
- Edge Act and agreement corporations

---

[85] FED. DEP'T OF INS. CORP., FORMAL ADMINISTRATIVE ACTIONS 8 (2016), *available at* https://www.fdic.gov/regulations/safety/manual/section15-1.pdf.

- Branches and agencies of foreign banking organizations operating in the United States and their parent banks
- Systemically important nonbank financial companies designated by the Financial Stability Oversight Council (FSOC) for supervision by the Federal Reserve
- Officers, directors, employees, and certain other categories of individuals or entities associated with the above banks, companies, and organizations (referred to as "institution-affiliated parties")

Generally, the Federal Reserve takes formal enforcement actions against the above entities and individuals for violations of laws, rules, or regulations, unsafe or unsound practices, breaches of fiduciary duty, and violations of final orders. Formal enforcement actions include cease and desist orders, written agreements, prompt corrective action directives, removal and prohibition orders, and orders assessing civil money penalties.

Since August 1989, the Federal Reserve has made all final enforcement orders public in accordance with the Financial Institutions Reform, Recovery, and Enforcement Act of 1989; since November 1990, it has made written agreements public in accordance with the Crime Control Act of 1990. Since July 21, 2011, the Federal Reserve has made public all final enforcement actions taken by the Federal Reserve regarding savings and loan holding companies. Formal enforcement actions taken by the Federal Reserve before August 1989 are not public.

Since 2008, the Federal Reserve has posted "Section 19 Letters" on the Board of Governors' public website. Reserve Banks send Section 19 Letters (referring to section 19 of the Federal Deposit Insurance Act, 12 U.S.C. § 1829) to individuals, generally institution-affiliated parties of entities supervised by the Federal Reserve, who have been convicted of a crime involving dishonesty, a breach of trust, or money laundering, or who have entered

> into a pretrial diversion or similar program in connection with a prosecution for such a crime. Section 19 prohibits any individual with such a conviction, or who has entered into such a program, from participating in the affairs of insured depository institutions, their holding companies, or credit unions without prior regulatory or judicial approval.[86]

3.6[C] National Credit Union Administration

The National Credit Union Administration (NCUA) also participates under the GBLA.

On June 6, 2000, the NCUA Board approved a proposal to revise 12 CFR part 748 to include requirements for administrative, technical, and physical safeguards for member records and information, as required by the GLB Act. 65 FR 37302, Jun. 14, 2000.[87]

> 12 CFR part 748 in relevant part:
>
> §748.0 Security program.
>
> (a) Each federally insured credit union will develop a written security program within 90 days of the effective date of insurance.
>
> (b) The security program will be designed to:
>
> (1) Protect each credit union office from robberies, burglaries, larcenies, and embezzlement;
>
> (2) Ensure the security and confidentiality of member records, protect against the anticipated threats or hazards to the security or integrity of such records, and protect against unauthorized access to or use of such records that could result in substantial harm or serious inconvenience to a member;

---

[86] *Enforcement Actions: About*, Board of Governors of the Fed. Res. Sys., https://www.federalreserve.gov/supervisionreg/enforcement-actions-about.htm (last visited May 16, 2021).

[87] Nat'l Credit Union Admin., 12 CFR Part 748: Guidelines for Safeguarding Member Information, *available at* https://www.ffiec.gov/exam/infobase/documents/02-ncu-12_cfr_748_app_a_safeguard_info-010100.pdf.

(3) Respond to incidents of unauthorized access to or use of member information that could result in substantial harm or serious inconvenience to a member;

(4) Assist in the identification of persons who commit or attempt such actions and crimes, and

(5) Prevent destruction of vital records, as defined in 12 CFR part 749.

(c) Each Federal credit union, as part of its information security program, must properly dispose of any consumer information the Federal credit union maintains or otherwise possesses, as required under §717.83 of this chapter.

[50 FR 53295, Dec. 31, 1985, as amended at 53 FR 4845, Feb. 18, 1988; 66 FR 8161, Jan. 30, 2001; 69 FR 69274, Nov. 29, 2004; 70 FR 22778, May 2, 2005][88]

Appendix A to Part 748 in relevant part:

Appendix A to Part 748—Guidelines for Safeguarding Member Information

The NCUA also enforces:

In working to protect the credit union system and the Share Insurance Fund from losses, NCUA employs several supervisory tools and enforcement actions depending on the severity of the situation. Some of these tools include letters of understanding and agreement, administrative orders and consent orders.

Administrative Orders

The NCUA issues Administrative Orders when it finds that a credit union or persons affiliated with a credit union have violated a law, a rule or regulation, or engaged in an unsafe or unsound practice.

[88] 12 C.F.R. § 748.0 (2019).

Letters of Understanding and Agreement

A Letters of Understanding is essentially a contract between the NCUA and a credit union, its officials or both, in which the credit union or officials agree to take, or not take, certain specified actions. NCUA also requires Letters of Understanding for newly chartered credit unions, and to grant permanent special assistance.

Consent Orders

NCUA assesses civil monetary penalties against credit unions that fail to file a Call Report on time. Here are lists of credit unions that agreed to civil monetary penalties for not submitting their quarterly Call Report information by the filing deadline.
https://www.ncua.gov/regulation-supervision/enforcement-actions

Administrative Orders are formal enforcement orders issued by the NCUA pursuant to Section 206 of the Federal Credit Union Act (FCUA) (12 U.S.C. § 1786). Generally, the NCUA issues Administrative Orders when it finds that a credit union or persons affiliated with a credit union have violated a law, rule or regulation, breached a fiduciary duty, or engaged in an unsafe or unsound practice.
The three most common orders issued by the NCUA include:

- An **Order to Cease and Desist**, which requires a party to take action (or refrain from taking action), including making restitution;

- An **Order or Notice of Prohibition**, which prohibits a party from ever working for a federally insured financial institution; and

- An **Order Assessing Civil Money Penalties**.

Prior to the issuance of an Administrative Order, the Federal Credit Union Act provides due process rights, which include the ability to have an administrative hearing before the Office of Financial Institution Adjudication, and to appeal the agency's decision to issue an order to the U.S. Circuit Court of Appeals.[89]

3.6[D] U.S. Commodity Futures Trading Commission

The U.S. Commodity Futures Trading Commission (CFTC) is another federal agency participating in the regulation of cybersecurity practices.

CFTC Press release last update on February 26, 2014:

> The U.S. Commodity Futures Trading Commission's (Commission) Division of Swap Dealer and Intermediary Oversight (Division) today issued a Staff Advisory that outlines recommended best practices for covered financial institutions to comply with Title V and Part 160 of the Commission's regulations concerning security safeguards.
>
> Congress enacted Title V of the Gramm-Leach-Bliley Act (GLBA) in 1999 to ensure that financial institutions respect the privacy of their customers and protect the security and confidentiality of nonpublic personal information. In enacting the GLBA, Congress directed certain Federal financial regulators to adopt and implement rules to achieve Title V's goals. These recommendations are consistent with guidelines and regulations issued by other Federal financial regulators.

---

[89] *Administrative Orders*, NAT'L CREDIT UNION ADMIN., https://www.ncua.gov/regulation-supervision/enforcement-actions/administrative-orders (last visited May 16, 2021) (emphasis added).

See CFTC Staff Advisory 14-21 under Related Links.[90]

3.6[E] Federal Financial Institutions Examination Council

Another Federal agency that is involved in financial institution cybersecurity standards is the Federal Financial Institutions Examination Council (FFIEC).

The Federal Financial Institutions Examination Council (FFIEC) was established on March 10, 1979, pursuant to title X of the Financial Institutions Regulatory and Interest Rate Control Act of 1978 (FIRA), Public Law 95-630. In 1989, title XI of the Financial Institutions Reform, Recovery and Enforcement Act of 1989 (FIRREA) established The Appraisal Subcommittee (ASC) within the Examination Council.

The Council is a formal interagency body empowered to prescribe uniform principles, standards, and report forms for the federal examination of financial institutions by the Board of Governors of the Federal Reserve System (FRB), the Federal Deposit Insurance Corporation (FDIC), the National Credit Union Administration (NCUA), the Office of the Comptroller of the Currency (OCC), and the Consumer Financial Protection Bureau (CFPB) and to make recommendations to promote uniformity in the supervision of financial institutions. To encourage the application of uniform examination principles and standards by the state and federal supervisory authorities, the Council established, in accordance with the requirement of the statute, the State Liaison Committee composed of five representatives of state supervisory agencies. In accordance with the Financial Services Regulatory Relief Act of 2006, a representative state regulator was added as a voting member of the Council in October 2006.

---

[90] Press Release, Commodity Futures Trading Comm'n, CFTC's Division of Swap Dealer and Intermediary. Oversight Issues a Staff Advisory on Best Practices for Complying with the Gramm-Leach-Bliley Act Security. Safeguards (Feb. 26, 2014).

The Council is responsible for developing uniform reporting systems for federally supervised financial institutions, their holding companies, and the nonfinancial institution subsidiaries of those institutions and holding companies. It conducts schools for examiners employed by the five federal member agencies represented on the Council and makes those schools available to employees of state agencies that supervise financial institutions.

The Council was given additional statutory responsibilities by section 340 of the Housing and Community Development Act of 1980 to facilitate public access to data that depository institutions must disclose under the Home Mortgage Disclosure Act of 1975 (HMDA) and the aggregation of annual HMDA data, by census tract, for each metropolitan statistical area (MSA).[91]

The Federal Financial Institutions Examination Council (FFIEC) members are taking a number of initiatives to raise the awareness of financial institutions and their critical third-party service providers with respect to cybersecurity risks and the need to identify, assess, and mitigate these risks in light of the increasing volume and sophistication of cyber threats.

Financial institutions are increasingly dependent on information technology and telecommunications to deliver services to consumers and business every day. Disruption, degradation, or unauthorized alteration of information and systems that support these services can affect operations, institutions, and their core processes, and undermine confidence in the nation's financial services sector.

In June 2013, the FFIEC announced the creation of the Cybersecurity and Critical Infrastructure Working Group to enhance communication among the FFIEC member agencies and build on existing efforts to strengthen the activities of other interagency and private sector groups. In addition, the FFIEC began assessing and enhancing the state of the industry preparedness and identifying gaps in the regulators' examination procedures and training that can be closed to strengthen the oversight of cybersecurity readiness.

---

[91] *About the FFIEC*, FED. FIN. INST. EXAMINATION COUNCIL, https://www.ffiec.gov/about.htm (last modified Apr. 15, 2020, 11:10 AM).

The National Institute of Standards and Technology defines cybersecurity as "the process of protecting information by preventing, detecting, and responding to attacks." As part of cybersecurity, institutions should consider management of internal and external threats and vulnerabilities to protect information assets and the supporting infrastructure from technology-based attacks.[92]

[92] *Cybersecurity Awareness*, FED. FIN. INST. EXAMINATION COUNCIL, https://www.ffiec.gov/cybersecurity.htm (last modified Aug. 13, 2020, 10:27 AM).

CHAPTER FOUR. U.S. Securities and Exchange Commission Cybersecurity

4.1 Introduction

Congress created the SEC through the Securities Act of 1934. Congress also passed the Securities Act of 1933. These congressional actions were designed to restore confidence during the Great Depression. As one might expect, cybersecurity was not on the minds of Congress during these actions. But with the advent of computers and computerized trading, the SEC has had to address cybersecurity.

This chapter includes an examination of regulations enforced by the SEC as well as that enforcement. Notably, the SEC recently adopted additional regulations concerning cybersecurity, specifically regarding disclosures concerning companies' cybersecurity programs and for material issues. An overview of the requirements of those regulations is provided. This chapter also reviews private litigation involving securities fraud and cybersecurity and disclosure issues related to cybersecurity.

4.2 Regulation S-P and Regulation SCI

The main regulations that the SEC relies on for cybersecurity are: 1) Privacy of Consumer Financial Information (Regulation S-P), 17 CFR PART 248; 2) Regulation SCI (Systems; Compliance; Integrity) plus Form SCI, 17 CFR PARTS 240, 242, and 249.

REGULATION S-P

Regulation S-P, which became effective on November 13, 2000, "requires registered broker-dealers, investment companies, and investment advisers to 'adopt written policies and procedures that address administrative, technical, and physical safeguards for the protection of customer records and information.'"[93]

The SEC promulgated Regulation S-P in response to "section 504 of the Gramm-Leach-Bliley Act." The SEC states that Section 504 places the onus on the SEC and other relevant agencies to create regulations directed to financial institutions and their stewardship over personal data. Regulation S-P is the SEC's product of that direction by Congress. The Regulation S-P is directed to "investment advisers registered with the Commission, brokers, dealers, and investment companies." The SEC has stated that:

> Under the Gramm-Leach-Bliley Act, a financial institution must provide its customers with a notice of its privacy policies and practices, and must not disclose nonpublic personal information about a consumer to nonaffiliated third parties unless the institution provides certain information to the consumer and the consumer has not elected to opt out of the disclosure. The Act also requires the Commission to establish for financial institutions appropriate standards to protect customer information.[94]

Amendments to Regulation S-P covering the Disposal of Consumer Report Information became effective on January 11, 2005. The SEC's amendments are intended to ensure the "proper disposal of consumer report information and records."[95] Those amendments require, "that any person who maintains or possesses consumer report information or any compilation of consumer report information derived from a consumer report for a business purpose must properly dispose of the information."[96] The amendments also

---

[93] 17 C.F.R. § 248.30 (2000).

[94] FINAL RULE: PRIVACY OF CONSUMER FINANCIAL INFORMATION, S.E.C. (Nov. 18, 2003), *available at* https://www.sec.gov/rules/final/34-42974.htm.

[95] Final Rule: Disposal of Consumer Report Information, S.E.C. (Dec. 2, 2004), *available at* https://www.sec.gov/rules/final/34-50781.htm.

[96] *Id.*

require that "policies and procedures adopted under the safeguard rule to be in writing."[97]

The relevant text of Regulation S-P can be found in section 248.30, entitled "Procedures to safeguard customer records and information; disposal of consumer report information." While confidentiality, integrity, and availability (CIA) are common goals of cybersecurity; administrative, technical, and physical safeguards are a common means to achieve those goals. And they can be thought of as providing a layered defense in depth. In other words, if the physical layer protections are breached then the perpetrator still has to get through the technical and administrative safeguard layers.

REGULATION SCI

In November 2014, the SEC adopted the Regulation Systems Compliance and Integrity and Form SCI. The goal was to "strengthen the technology infrastructure of the U.S. securities markets."

The rules were "designed to:

- Reduce the occurrence of systems issues;
- Improve resiliency when systems problems do occur;
- Enhance the Commission's oversight and enforcement of securities market technology infrastructure."

The regulation covers "SCI entities" that "includes self-regulatory organizations ('SROs'), including stock and options exchanges, registered clearing agencies, FINRA and the MSRB, alternative trading systems ('ATSs'), that trade NMS and non-NMS stocks exceeding specified volume thresholds, disseminators of consolidated market data ('plan processors'), and certain exempt clearing agencies."[98]

---

[97] *Id.*

[98] *Spotlight on Regulation SCI*, U.S. SECURITIES AND EXCHANGE COMMISSION, https://www.sec.gov/spotlight/regulation-sci.shtml (last modified Dec. 9, 2016).

The regulation primarily covers "the systems of SCI entities that directly support any one of six key securities market functions – trading, clearance and settlement, order routing, market data, market regulation, and market surveillance . . ."[99] Section 242.1001 covers obligations related to policies and procedures of SCI entities and lays out the requirements for the capacity, integrity, resiliency, availability, and security for SCI systems.

Capacity, integrity, resiliency, availability, and security are very close to the CIA basic security tenants of confidentiality, integrity, and availability. These requirements are all about preventing system down-time because the financial markets would react negatively to systems not being available. Also, notice that these requirements are similar to that of a private corporation, who's lifeblood may depend on its systems and where down systems can equate to lost revenue and lowered public opinion. So, basically, the SEC is giving notice that if a company wants to operate in this space, it must establish excellent business continuity planning. One interesting departure from CIA is capacity. Here the SEC is concerned about having enough capacity within the system, probably to handle high-volume situations that could cause market panic if the systems do not have enough capacity to handle all requests.

Section 242.1002 describes obligations related to SCI events. An SCI event per section 242.1000 "means and event at an SCI entity that constitutes:

(1) A systems disruption;
(2) A systems compliance issue; or
(3) A systems intrusion."

Section 242.1006 covers electronic filing and submission requirements including the use of Form SCI (found in section 249.1900).

It is worth noting at this point that Regulation S-P is focused on customer data, whereas Regulation SCI is focused on an

[99] *Id.*

entities' SCI systems. Accordingly, a company may be regulated under Regulation S-P because of its business plan and customer data, but not be regulated under Regulation SCI because its business model does not make it an SCI entity.

4.3 SEC Enforcement

Now that we have covered the SEC security regulations, we will examine how the SEC enforces those regulations. The SEC, through the Division of Enforcement's Cyber Unit, can file actions enforcing cybersecurity related provisions directed to regulated entities. The SEC's enforcement action authority is broader than that and can include violations involving "digital assets, initial coin offerings and cryptocurrencies; cybersecurity controls at regulated entities; issuer disclosures of cybersecurity incidents and risks; trading on the basis of hacked nonpublic information; and cyber-related manipulations, such as brokerage account takeovers and market manipulations using electronic and social media platforms."[100]

The Cyber Unit was created in September 2017. However, SEC enforcement actions related to cyber security predate the creation of the Cyber Unit thus, it is apparent that the SEC was active in the cybersecurity law enforcement space long before it created the Cyber Unit. Apparently, the creation of the Cyber Unit was a way to maintain focus on Cyber Security.[101]

---

[100] *See Spotlight on Cybersecurity, the SEC and You*, U.S. SECURITIES AND EXCHANGE COMMISSION, https://www.sec.gov/spotlight/cybersecurity (last modified Feb. 26, 2021).

[101] The Financial Industry Regulatory Authority (FINRA) is a nonprofit which Congress has authorized to regulate brokers and dealers, and enforces SEC regulations concerning cybersecurity. See FINRA, *Cybersecurity*, available at Cybersecurity | FINRA.org. Notably, in 2016, FINRA fined 12 securities dealers around $14.4 million for cybersecurity related issues. See FINRA, *FINRA Fines 12 Firms a Total of $14.4 Million for Failing to Protect Records From Alteration*, (Dec. 26, 2016), available at FINRA Fines 12 Firms a Total of $14.4 Million for Failing to Protect Records From Alteration | FINRA.org.

4.3[A] OVERVIEW OF SEC ENFORCEMENT ACTIONS

The SEC categorizes its cybersecurity enforcement actions as one of:

1) digital assets / initial coin offerings;
2) account intrusions;
3) hacker / insider trading;
4) market manipulation / false tweets / fake websites;
5) regulated entities – cybersecurity controls and safeguarding customer information;
6) public company disclosure and controls
7) trading suspensions

The SEC charts actions brought by the SEC across the different potential categories of actions.[102]

4.3[B] SEC ENFORCEMENT ACTIONS

In the Matter of Virtu America's LLC (September 30, 2019),[103] the SEC relied on the Regulation Systems Compliance and Integrity (Regulation SCI) that went into effect on February 3, 2015 in bringing its enforcement action to issue an "Order Instituting Administrative and Cease-and-Desist proceedings . . . and Imposing Remedial Sanctions and a Cease-and-Desist Order."[104]

The SEC identified cyber security deficiencies with policies and procedures found after a break-in that compromised customer data.[105] The Commission found that the defendant failed to "comply with Regulation Systems Compliance and Integrity ('Regulation SCI')" when its alternative trading system ("ATS") exceeded a

---

[102] *See Cyber Enforcement Actions*, U.S. SECURITIES AND EXCHANGE COMMISSION, https://www.sec.gov/spotlight/cybersecurity-enforcement-actions.

[103] *In the Matter of Virtu America's LLC*, Release No. 34-87155 (September 30, 2019).

[104] Order Instituting Administrative and Cease-and-Desist Proceedings, Virtu Americas LLC., No. 3-19563 (Sept. 30, 2019).

[105] *SEC Charges Firm with Deficient Cybersecurity Procedures*, U.S. SECURITIES AND EXCHANGE COMMISSION (SEPT. 26, 2018), https://www.sec.gov/news/press-release/2018-213.

trading volume threshold that recategorized the ATS as an SCI ATS, thus requiring it to comply with "substantive provisions of Regulation SCI." The Commission claimed that the defendant did not comply with required provisions of Regulation SCI. The defendant was ordered to "cease and desist from committing or causing any violations and any future violations of Rules 1001, 1003, 1004, and 1005 of Regulation SCI, promulgated under the Exchange Act." The defendant also had to "pay a civil money penalty in the amount of $1,500,000.00 to the Securities and Exchange Commission for transfer to the general fund of the United States Treasury, subject to Exchange Act Section 21F(g)(3). If timely payment is not made, additional interest shall accrue pursuant to 31 U.S.C. §3717."

In the Matter of Voya Financial Advisors (September 26, 2018)[106], the Securities and Exchange Commission found that VFA, "a dually registered broker-dealer and investment advisor," failed "to adopt written policies and procedures reasonably designed to protect customer records and information, in violation of Rule 30(a) of Regulation S-P (17 C.F.R. § 248.30(a)) (the 'Safeguards Rule')" and also failed "to develop and implement a written Identity Theft Prevention Program as required by Rule 201 of Regulation S-ID (17 C.F.R. § 248.201) (the 'Identity Theft Red Flags Rule')." VFA "gave its independent contractor representatives ("contractor representatives") access to its brokerage customer and advisory client (hereinafter, "customer") information through a proprietary web portal." Of note, the Commission found that Voya's policies and procedures that were in place before the intrusion were deficient because VFA did not have its own cybersecurity staff and "outsourced most of its cybersecurity functions and some of its information technology functions to its parent company, Voya."

The Commission found that through its conduct, "VFA willfully violated Rule 30(a) of Regulation S-P (17 C.F.R. § 248.30(a)), which requires every broker-dealer and every investment adviser registered with the Commission to adopt written policies and procedures that are reasonably designed to safeguard customer records and information." The Commission also found that "VFA willfully violated Rule 201 of Regulation S-ID

---

[106] *In the Matter of Voya Financial Advisors*, Release No. 84288 (September 26, 2018).

(17 C.F.R. § 248.201), which requires registered broker-dealers and investment advisers that offer or maintain covered accounts to develop and implement a written Identity Theft Prevention Program that is designed to detect, prevent, and mitigate identity theft in connection with the opening of a covered account or any existing covered account." For its violations, VFA was ordered to "cease and desist from committing or causing any violations and any future violations of Rule 30(a) of Regulation S-P (17 C.F.R. § 248.30(a)) and of Rule 201 of Regulation S-ID (17 C.F.R. § 248.201)." VFA was also censured and ordered to "pay, within 10 (ten) business days of the entry of this Order, a civil money penalty in the amount of $1,000,000 to the Securities and Exchange Commission for transfer to the general fund of the United States Treasury, subject to Exchange Act Section 21F(g)(3). If timely payment is not made, additional interest shall accrue pursuant to 31 U.S.C. § 3717."

In the Matter of Morgan Stanley Smith Barney,[107] the Commission found that Morgan Stanley Smith Barney ("MSSB") failed "to adopt written policies and procedures reasonably designed to protect customer records and information, in violation of Rule 30(a) of Regulation S-P (17 C.F.R. § 248.30(a)) (the 'Safeguards Rule')." Specifically, MSSB "failed to ensure the reasonable design and proper operation of its policies and procedures in safeguarding confidential customer data."

"MSSB maintained customer PII in numerous internal databases accessible by both the BIS Portal and the FID Select Portal. Although MSSB had adopted written policies and procedures relating to the protection of customer PII, those policies and procedures were not reasonably designed to safeguard its customers' PII as required by the Safeguards Rule. For example, MSSB's written policies and procedures failed to adequately address certain key administrative, technical and physical safeguards, such as: reasonably designed and operating authorization modules for the BIS Portal and the FID Select Portal to restrict employee access to only the confidential customer data as to which such employees had a legitimate business need; auditing and/or testing of the effectiveness of such authorization

[107] *In the Matter of Morgan Stanley Smith Barney*, Release No. 4415 (June 8, 2016).

modules; and monitoring and analyzing of employee access to and use of the Portals." This behavior resulted in "MSSB willfully violated Rule 30(a) of Regulation S-P (17 C.F.R. § 248.30(a)), which requires every broker-dealer and investment adviser registered with the Commission to adopt written policies and procedures that are reasonably designed to safeguard customer records and information." The Commission ordered that "MSSB cease and desist from committing or causing any violations and any future violations of Rule 30(a) of Regulation S-P (17 C.F.R. § 248.30(a))" MSSB was also censured and instructed to, "within ten days of the entry of this Order, pay a civil money penalty in the amount of $1,000,000 to the Securities and Exchange Commission for transfer to the general fund of the United States Treasury, subject to Exchange Act Section 21F(g)(3). If timely payment is not made, additional interest shall accrue pursuant to 31 U.S.C. § 3717."

4.4 Private Litigation Concerning Securities Fraud for Data Breach

The following case concerns a major litigation brought by private parties concerning securities fraud for a significant data breach.

The *In re Equifax Securities Litigation*[108] case centers around the September 7, 2017 disclosure of the hack of the Equifax computer network by criminal hackers that resulted in the compromise of personally identifiable information. Among other allegations, the plaintiff alleged that defendants "made false or misleading statements on Equifax's website, in Equifax's SEC filings, and at Equifax Investor Conferences and Presentations. According to the Plaintiff, these false or misleading statements concerned the state of Equifax's cybersecurity, Equifax's compliance with data protection laws, regulations, and industry best practices, and Equifax's internal controls." The defendants responded that plaintiff does not have a case for securities fraud because the allegations "concern mere corporate mismanagement." The court did not find this response persuasive because "[t]he Plaintiff does not argue that the Defendants violated section 10(b) by failing to implement better cybersecurity practices. Instead, the Plaintiff contends that the Defendants violated section 10(b) by

[108] *In re Equifax Securities Litigation*, 357 F.Supp.3d 1189 (2019).

making false or misleading statements as to the strength and quality of Equifax's cybersecurity." The defendants also argued "that the statements touting the strength of Equifax's data security systems and the adequacy of Equifax's efforts to promote cybersecurity do not constitute material misrepresentations." Defendants argued that these are not material misrepresentations because "the alleged statements are not actually false or misleading because the facts pleaded do not show that Equifax's data security was actually inadequate"; and "these statements constitute inactionable puffery." Cybersecurity experts offered an opinion "that Equifax's data security failures flowed from an inadequate 'tone at the top' and that 'the real problem was a very poor focus on information security at the highest levels of the company.'"

The plaintiff alleged that Equifax's cybersecurity shortcomings included failures to "implement adequate patching processes . . . to create adequate encryption measures to protect the information in its custody . . . implement adequate authentication measures to ensure that parties attempting to access its networks were authorized to do so . . . establish mechanisms for monitoring its networks for security breaches . . . warehouse obsolete personal information." Also alleged were that Equifax "stored personal data in easily accessible public channels" and "relied on outdated and obsolete software." The court found that "[g]iven the dangerously deficient state of Equifax's cybersecurity" Equifax's cybersecurity statements were "false, or at least misleading" and were "not inactionable puffery." The court agreed with the Defendants that they "were under no duty to disclose the existence of the Data Breach before they knew it had occurred." Regarding Plaintiff's claims on Equifax's compliance with data protection laws, regulations, and best practices, the court sided with the Plaintiff because "[t]he Plaintiff does not allege that the Defendants violated section 10(b) by failing to comply with cybersecurity laws, regulations, and best practices. Instead, the Plaintiff argues that they violated section 10(b) by stating that Equifax was in compliance with these laws and regulations, when in fact it was not." The court agreed with defendants that the Plaintiff failed to plead the falsity of the Defendants' statements about Equifax's internal controls because the statements addressed Equifax's internal controls over financial reporting, instead of controls over data security.

4.5 New SEC Regulations Concerning Disclosures

On July 26, 2023, the Securities and Exchange Commission (SEC) adopted the Cybersecurity Risk Management, Strategy, Governance, and Incident Disclosure that will be included in 17 CFR Parts 229, 232, 240, and 249.[109] The rule has significant requirements for public companies on reporting security incidents and reporting on cybersecurity processes.

The new rule removes the word "breach" from the reporting equation and instead focuses on security incidents that would be "material" to an investor. With the new standard of materiality, companies can no longer argue that they did not have a breach because the incident was not reportable under state "breach" notification laws. The threshold for reporting under those laws is rather high, requiring covered information of the nature of a social security number, driver's license, or financial account information. Such covered information has long been characterized as personally identifiable information (PII). New state privacy laws have broadened this concept to any information connected to a person and labeled it as personal information or personal data. One could argue that because the definition of protected personal information has greatly broadened, that so too has the importance of cybersecurity. We will see in the state chapter that the new state privacy laws are actually privacy and cybersecurity laws. The second part of the new SEC rule is squarely centered on cybersecurity.

An additional issue concerns the extent of the disclosure. Prior SEC guidance warned against disclosing a roadmap to enable other cyber attackers to successfully breach other companies' systems which may have the same exploitable vulnerability. It is unclear how much disclosure will be enough to satisfy the SEC's desire to have the public adequately assess the impact on the value of a company based on a breach while at the same time not providing enough information which may cause more harm than benefit. Because companies have not wanted to disclose breach

---

[109] Securities and Exchange Commission, Cybersecurity Risk Management, Strategy, Governance, and Incident Disclosure Report (July 26, 2023), available at https://www.sec.gov/files/rules/final/2023/33-11216.pdf

information, the SEC may err on the side of requiring more disclosure rather than less. However, companies should be careful not to disclose technical details allowing hackers to understand how to successfully breach companies' systems.

Part C of the new rule requires "Disclosure of a Registrant's Risk Management, Strategy and Governance. The SEC made two important points in the new rule: (1) "that extensive public disclosure on how a company plans for, defends against, and responds to cyberattacks has the potential to advantage threat actors", and (2) "we confirm that the purpose of the rules is, and was at proposal, to inform investors, not to influence whether and how companies manage their cybersecurity risk."

Both points are interesting because threat actors are constantly using any information they can find to give them and advantage and these will be public disclosures. The FTC and state attorney generals may not have the same goal. The SEC noted:

> As adopted, 17 CFR 229.106(b)(1) (Regulation S-K 'Item 106(b)(1)') requires a description of 'the registrant's processes, if any, for assessing, identifying, and managing material risks from cybersecurity threat in sufficient detail for a reasonable investor to understand those processes'. We believe this revised formulation of the rule should help avoid levels of detail that may go beyond information that is material to investors and address commenters' concerns that those details could increase a company's vulnerability to cyberattack. We have also substituted the term "processes" for the proposed "policies and procedures" to avoid requiring disclosure of the kinds of operational details that could be weaponized by threat actors, and because the term "processes" more fully compasses registrants' cybersecurity practices than "policies and procedures," which suggest formal codification.[110]

[110] *Id.* at 60-61.

If this leaves you scratching your head as to how processes are any less revealing than policies and procedures, you are not alone. One can normally reverse engineer processes into policies and procedures. And, the SEC agrees, "the term 'processes' more fully compasses registrants' cybersecurity practices than 'policies and procedures'." Regardless of what it is called, a threat actor can gain an advantage from any internal knowledge that is not public. That is why companies require non-disclosure agreements with their customers before providing SOC 2 reports and audit findings. Companies are left to figure out where the line is between avoiding advantaging threat actors and being taken to task for under reporting by the SEC.

The enumerated elements that a registrant should address in its Item 106(b) disclosure, as applicable, are:

> - Whether and how the described cybersecurity processes in Item 106(b) have been integrated into the registrant's overall risk management system or processes;
> - Whether the registrant engages assessors, consultants, auditors, or other third parties in connection with any such processes; and
> - Whether the registrant has processes to oversee and identify material risks from cybersecurity threats associated with its use of any third-party service provider.
>
> We have also revised the rule text to clarify that the above elements compose a non-exclusive list of disclosures; registrants should additionally disclose whatever information is necessary, based on their facts and circumstances, for a reasonable investor to understand their cybersecurity processes.[111]

Some have asked if it is sufficient to state that they are aligned with NIST CSF or ISO:27001 or another commercially available risk framework. Maybe. Some have projected that this disclosure we become boiler plate like the standard security measures paragraph found in many privacy policies. Time will tell.

---

[111] *Id.* at 63-63.

4.6 SEC Order for Failure to Disclose Breach Under Securities Reporting Laws

The following order, *In the Matter of ALTABA INC., f/d/b/a YAHOO! INC.*,[112] concerns Yahoo!'s failure to disclose a cybersecurity breach under securities laws:

This matter concerned material misstatements and omissions by Yahoo, one of the world's largest Internet media companies, regarding a 2014 data breach affecting more than 500 million of its user accounts.

It wasn't until around September 22, 2016 that Yahoo disclosed, in a press release, the 2014 data breach that involved 500 million user accounts. This was a particularly egregious failure to disclose relevant information to investors. Yahoo was apparently attempting to protect its value in light of its eventual acquisition by Verizon. After the breach was finally disclosed, Yahoo's market value and the price for acquisition dropped significantly. The Commission found it appropriate to order the following:

> A. Pursuant to Section 8A of the Securities Act and Section 21C of the Exchange Act, Respondent cease and desist from committing or causing any violations and any future violations of Sections 17(a)(2) and 17(a)(3) of the Securities Act, Section 13(a) of the Exchange Act, and Rules 12b-20, 13a-1, 13a-11, 13a-13, and 13a-15 thereunder.
>
> B. Respondent shall, within ten (10) days of the entry of this Order, pay a civil money penalty in the amount of $35,000,000.00 to the Securities and Exchange Commission for transfer to the general fund of the United States Treasury, subject to Exchange Act Section 21F(g)(3). If timely payment is not made, additional interest shall accrue pursuant to 31 U.S.C. §3717.

---

[112] *In the Matter of ALTABA INC., f/d/b/a YAHOO! INC.*, Release No. 3937 (SEC, April 24, 2018), available at https://www.sec.gov/litigation/admin/2018/33-10485.pdf.

CHAPTER FIVE. Health Insurance Portability and Accountability Act

5.1 Introduction

HIPAA is the Health Insurance Portability and Accountability Act of 1996. Most Americans are familiar with the term HIPAA and would probably classify it as a privacy law that protects their medical data. In addition to the privacy side of HIPAA, the U.S. Department of Health and Human Services (HHS) also provides a Security Rule for the protection of electronic health information. This chapter reviews the Security Rule, its enforcement and private litigation concerning HIPAA in the cybersecurity context.

5.2 The HIPAA Security Rule and Breach Notification Rules

The U.S. Department of Health and Human Services (HHS) has recognized both a Privacy Rule and a Security Rule. The privacy side of HIPAA has been well documented and analyzed in various texts, memorandums, and forums. In this chapter we will focus on the Security Rule. The text of the Security Rule is contained in 45 CFR Part 160 and Part 164. The HHS has stated that the Security Rule is directed to providing "technical and non-technical safeguards" for "covered entities" "to secure individuals' "electronic protected health information." (e-PHI). The Security Rule provides a nationwide standard and is enforced by the HHS's Office for Civil Rights. The Office of Civil Rights has the authority to issue civil money penalties and engage in "voluntary compliance activities."[113] Notably, state attorney generals also can enforce the HIPAA Security Rule.

The HHS has stated that the Security Rule is designed to facilitate the adoption of technology to make the provision of healthcare more efficient and productive. Importantly, the Rule is

---

[113] *See Summary of the HIPAA Security Rule*, U.S. DEPARTMENT OF HEALTH & HUMAN SERVICES, https://www.hhs.gov/hipaa/for-professionals/security/laws-regulations/index.html (last reviewed July 26, 2013).

flexible in nature, "so a covered entity can implement policies, procedures, and technologies that are appropriate for the entity's particular size, organizational structure, and risks to consumers' e-PHI."[114] However, as you shall soon see, you may disagree with that the Security Rule is as flexible in practice as perhaps intended by HHS.

The Security Rule, which applies to only certain entities, relies on administrative, technical, and physical security procedures to maintain the confidentiality, integrity, and availability of electronic Personal Health Information (e-PHI). The entities to which the Security Rule applies are:

> health plans, health care clearinghouses, and to any health care provider who transmits health information in electronic form in connection with a transaction for which the Secretary of HHS has adopted standards under HIPAA (the "covered entities") and to their business associates.[115]

Health plans would include:

- Health insurance companies
- HMOs, or health maintenance organizations
- Employer-sponsored health plans
- Government programs that pay for health care, like Medicare, Medicaid, and military and veterans' health programs.[116]

Health care clearinghouses include "organizations that process nonstandard health information to conform to standards for data content or format, or vice versa, on behalf of other organizations."[117] Providers include entities that submit HIPAA transactions electronically such as:

---

[114] *Id.*
[115] *Id.*
[116] *Are You a Covered Entity?*, CENTERS FOR MEDICARE & MEDICAID SERVICES, https://www.cms.gov/Regulations-and-Guidance/Administrative-Simplification/HIPAA-ACA/AreYouaCoveredEntity (last modified Aug. 2, 2020).
[117] *Id.*

- Doctors
- Clinics
- Psychologists
- Dentists
- Chiropractors
- Nursing homes
- Pharmacies.[118]

Business Associates include:

- Third-party administrator that assists a health plan with claims processing
- Consultant that performs utilization reviews for a hospital
- Health care clearinghouse that translates a claim from a nonstandard format into a standard transaction on behalf of a health care provider, and forwards the processed transaction to a payer
- Independent medical transcriptionist that provides transcription services to a physician.[119]

Health Information Technology for Economic and Clinical Health (HITECH)

Privacy and security protections for e-PHI were further expanded when in 2009 the U.S. Department of Health and Human Services (HHS) Office for Civil Rights (OCR) enacted HITECH as part of the American Recovery and Reinvestment Act of 2009.[120] On January 25, 2013, a final rule was announced by HHS that "implemented a number of provisions of the HITECH Act to strengthen the privacy and security protections for health information established under HIPAA."[121]

---

[118] *Id.*
[119] *Id.*
[120] *Omnibus HIPAA Rulemaking*, U.S. DEPARTMENT OF HEALTH & HUMAN SERVICES, https://www.hhs.gov/hipaa/for-professionals/privacy/laws-regulations/combined-regulation-text/omnibus-hipaa-rulemaking/index.html (last reviewed Sept. 13, 2019).
[121] *See Combined Regulation Text of All Rules*, U.S. DEPARTMENT OF HEALTH & HUMAN SERVICES, https://www.hhs.gov/hipaa/for-professionals/privacy/laws-regulations/combined-regulation-text/index.html?language=es (last reviewed May 17, 2017).

SECURITY RULE STANDARDS

The security standards of the Security Rule contain the familiar administrative (45 CFR 164.308), physical (45 CFR 164.310), and technical (45 CFR 164.312) safeguards categories to ensure confidentiality, integrity, and availability (CIA) of e-PHI.[122]

---

[122] 45 C.F.R. §164.304 contains definitions for terms included in the Security Rule Standards section:
"As used in this subpart, the following terms have the following meanings:

Access means the ability or the means necessary to read, write, modify, or communicate data/information or otherwise use any system resource. (This definition applies to "access" as used in this subpart, not as used in subparts D or E of this part.)

Administrative safeguards are administrative actions, and policies and procedures, to manage the selection, development, implementation, and maintenance of security measures to protect electronic protected health information and to manage the conduct of the covered entity's or business associate's workforce in relation to the protection of that information.

Authentication means the corroboration that a person is the one claimed.

Availability means the property that data or information is accessible and useable upon demand by an authorized person.

Confidentiality means the property that data or information is not made available or disclosed to unauthorized persons or processes.

Encryption means the use of an algorithmic process to transform data into a form in which there is a low probability of assigning meaning without use of a confidential process or key.

Facility means the physical premises and the interior and exterior of a building(s).

Information system means an interconnected set of information resources under the same direct management control that shares common functionality. A system normally includes hardware, software, information, data, applications, communications, and people.

Integrity means the property that data or information have not been altered or destroyed in an unauthorized manner.

Malicious software means software, for example, a virus, designed to damage or disrupt a system.

This section will discuss each safeguards category. Given the sensitive nature of personal health information, the Security Rule sets forth a significant amount of detail concerning compliance compared to other industry sectors previously reviewed.[123]

Password means confidential authentication information composed of a string of characters.

Physical safeguards are physical measures, policies, and procedures to protect a covered entity's or business associate's electronic information systems and related buildings and equipment, from natural and environmental hazards, and unauthorized intrusion.

Security or Security measures encompass all of the administrative, physical, and technical safeguards in an information system.

Security incident means the attempted or successful unauthorized access, use, disclosure, modification, or destruction of information or interference with system operations in an information system.

Technical safeguards means the technology and the policy and procedures for its use that protect electronic protected health information and control access to it.

User means a person or entity with authorized access.

Workstation means an electronic computing device, for example, a laptop or desktop computer, or any other device that performs similar functions, and electronic media stored in its immediate environment." *Id.*

[123] Despite this added level of detail and guidance, some critique HIPAA's ability to protect sensitive information, particularly after a pandemic. See Letter from Russell P. Branzwell, President and CEO of Chime, and John Kravitz, Chair of the CHIME Board of Trustees, to the Honorable Lamar Alexander, Chairman of the Sen. Comm. on Health, Educ., Labor & Pensions (June 20, 2020), *available at* https://chimecentral.org/wp-content/uploads/2020/06/CHIME-Comments-for-Preparing-for-the-Next-Pandemic-White-Paper.pdf. That letter states, in relevant part:

> III. Strengthen Cybersecurity Infrastructure
>
> Healthcare is deemed a critical infrastructure by the Department of Homeland Security (DHS) and as such, patient safety and patient data should be viewed as a public good; protecting those things should be a national priority. As we increase interoperability, additional threats to data integrity and patient safety will arise. Without proper safeguards, the

Importantly, the "HHS recognizes that covered entities range from the smallest provider to the largest, multi-state health plan."[124] "[T]he Security Rule is flexible and scalable to allow covered entities to analyze their own needs and implement solutions appropriate for their specific environments."[125] The adoption of measures will depend on the "appropriate[ness] for a particular covered entity . . . depend[ing] on the nature of the covered entity's business, as well as the covered entity's size and resources."[126] Covered entities ad business associates may consider the following in "deciding which security measures to use:

1. Its size, complexity, and capabilities,

> safe and secure transmission of sensitive data will continue to be a challenge and will hinder efforts to improve outcomes.
>
> The healthcare sector, despite making progress over the past several years, is ill-equipped to handle a concurrent pandemic and cyberattack. Unfortunately, that is what our nation's healthcare system could very well experience. Cyber criminals are fully aware of our vulnerabilities and experts are predicting they will capitalize on those vulnerabilities. Given the complexity of the ever-growing number of interconnected devices, it is important to guarantee the security of those devices and the networks they reside on. As 5G utilization grows, the industry must monitor its adoption for additional risks that may arise as the Internet of Medical Things (IoMT) continues to rapidly expand.
>
> The added stress to our nation's healthcare providers as they treat those with or suspected to have COVID-19 brings heightened importance to fortifying their ability to maintain continuity of operations. One industry estimate found that since January there has been a "30,000% increase in phishing, malicious websites, and malware targeting remote users—all related to COVID-19" (Zscaler, April 2020).
>
> Providers need additional support to fend off the growing and sophisticated attacks aimed at stealing intellectual property, extorting ransoms, threatening patients by targeting medical devices connected to patients and hindering their ability to deliver care overall. *Id.*

[124] *See Summary of HIPAA Security Rule*, U.S. Department of Health & Human Services, https://www.hhs.gov/hipaa/for-professionals/security/laws-regulations/index.html (last reviewed July 26, 2013).

[125] *Id.*

[126] *Id.*

2. Its technical, hardware, and software infrastructure,
3. The costs of security measures, and
4. The likelihood and possible impact of potential risks to e-PHI.[127]

Section 164.306 specifically provides general requirements for covered entities and business associates including:

> **(1)** Ensure the confidentiality, integrity, and availability of all electronic protected health information the covered entity or business associate creates, receives, maintains, or transmits.
>
> **(2)** Protect against any reasonably anticipated threats or hazards to the security or integrity of such information.
>
> **(3)** Protect against any reasonably anticipated uses or disclosures of such information that are not permitted or required under subpart E of this part.
>
> **(4)** Ensure compliance with this subpart by its workforce.

Section 164.308 provides for administrative safeguards by setting forth eight standards and provisions concerning business associate contracts. The eight standards are discussed first and the business associate contracts provisions second.

The eight administrative standards include implementation specifications for each standard. Notably, some implementation specifications are designated as "Required" or "Addressable." The difference between the two types are designed to provide covered entities with flexibility. The Health and Human Services Agency has provided some additional information concerning the meaning of the two terms in the Security Rule:

If an implementation specification is described as "required," the specification must be implemented. The concept of

---

127 *Id.*

"addressable implementation specifications" was developed to provide covered entities additional flexibility with respect to compliance with the security standards. In meeting standards that contain addressable implementation specifications, a covered entity will do one of the following for each addressable specification: (a) implement the addressable implementation specifications; (b) implement one or more alternative security measures to accomplish the same purpose; (c) not implement either an addressable implementation specification or an alternative. The covered entity's choice must be documented. The covered entity must decide whether a given addressable implementation specification is a reasonable and appropriate security measure to apply within its particular security framework. For example, a covered entity must implement an addressable implementation specification if it is reasonable and appropriate to do so, and must implement an equivalent alternative if the addressable implementation specification is unreasonable and inappropriate, and there is a reasonable and appropriate alternative. This decision will depend on a variety of factors, such as, among others, the entity's risk analysis, risk mitigation strategy, what security measures are already in place, and the cost of implementation. The decisions that a covered entity makes regarding addressable specifications must be documented in writing. The written documentation should include the factors considered as well as the results of the risk assessment on which the decision was based.[128]

The eight administrative safeguards standards in section 164.308 include: (1) Security management process; (2) Assigned security responsibility; (3) Workforce security; (4) Information access management; (5) Security awareness and training; (6) Security incident procedures; (7) Contingency plan; and (8) Evaluation. Subsection (1) security management process requires implementation of "policies and procedures to prevent, detect, contain, and correct security violations." Specifically, subsection (1) provides four implementation specifications which are all designated as "Required," including: risk analysis, risk

[128] *What is the difference between addressable and required implementation specifications in the Security Rule?*, U.S. DEPARTMENT OF HEALTH & HUMAN SERVICES, https://www.hhs.gov/hipaa/for-professionals/faq/2020/what-is-the-difference-between-addressable-and-required-implementation-specifications/index.html (last reviewed July 26, 2013).

management, sanction policy and information system review. Risk analysis includes "[c]onduct[ing] an accurate and thorough assessment of the potential risks and vulnerabilities to the confidentiality, integrity, and availability of electronic protected health information held by the covered entity or business associate." Risk management includes "[i]mplement[ing] security measures sufficient to reduce risks and vulnerabilities to a reasonable and appropriate level to comply with § 164.306(a)." Sanction policy includes "[a]pply[ing] appropriate sanctions against workforce members who fail to comply with the security policies and procedures of the covered entity or business associate." Finally, information system review includes "[i]mplement[ing] procedures to regularly review records of information system activity, such as audit logs, access reports, and security incident tracking reports."

The second administrative safeguards standard is assigned security responsibility. The implementation of this standard fixes responsibility on a security official. Specifically, the implementation requirement states that the security official "is responsible for the development and implementation of the policies and procedures required by this subpart for the covered entity or business associate."

The third administrative standard is workforce security. This standard covers the administrative security measures applicable to workforce access to protected information from access to termination of the relationship with the covered entity or business associate. For implementation, the standard states that the covered entity or business associate must "[i]mplement policies and procedures" that segment access to protected information to only those "workforce members" who need "appropriate access" and restrict those "workforce members" from access who do not need that information. There are three implementation standards that are designated as "addressable": authorization and/or supervision; workforce clearance procedure; and termination procedure. The first, authorization and/or supervision provides, "[i]mplement[ing] procedures for the authorization and/or supervision of workforce members who work with electronic protected health information or in locations where it might be accessed." The second, workforce clearance procedure states: "[i]mplement[ing] procedures to determine that the access of a workforce member to electronic protected health information is appropriate." Finally, termination procedures provides: "[i]mplement[ing] procedures for terminating access to electronic protected health information when the employment of, or other arrangement with, a workforce member ends or as required by determinations made as specified in paragraph (a)(3)(ii)(B) of this section."

The fourth administrative standard is information access management. This standard states that, "policies and procedures [must be implemented] for authorizing access to electronic protected health information that are consistent with the applicable requirements of subpart E of this part." This administrative standard concerns policies and procedures concerning access to personal health information. There are three implementation specifications: isolating health care clearinghouse functions; access authorization; and access establishment and modification. Isolating health care clearinghouse functions is required. Access authorization and access establishment and modification are designated as addressable. Isolating health care clearinghouse functions requires, "[i]f a health care clearinghouse is part of a larger organization, the clearinghouse must implement policies and procedures that protect the electronic protected health information of the clearinghouse from unauthorized access by the larger organization." Access authorization states, "[i]mplement[ing] policies and procedures for granting access to electronic protected health information, for example, through access to a workstation, transaction, program, process, or other mechanism." Access establishment and modification provides, "[i]mplement[ing] policies and procedures that, based upon the covered entity's or the business associate's access authorization policies, establish, document, review, and modify a user's right of access to a workstation, transaction, program, or process."

The fifth standard is security awareness and training. The standard clarifies that "implement[ing] a security awareness and training program for all members of its workforce (including management)." There are four implementation specifications: security reminders; protection from malicious software; log-in monitoring; and password management. All four are designated as addressable. Security reminders are simply "[p]eriodic security updates." Protection from malicious software includes adopting "[p]rocedures for guarding again, detecting, and reporting malicious software." Log-in monitoring includes having "[p]rocedures for monitoring log-in attempts and reporting discrepancies. Finally, password management including adopting "[p]rocedures for creating, changing, and safeguarding passwords."

The sixth standard is security incident procedures. The standard requires "[i]mplement[ing] policies and procedures to address security incidents. There is only one required implementation specification which is response and reporting. Response and reporting requires "identify[ing] and respond[ing] to suspected or known security incidents; mitigate, to the extent practicable, harmful effects of security incidents that are known to the covered entity or business associate; and document security incidents and their outcomes."

The seventh standard is a contingency plan. Specifically, the contingency plan includes, "[e]stablish[ing] (and implement[ing] as needed) policies and procedures for responding to an emergency or other occurrence (for example, fire, vandalism, system failure, and natural disaster) that damages systems that contain electronic protected health information." There are five implementation specifications: data back up plan; disaster recovery plan; emergency mode operation plan; and testing and revision procedures. The first three are required and the last two are addressable. The data backup plan requires, "[e]stablish[ing] and implement[ing] procedures to create and maintain retrievable exact copies of electronic protected health information." The disaster recovery plan requires, "[e]stablish[ing] (and implement[ing] as needed) procedures to restore any loss of data." The emergency mode operation plan requires, "[e]stablish[ing] (and implement[ing] as needed) procedures to enable continuation of critical business processes for protection of the security of electronic protected health information while operating in emergency mode." The testing and revision procedures provide for "[i]mplement[ing] procedures for periodic testing and revision of contingency plans." Finally, applications and data criticality analysis states that, "[a]ssess[ing] the relative criticality of specific applications and data in support of other contingency plan components."

The eighth standard is evaluation. Simply put, this administrative standard requires ongoing review to "establish the extent to which a covered entity's or business associate's security policies and procedures meet the requirements of this subpart."

Notably, this is a "periodic technical and nontechnical evaluation" that considers "environmental or operational changes affecting the security of electronic protected health information."

The second main part of this section discusses business associate contracts and other arrangements. There are two main provisions and one part on implementation specifications. The provisions essentially concern the creation of information and movement of information between entities, including covered entities and business associates and between business associates. The first part (b)(1) provides, in relevant part, that, "A covered entity may permit a business associate to create, receive, maintain, or transmit electronic protected health information on the covered entity's behalf only if the covered entity obtains satisfactory assurances, in accordance with § 164.314(a), that the business associate will appropriately safeguard the information." Notably, "A covered entity is not required to obtain such satisfactory assurances from a business associate that is a subcontractor." The second part b(2) states, "A business associate may permit a business associate that is a subcontractor to create, receive, maintain, or transmit electronic protected health information on its behalf only if the business associate obtains satisfactory assurances, in accordance with § 164.314(a), that the subcontractor will appropriately safeguard the information." The implementation specification is written contract or other arrangement and is designated as required. That specification requires "[d]ocument[ing] the satisfactory assurances required by paragraph (b)(1) or (b)(2) of this section through a written contract or other arrangement with the business associate that meets the applicable requirements of § 164.314(a)."

Section 164.310 concerns physical safeguards for covered entities and business associations, and the section contains four standards: facility access controls; workstation use; workstation security; and device and media controls. Each standard has implementation specifications. The first standard, facility access controls, states, "[i]mplement[ing] policies and procedures to limit physical access to its electronic information systems and the facility or facilities in which they are housed, while ensuring that properly authorized access is allowed." There are four implementation specifications: contingency operations; facility security plan; access control and validation procedures; and maintenance records. All four are addressable and not required. The first, contingency operations, states, “[e]stablish[ing] (and implement[ing] as needed) procedures that allow facility access in support of restoration of lost data under the disaster recovery plan and emergency mode operations plan in the event of an emergency.” Second, facility security plan provides “[i[mplement[ing] policies and procedures to safeguard the facility and the equipment therein from unauthorized physical access, tampering, and theft.” Third, access control and validation procedures states, “[i]mplement[ing] procedures to control and validate a person's access to facilities based on their role or function, including visitor control, and control of access to software programs for testing and revision.” Fourth, maintenance records provides, “[i]mplement[ing] policies and procedures to document repairs and modifications to the physical components of a facility which are related to security (for example, hardware, walls, doors, and locks).”

The second standard is workstation use. There is one implementation standard: “[i[mplement policies and procedures that specify the proper functions to be performed, the manner in which those functions are to be performed, and the physical attributes of the surroundings of a specific workstation or class of workstation that can access electronic protected health information.” The third standard is workstation security. There is one implementation standard: [i]mplement physical safeguards for all workstations that access electronic protected health information, to restrict access to authorized users.”

The fourth standard is device and media controls. This fourth standard states: “[i]mplement policies and procedures that govern the receipt and removal of hardware and electronic media that contain electronic protected health information into and out of a facility, and the movement of these items within the facility.” There are four implementation specifications: disposal, media re-use, accountability, and data backup and storage. The first two are required and the second two are addressable. Disposal requires, “[i]mplement[ing] policies and procedures to address the final disposition of electronic protected health information, and/or the hardware or electronic media on which it is stored.” Media re-use requires, “[i]mplement[ing] procedures for removal of electronic protected health information from electronic media before the media are made available for re-use.” Accountability states, "[m]aintain[ing] a record of the movements of hardware and electronic media and any person responsible therefore." Data backup and storage provides, "[c]reat[ing] a retrievable, exact copy of electronic protected health information, when needed, before movement of equipment.

Section 164.312 sets for the requirements for technical safeguards . There are five standards: access control; audit controls; integrity; person or entity authentication; and transmission security. The standard for access control states, "[i]mplement[ing] technical policies and procedures for electronic information systems that maintain electronic protected health information to allow access only to those persons or software programs that have been granted access rights as specified in § 164.308(a)(4)." The implementation specifications include: unique user identification, emergency access procedure, automatic logoff, and encryption and decryption. The first two are required and the next two are addressable. Unique user identification requires "[a]ssign[ing] a unique name and/or number for identifying and tracking user identity." Emergency access procedure requires "[e]stablish[ing] (and implement[ing] as needed) procedures for obtaining necessary electronic protected health information during an emergency." Automatic logoff states "[i]mplement[ing] electronic procedures that terminate an electronic session after a predetermined time of inactivity." Encryption and decryption provides, "[i]mplement[ing] a mechanism to encrypt and decrypt electronic protected health information."

The second standard is audit controls. Audit controls requires "[i]mplement[ing] hardware, software, and/or procedural mechanisms that record and examine activity in information systems that contain or use electronic protected health information." The third standard is integrity. Integrity requires "[i]mplement[ation of] policies and procedures to protect electronic protected health information from improper alteration or destruction." The implementation specification is titled, "Mechanism to authenticate electronic protected health information." It is designated as addressable and states, "[i]mplement[ing] electronic mechanisms to corroborate that electronic protected health information has not been altered or destroyed in an unauthorized manner."

The fourth standard is person or entity authentication. Person or entity authentication requires "[i]mplement[ing] procedures to verify that a person or entity seeking access to electronic health information is the one claimed." The final standard is transmission security. Transmission security requires "[i]mplement[ing] technical security measures to guard against unauthorized access to electronic protected health information that is being transmitted over an electronic communications network." The implementation specifications are designated as addressable, and are integrity controls and encryption. Integrity controls states, "[i]mplement[ing] security measures to ensure that electronically transmitted electronic protected health information is not improperly modified without detection until disposed of." Encryption provides, "[i]mplement[ing] a mechanism to encrypt electronic protected health information whenever deemed appropriate."

The term implementation specification as used in the appendix, equates to "specific requirements or instruction for implementing a standard.[129] **Appendix A to Subpart C of Part 164 - Security Standards: Matrix[130]**

HHS Summary of HIPAA Security Rule

The HHS has provided a document titled, "Summary of HIPAA Security Rule," on the operation of the Security Rule on the HHS website. Importantly, that document notes that state law is preempted if it is "contrary" with HIPAA regulations. The federal law will trump the state law. "Contrary" is defined to mean "it would be impossible for a covered entity to comply with both the State and federal requirements, or that the provision of State law is an obstacle to accomplishing the full purposes and objectives of the Administrative Simplification provisions of HIPAA.[131]

---

[129] *See* 45 C.F.R. § 160.103.

[130] 45 C.F.R. Appendix A to Subpart C of Part 164—Security Standards: Matrix, *available at* https://www.law.cornell.edu/cfr/text/45/appendix-A_to_subpart_C_of_part_164.

[131] *See Summary of HIPAA Security Rule*, U.S. DEPARTMENT OF HEALTH & HUMAN SERVICES, https://www.hhs.gov/hipaa/for-professionals/security/laws-regulations/index.html (last reviewed July 26, 2013).

Breach Notification Rules

HIPAA also requires breach notification to patients, the media and HHS. The following regulations concern breach notification.[132] The

[132] 45 C.F.R. § 164.402 contains definitions concerning the breach notification part:

"As used in this subpart, the following terms have the following meanings:

Breach means the acquisition, access, use, or disclosure of protected health information in a manner not permitted under subpart E of this part which compromises the security or privacy of the protected health information.
(1) Breach excludes:
(i) Any unintentional acquisition, access, or use of protected health information by a workforce member or person acting under the authority of a covered entity or a business associate, if such acquisition, access, or use was made in good faith and within the scope of authority and does not result in further use or disclosure in a manner not permitted under subpart E of this part.
(ii) Any inadvertent disclosure by a person who is authorized to access protected health information at a covered entity or business associate to another person authorized to access protected health information at the same covered entity or business associate, or organized health care arrangement in which the covered entity participates, and the information received as a result of such disclosure is not further used or disclosed in a manner not permitted under subpart E of this part.
(iii) A disclosure of protected health information where a covered entity or business associate has a good faith belief that an unauthorized person to whom the disclosure was made would not reasonably have been able to retain such information.
(2) Except as provided in paragraph (1) of this definition, an acquisition, access, use, or disclosure of protected health information in a manner not permitted under subpart E is presumed to be a breach unless the covered entity or business associate, as applicable, demonstrates that there is a low probability that the protected health information has been compromised based on a risk assessment of at least the following factors:
(i) The nature and extent of the protected health information involved, including the types of identifiers and the likelihood of re-identification;
(ii) The unauthorized person who used the protected health information or to whom the disclosure was made;
(iii) Whether the protected health information was actually acquired or viewed; and
(iv) The extent to which the risk to the protected health information has been mitigated.

Unsecured protected health information means protected health information that is not rendered unusable, unreadable, or indecipherable to unauthorized persons through the use of a technology or methodology specified by the Secretary in the guidance issued under section 13402(h)(2) of Public Law 111–5." *Id.*

requirements for notification to individual is covered by 45 C.F.R. § 164.404. The requirements for the notification to the media is covered by 45 C.F.R. § 164.406 Notification to the media. The requirements for notification to the secretary is covered by 45 C.F.R. § 164.408.

5.3 Office of Civil Rights Enforcement Actions Concerning HIPAA

The OCR is tasked with enforcing the Privacy and Security Rules. The OCR uses the following methods:

- investigation of complaints filed with the OCR;
- determining if covered entities are in compliance by conducting compliance interviews;
- education and outreach programs to encourage compliance.[133]

Cases closed by the OCR fall into five categories:

1) Resolved after intake and review without investigation;
2) Technical Assistance without investigation;
3) After investigation, no violation is determined;
4) After investigation, corrective action is obtained;
5) Other because OCR may have decided not to investigate based on:

a) referral to DOJ for prosecution;
b) case was part of a natural disaster;
c) case was resolved by prosecution by state authorities;
d) steps were taken to comply and OCR decides not to use resources to pursue.

As we have seen with other federal agencies that enforce cybersecurity, the accused normally has the choice to come to terms

---

[133] *Enforcement Process*, U.S. DEPARTMENT OF HEALTH & HUMAN SERVICES, https://www.hhs.gov/hipaa/for-professionals/compliance-enforcement/enforcement-process/index.html (last reviewed June 7, 2017).

with the OCR accusations and enter into a resolution agreement. With such an agreement, "the covered entity or business associate agrees to perform certain obligations and make reports to HHS, generally for a period of three years. During the period, HHS monitors the covered entity's compliance with its obligations. A resolution agreement may include the payment of a resolution amount."[134] The list of enforcement matters brought by the OCR can be found online.[135]

The Health and Human Services Office of Civil Rights submitted a document to Congress which includes a discussion of the responsibilities and duties of the OCR in enforcement:

Health and Human Services Office of Civil Rights, Report to Congress on HIPAA Privacy, Security, and Breach Notification Rule Compliance For Calendar Years 2015, 2016

Enforcement Process

> OCR enforces the HIPAA Rules by investigating written complaints filed with OCR, either on paper, by e-mail, or through its complaint portal. OCR also conducts compliance reviews of circumstances brought to its attention, to determine if covered entities or business associates are in compliance with the Rules. In addition, OCR's compliance activities include conducting audits and providing education and outreach to foster compliance with the Rules' requirements, which are discussed later in the report. When necessary, OCR has authority to issue subpoenas to compel cooperation with an investigation.

---

[134] *See Resolution Agreements*, U.S. DEPARTMENT OF HEALTH & HUMAN SERVICES, https://www.hhs.gov/hipaa/for-professionals/compliance-enforcement/agreements/index.html (last reviewed Mar. 26, 2021).

[135] *Resolution Agreements*, U.S. DEPARTMENT OF HEALTH & HUMAN SERVICES, https://www.hhs.gov/hipaa/for-professionals/compliance-enforcement/agreements/index.html.

The report also details conditions for taking action on Complaints, how it conducts Compliance Reviews, and Civil Money Penalties.

Health and Human Services and Metropolitan Health Community Health Services Matter

One matter concerning enforcement of HIPAA requirements involved Metropolitan Community Health Services. Please note that the target entity of the HHS is a relatively small health provider with very limited resources. From the HHS perspective, this did not seem to factor in very much with respect to whether there is liability. An interesting question is whether the penalty was appropriate given the resources and mission of the target. HHS released the following on its website describing the HHS and Metropolitan Community Health Services Matter:

> "Small Health Care Provider Fails to Implement Multiple HIPAA Security Rule Requirements
>
> Metropolitan Community Health Services (Metro), doing business as Agape Health Services, has agreed to pay $25,000 to the Office for Civil Rights (OCR) at the U.S. Department of Health and Human Services (HHS) and to adopt a corrective action plan to settle potential violations of the Health Insurance Portability and Accountability Act (HIPAA) Security Rule. Metro is a Federally Qualified Health Center that provides a variety of discounted medical services to the underserved population in rural North Carolina and these facts were taken into account in reaching this agreement.
>
> On June 9, 2011, Metro filed a breach report regarding the impermissible disclosure of protected health information to an unknown email account. The breach affected 1,263 patients. OCR's investigation revealed longstanding, systemic noncompliance with the HIPAA Security Rule. Specifically, Metro failed to conduct any risk

analyses, failed to implement any HIPAA Security Rule policies and procedures, and neglected to provide workforce members with security awareness training until 2016.

'Health care providers owe it to their patients to comply with the HIPAA Rules. When informed of potential HIPAA violations, providers owe it to their patients to quickly address problem areas to safeguard individuals' health information,' said Roger Severino, OCR Director."[136]

The following is an example of a resolution agreement.

Resolution Agreement and Corrective Action Plan between Health and Human Services and Metropolitan Health Community Health Services (2020)[137]

Important to these resolution agreements is that "HHS has the authority to conduct compliance reviews and investigations of complaints alleging violations of the Privacy, Security, and Breach Notification Rules (the 'HIPAA Rules') by covered entities and business associates, and covered entities and business associates must cooperate with HHS compliance reviews and investigations. See 45 C.F.R. §§ 160.306(c), 160.308. and 160.310(b)."

Metropolitan Community Health Services, Inc. ("MCHS"), a covered entity, is a 501 (c)(3) (nonprofit) Federally Qualified Health Center ("FQHC"). An investigation of MCHS occurred after the OCR received a breach report from MCHS on June 9, 2011. That investigation uncovered "widespread compliance issues" with regard to the HIPAA Security Rule including:

---

[136] *Small Health Care Provider Fails to Implement Multiple HIPAA Security Rule Requirements*, U.S. DEPARTMENT OF HEALTH & HUMAN SERVICES (July 23, 2020), https://www.hhs.gov/about/news/2020/07/23/small-health-care-provider-fails-to-implement-multiple-hipaa-security-rule-requirements.html.

[137] RESOLUTION AGREEMENT AND CORRECTIVE ACTION PLAN BETWEEN HEALTH AND HUMAN SERVICES AND METROPOLITAN HEALTH COMMUNITY HEALTH SERVICES, U.S. DEPARTMENT OF HEALTH & HUMAN SERVICES (2020), *available at* https://www.hhs.gov/sites/default/files/metro-signed-agreement.pdf.

A. MCHS failed to implement HIPAA Security Rule policies and procedures. See 45 C.F.R. §164.316.

B. Until June 30, 2016, MCHS failed to provide its workforce with HIPAA Security Awareness and Training. See 45 C.F.R. §164.308(a)(5).

C. MCHS failed to conduct an accurate and thorough assessment of the potential risks and vulnerabilities to the confidentiality, integrity, and availability ePHI held by it. See 45 C.F.R. § 164.308(a)(l)(ii)(A). . . .

The following are the terms and conditions of the resolution agreement:

1. Payment. MCHS agrees to pay to HHS the amount of $25,000 ("Resolution Amount"). MCHS agrees to pay the Resolution Amount on or before April 10, 2020, pursuant to written instructions to be provided by HHS.

2. Corrective Action Plan. MCHS has entered into and agrees to comply with the Corrective Action Plan ("CAP"), attached as Appendix A, which is incorporated into this Agreement by reference. If MCHS breaches the CAP, and fails to cure the breach as set forth in the CAP, then MCHS will be in breach of this Agreement and HHS will not be subject to the Release set forth in Section II, Paragraph 3 of this Agreement.

3. Release by HHS. In consideration and conditioned upon HHS's performance of its obligations under this Agreement. HHS releases MCHS from any actions it may have against MCHS under the HIPAA Rules for the Covered Conduct identified in Section I, Paragraph 2. HHS does not release MCHS from, nor waive any rights, obligations, or causes of action other than those specifically referred to or in that paragraph. This release does not extend to actions that may be brought under section 1177 of the Social Security Act, 42 C.S.C. § 1320d-6.

The National Institute of Standards and Technology (NIST) has a special publication for providing guidance on implementing the HIPAA Security Rule and is in the process of drafting a second revision of that special publication:

SP 800-66 Rev. 1: An Introductory Resource Guide for Implementing the Health Insurance Portability and Accountability Act (HIPAA) Security Rule

> NIST is planning to update NIST Special Publication (SP) 800-66, Revision 1, *An Introductory Resource Guide for Implementing the Health Insurance Portability and Accountability Act (HIPAA) Security Rule* ("Resource Guide"). NIST's cybersecurity resources have evolved since SP 800-66, Revision 1, was published in 2008, and stakeholders will benefit from guidance that includes references to these updated resources. The public is invited to provide input by **June 15, 2021** for consideration in the update.[138]

5.4 Private Litigation and HIPAA

In the *In re Premera Blue Cross Customer Data Security Breach Litigation* matter,[139] the district court found that representations by a health insurer concerning compliance with HIPAA privacy and security requirements could give rise to some tort, state statutory and contract claims in the data breach context.

Plaintiffs brought the above-named case as a putative class action against Defendant Premera Blue Cross ("Premera"). Premera is a healthcare benefits servicer and provider. On March 17, 2015, Premera publicly disclosed a breach of its computer network. "Plaintiffs allege that this breach compromised the confidential information of approximately 11 million current and former members, affiliated members, and employees of Premera." The confidential information included "names, dates of birth, Social Security Numbers, member identification numbers, mailing addresses, telephone numbers, email addresses, medical claims information, financial information, and other protected health

---

[138] https://csrc.nist.gov/publications/detail/sp/800-66/rev-2/draft (last visited May 21, 2021).

[139] *In re Premera Blue Cross Customer Data Security Breach Litigation*, 2017 WL 539578 (D. Or. 2017).

information." (collectively, "Sensitive Information"). Plaintiffs contend that the "breach began in May 2014 and went undetected for nearly a year." Plaintiffs also contend "that after discovering the breach, Premera unreasonably delayed in notifying all affected individuals." "Based on these allegations, among others, Plaintiffs bring various state common law claims and state statutory claims." Premera then moved to dismiss the fraud-based and contract claims. "Premera argues that Plaintiffs' claims that "sound in fraud" continue to fail to comply with the heightened pleading requirements of Rule 9(b) of the Federal Rules of Civil Procedure and should be dismissed." The court concluded that "Plaintiffs sufficiently allege a claim for fraud by omission and claims based on alleged misrepresentations in statements made in Premera's Preferred Select policy booklet, Privacy Notice, and Code of Conduct."

For its contract-based claims, the plaintiffs relied on express contract terms regarding the policy booklets, privacy notice, and code of conduct in addition to implied terms in the express contract, and breach of implied-in-fact contract. The court concluded that the Plaintiffs "have sufficiently alleged claims for breach of express contract for alleged breach of Premera's obligations contained in the Preferred Select policy and Privacy Notice" but "have not sufficiently alleged claims for breach of express contract for promises or obligations contained in the Preferred Bronze policy or Code of Conduct."

In the following case, *In re Anthem, Inc. Data Breach Litigation,*[140] the district court rejected the plaintiffs breach of contract claims but found that the plaintiffs sufficiently alleged unfair business practices under California law in the data breach context based on violations of HIPAA.

In this case, the plaintiffs brought a putative class action suit "against Anthem, Inc., 28 Anthem affiliates, [Anthem Defendants] Blue Cross Blue Shield Association, and 17 non-Anthem Blue Cross Blue Shield Companies [Non-Anthem Defendants]." Each brought a separate motion to dismiss. Both defendants promised to protect members PII. Anthem announced

[140] *In re Anthem, Inc. Data Breach Litigation*, 162 F.Supp.3d 953 (N.D. Cal. 2016).

in February 2015, that "cyberattackers had breached the Anthem Database, and [had] accessed [the PII of] individuals in the Anthem Database." Anthem had other data security issues dating back to late 2009 that resulted in HHS fines and advisories. Plaintiffs alleged "that Defendants did not sufficiently heed these warnings, which allowed cyberattackers to extract massive amounts of data from Anthem's database between December 2014 and January 2015." Plaintiffs asserted "against the Anthem Defendants a breach of contract claim under California law.'"

The Court found that plaintiffs allegations failed "based on a review of (1) the language in the consolidated amended complaint, (2) the language on Anthem's public websites and in various privacy notices, (3) the exhibits submitted in connection with the consolidated amended complaint." But plaintiffs also had a remaining claim under California Unfair Competition Law ("UCL"), which "provides a cause of action for business practices that are (1) unlawful, (2) unfair, or (3) fraudulent. Cal. Bus & Prof. Code § 17200, et seq." The court found that Plaintiffs "by demonstrating both causation and economic loss, Plaintiffs have sufficiently established standing under the UCL." The court found that the Plaintiffs survived the unlawful prong of the UCL because the Plaintiffs' allegations "identify the particular section of the statute that was violated, and other allegations in the consolidated amended complaint "describe with reasonable particularity the facts supporting the violation." Under the unfair prong, the court concluded that "[w]hether Defendants' public policy violation is outweighed by the utility of their conduct under the balancing test is a question to be resolved at a later stage in this litigation." Under the fraudulent claim, the court found "that Plaintiffs have not stated a fraud claim under the UCL, but that Plaintiffs may be able to do so after amendment."

CHAPTER SIX. Family Education Rights and Privacy Act

6.1 Introduction

The Family Education Rights and Privacy Act (FERPA) is another act that appears on the surface to be all about privacy, but a closer look reveals a "reasonable methods" standard for cybersecurity controls. Some educational institutions are also governed by the Graham-Leach Bliley Act, which is mostly enforced by the Federal Trade Commission. Additionally, the Department of Education, Office of the Inspector General has overlapping responsibility concerning FERPA. The Department of Education notes that "specific security controls" are not mandated, but the flexible "reasonable methods" standard is required to prevent breaches that may lead to "a host of negative consequences such as identity theft, fraud, and extortion."[141]

6.2 FERPA

The DOE provides an overview of FERPA:

> The Family Educational Rights and Privacy Act (FERPA) (20 U.S.C. § 1232g; 34 CFR Part 99) is a Federal law that protects the privacy of student education records. The law applies to all schools that receive funds under an applicable program of the U.S. Department of Education.
>
> FERPA gives parents certain rights with respect to their children's education records. These rights transfer to the student when he or she reaches the age of 18 or attends a school beyond the high school level. Students to whom the rights have transferred are "eligible students."
>
> - Parents or eligible students have the right to inspect and review the student's education records maintained by the school. Schools are

[141] *See Data Security: K-12 and Higher Education*, U.S. DEPARTMENT OF EDUCATION, https://studentprivacy.ed.gov/Security (last visited May 18, 2021).

not required to provide copies of records unless, for reasons such as great distance, it is impossible for parents or eligible students to review the records. Schools may charge a fee for copies.

- Parents or eligible students have the right to request that a school correct records which they believe to be inaccurate or misleading. If the school decides not to amend the record, the parent or eligible student then has the right to a formal hearing. After the hearing, if the school still decides not to amend the record, the parent or eligible student has the right to place a statement with the record setting forth his or her view about the contested information.
- Generally, schools must have written permission from the parent or eligible student in order to release any information from a student's education record. However, FERPA allows schools to disclose those records, without consent, to the following parties or under the following conditions (34 CFR § 99.31):
  - School officials with legitimate educational interest;
  - Other schools to which a student is transferring;
  - Specified officials for audit or evaluation purposes;
  - Appropriate parties in connection with financial aid to a student;
  - Organizations conducting certain studies for or on behalf of the school;
  - Accrediting organizations;
  - To comply with a judicial order or lawfully issued subpoena;
  - Appropriate officials in cases of health and safety emergencies; and
  - State and local authorities, within a juvenile justice system, pursuant to specific State law.

Schools may disclose, without consent, "directory" information such as a student's name, address, telephone number, date and place of birth, honors and awards, and dates of attendance. However, schools must tell parents and eligible students about directory information and allow parents and eligible students a

> reasonable amount of time to request that the school not disclose directory information about them. Schools must notify parents and eligible students annually of their rights under FERPA. The actual means of notification (special letter, inclusion in a PTA bulletin, student handbook, or newspaper article) is left to the discretion of each school.[142]

34 CFR Part 99.31(a)(1)(ii) requires a minimum of effective administrative policy for controlling access to education records:

> **(ii)** An educational agency or institution must use reasonable methods to ensure that school officials obtain access to only those education records in which they have legitimate educational interests. An educational agency or institution that does not use physical or technological access controls must ensure that its administrative policy for controlling access to education records is effective and that it remains in compliance with the legitimate educational interest requirement in paragraph (a)(1)(i)(A) of this section.[143]

Paragraph (a)(1)(i)(A) states:

> **(A)** The disclosure is to other school officials, including teachers, within the agency or institution whom the agency or institution has determined to have legitimate educational interests.

The authors find it interesting that an educational agency or institution is permitted to rely on administrative policy without physical or technological controls. Moreover, there is not a data breach notification requirement for students in FERPA. Additionally, FERPA does not include a private right of action.

---

[142] *Family Educational Rights and Privacy Act (FERPA),* U.S. DEPARTMENT OF EDUCATION, https://www2.ed.gov/policy/gen/guid/fpco/ferpa/index.html (last modified Dec. 15, 2020).

[143] 34 C.F.R. § 99.31.

6.2[A] DOE GUIDANCE FROM THE PRIVACY TECHNICAL ASSISTANCE CENTER

The following documents are from the DOE Privacy Technical Assistance Center and provide guidance concerning data security. The Privacy Technical Assistance Center of the DOE released several documents including:

- a document[144] setting forth information for training personnel concerning data security
- a document[145] setting forth best practices for identify authentication
- a document[146] stating Data Security Checklist
- a document[147] titled Protecting Student Privacy While Using Online Educational Services: Model Terms of Service
- a document[148] titled Frequently Asked Questions: Cloud Computing
- a document[149] titled Best Practices for Data Destruction

---

[144] PRIVACY TECHNICAL ASSISTANCE CENTER, DATA SECURITY AND MANAGEMENT TRAINING: BEST PRACTICE CONSIDERATIONS 3 (2015), *available at* https://studentprivacy.ed.gov/sites/default/files/resource_document/file/Data%20Security%20and%20Management%20Training_1.pdf.

[145] PRIVACY TECHNICAL ASSISTANCE CENTER, IDENTITY AUTHENTICATION BEST PRACTICES: BEST PRACTICE CONSIDERATIONS 4–6 (2015), *available at* https://studentprivacy.ed.gov/sites/default/files/resource_document/file/Identity_Authentication_Best_Practices_0.pdf.

[146] PRIVACY TECHNICAL ASSISTANCE CENTER, DATA SECURITY CHECKLIST 1–4 (2015), available at https://studentprivacy.ed.gov/sites/default/files/resource_document/file/Data%20Security%20Checklist_0.pdf.

[147] PRIVACY TECHNICAL ASSISTANCE CENTER, PROTECTING STUDENT PRIVACY WHILE USING ONLINE EDUCATIONAL SERVICES: MODEL TERMS OF SERVICE 8 (2016), *available at* https://studentprivacy.ed.gov/sites/default/files/resource_document/file/TOS_Guidance_Mar2016.pdf.

[148] PRIVACY TECHNICAL ASSISTANCE CENTER, FREQUENTLY ASKED QUESTIONS: CLOUD COMPUTING 2–4 (2015), *available at* https://studentprivacy.ed.gov/sites/default/files/resource_document/file/FAQ_Cloud_Computing_0.pdf.

[149] PRIVACY TECHNICAL ASSISTANCE CENTER, BEST PRACTICES FOR DATA DESTRUCTION 2–8 (2014), *available at* https://studentprivacy.ed.gov/sites/default/files/resource_document/file/Best%20Practices%20for%20Data%20Destruction%20%282019-3-26%29.pdf.

6.2[B] Additional Cybersecurity Requirements for Title IV Schools

There are additional cyber security requirements for Title IV schools. Title IV schools are essentially schools that process federal financial aid.

Title IV schools should be aware that:

- "Under their Program Participation Agreement (PPA) and the Gramm-Leach-Bliley Act (15 U.S. Code § 6801), they must protect student financial aid information, with particular attention to information provided to institutions by the Department of Education or otherwise obtained in support of the administration of the Title IV Federal student financial aid programs authorized under Title IV of the Higher Education Act, as amended (the HEA). Summary information about the GLBA requirements is provided later in this letter; and
- Under their Student Aid Internet Gateway (SAIG) Enrollment Agreement, they *"[m]ust ensure that all users are aware of and comply with all of the requirements to protect and secure data from Departmental sources using SAIG."*[150]

20 U.S. Code 1094 covers program participation agreements.[151]

The GLBA requires institutions to, among other things:

- Develop, implement, and maintain a written information security program;

---

[150] Letter from Ted Mitchell, Undersecretary, Fed. Student Aid, U.S. Dep't. of Educ., to colleagues (July 1, 2016), *available at* https://ifap.ed.gov/dear-colleague-letters/07-01-2016-gen-16-12-subject-protecting-student-information.

[151] *See* 20 U.S.C. § 1094.

- Designate the employee(s) responsible for coordinating the information security program;
- Identify and assess risks to customer information;
- Design and implement an information safeguards program;
- Select appropriate service providers that are capable of maintaining appropriate safeguards; and
- Periodically evaluate and update their security program.

Under these GLBA requirements, Presidents and Chief Information Officers of institutions should have, at a minimum, evaluated and documented their current security posture against the requirements of GLBA and have taken immediate action to remediate any identified deficiencies.[152]

The Department of Education encourages Title IV schools to use NIST SP 800-171 for cyber security guidance:

> The Department strongly encourages institutions to review and understand the standards defined in the NIST SP 800-171, the recognized information security publication for protecting "Controlled Unclassified Information (CUI)," a subset of Federal data that includes unclassified information that requires safeguarding or dissemination controls pursuant to and consistent with law, regulations, and Federal policies. NIST SP 800-171 identifies specific recommended requirements for non-Federal entities that handle CUI. Some examples of the recommended requirements are:
>
> - Create information system audit records (Audit and Accountability Requirements);

---

[152] Letter from Ted Mitchell, Undersecretary, Fed. Student Aid, U.S. Dep't. of Educ., to colleagues (July 1, 2016), *available at* https://ifap.ed.gov/dear-colleague-letters/07-01-2016-gen-16-12-subject-protecting-student-information

- Establish baseline configurations and inventories of systems (Configuration Management Requirements);
- Identify and authenticate users appropriately (Identification and Authentication Requirements);
- Perform appropriate maintenance on information systems (Maintenance Requirements);
- Screen individuals prior to authorizing access (Personnel Security Requirements);
- Conduct risk assessments (Risk Assessment Requirements);
- Assess security controls periodically and implement action plans (Security Assessment Requirements);
- Monitor, control, and protect organizational communications (System and Communications Protection Requirements); and
- Identify, report, and correct information flaws in a timely manner (System and Information Integrity Requirement).[153]

We will cover National Institute of Standards and Technology (NIST) in detail.

6.2[C] Office of Inspector General U.S. Department of Education Technology Crimes Division

The mission and jurisdiction of the Technology Crimes Division goes beyond just Title IV schools. The Office of Inspector General (OIG) is an "independent component of Federal agencies created by Congress" that "reports to [the] Head of the Agency and

[153] *Id.*

Congress."[154] After the President appoints an Inspector General (IG), the IG is confirmed by the Senate. The Technology Crimes Division of the U.S. Department of Education investigates "crimes and criminal cyber threats against" the U.S. Department of Education's "IT infrastructure, or criminal activity in cyber space that threatens the Department's administration of Federal education assistance funds."[155] The Technology Crimes Division's "investigative jurisdiction encompasses any IT system used in the administration of Federal money originating from the Department of Education."[156]

The case examples include:

- Grade hacking
- Computer Intrusions
- Criminal Forums online selling malware
- ID/Credential theft to hijack Student Aid applications
- Misuse of Department systems to obtain personal information
- Falsifying student aid applications by U.S. government employees
- Child Exploitation material trafficking[157]

The Department of Justice describes the responsibilities of the Technology Crimes Division as follows:

> **Technology Crimes Division**
>
> The Technology Crimes Division (TCD) is the OIG component responsible for investigating computer security incidents within ED, as well as, conducting

[154] *See* OFFICE OF THE INSPECTOR GENERAL, US DEP'T. OF EDUC., CYBER SECURITY FOR TITLE IV SCHOOLS, *available at* https://www.ren-isac.net/events/attachments/TB_Apr21_2017.pdf .
[155] *Id.*
[156] *Id.*
[157] *Id.*

forensic analysis of computer systems and other electronic media in support of criminal investigations. In addition, it is responsible for the coordination, tracking, and conduct of proactive data mining activities and projects; referring the results of those efforts to the field for investigation. TCD is comprised of full-time Computer Crime Investigators (CCIs), technical professionals, and program analysts. All CCIs have full statutory law enforcement authority as granted by Congress.

In performing its responsibilities, the Division:

- Perform cybercrime investigations in response to attacks against, as well as unauthorized access of, Department of Education information systems, networks, computer systems, or databases.
- Investigates the criminal misuse of Departmental computers, which could include the accessing of child pornography.
- Performs forensic analysis of computer media in support of criminal investigations by both TCD and OIG Investigation Services.
- Develop policies and procedures on the application of advanced evidence collection, preservation, and analysis techniques.
- Performs the intermediate step of validation of data query results to reduce or eliminate false positives, cross-checking data with other publicly and privately available databases, conducting sophisticated link analysis, and ultimately generating productive investigative referrals for Investigation Services field offices.
- Conducts proactive data mining initiatives and is responsible for the project management of those products, which includes coordination with field offices, tracking efforts, and reporting results.[158]

---

[158] *Archived Information: US Department of Education Principal office Functional Statements*, U.S. DEPARTMENT OF EDUCATION, https://www2.ed.gov/about/offices/list/om/fs_po/oig/it.html (last modified May 20, 2020).

CHAPTER SEVEN. Additional Federal Regulation Concerning Cybersecurity

7.1 Introduction

This chapter provides an overview of the additional federal regulation and guidance concerning cybersecurity. Notably, as discussed previously, the U.S. government has a sectoral approach to the regulation of cybersecurity for the most part. For example, there are numerous laws and regulations directed to the health care, educational and financial industries as previously reviewed. There are also additional federal regulations concerning transportation, medical devices, communications and retirement plans, for example.

In recent years, the federal government has focused on directing federal agencies to increase their level of required cybersecurity protection. Moreover, the federal government is not only focused on federal agency cybersecurity, but is attempting to influence private contractors for the federal government. Private contractors provide numerous products and services for the government, including software and cloud services. Moreover, a significant amount of critical infrastructure is owned and operated by the private sector. The goal is to raise cybersecurity requirements for private contractors dealing with the federal government which may change behavior amongst private companies generally participating in the supply chain. Additionally, the federal government is attempting to leverage once in a generation spending legislation such as the CHIPS Act and Infrastructure Investment and Jobs Act to raise cybersecurity levels of protection.[159] Finally, a key goal of the federal government

[159] *See* Casey Dolen and Glen Grimshaw, Opportunities For Cybersecurity Investment In The Bipartisan Infrastructure Investment And Jobs Act, National Governors Association (August 24, 2022) ("In an increasingly modernized and interconnected world, the cybersecurity risk continues to grow, and our nation's infrastructure is not impervious. . . . The IIJA recognizes this by including a number of cybersecurity-specific programs, as well as allowing spending from numerous other programs on cybersecurity preparedness and response, which can be integrated into other infrastructure investments."). Dolen and Grimshaw outline the numerous opportunities for states to receive funding under the Infrastructure Investment and Jobs Act and other laws. *Id.* (for example, U.S.

is to increase collaboration amongst industry participants and the government. Collaboration is key to information sharing to detect and stop threats as well as mitigate the harm from incidents.

The Executive Branch is utilizing Executive Orders as well as other policy documents to increase cybersecurity requirements. The Biden Administration's 2021 Executive Order is important as well as the subsequent updated National Cybersecurity Strategy released in 2023. Since the issuance of the 2021 Executive Order, federal agencies have been acting to address cybersecurity issues.[160] First, this chapter reviews the 2023 Biden Executive Order on cybersecurity and some agency activity concerning implementing the direction from that Order. Second, the National Cybersecurity Strategy is reviewed. Third, an overview is provided of the Cyber Incident Reporting for Critical Infrastructure Act of 2022. Finally, cybersecurity regulations and guidance for other industries is analyzed.

7.2. Biden Administration 2021 Executive Order

On May 12, 2021, the Biden Administration issued an Executive Order titled, "Executive Order on Improving the Nation's Cybersecurity." The Executive Order is an important attempt to increase cybersecurity levels across the federal government as well as private industry. In August of 2021, Senators Portman and Peters released a bipartisan report building on prior reports that found that numerous federal agencies have deficient

---

Department of Homeland Security Cybersecurity Programs, U.S. Department of Energy Programs, U.S. Department of Transportation, and the U.S. Environmental Protection Agency).

[160] In August of 2023, the Cybersecurity and Infrastructure Security Agency released its FY 2024-2026 Cybersecurity Strategic Plan. CISA, FY 2024-2026 CISA Cybersecurity Strategic Plan, available at https://www.cisa.gov/cybersecurity-strategic-plan. The Plan has three goals:

> GOAL 1: Address Immediate Threats: Our understanding of immediate and emerging threats will enable us to prioritize investment in the security controls, product attributes, and services that most effectively reduce risks. GOAL 2. Harden the Terrain: As we provide guidance and services that help organizations prioritize reductions in enterprise risk, we will more clearly define the risks that can be most effectively addressed by safer products. GOAL 3. Drive Security at Scale: As we advance security across the product lifecycle, we will force threat actors to adopt more time-consuming and expensive tactics, reducing the prevalence of attacks. Id. at 6.

cybersecurity.[161] Notably, the Government Accountability Office recently determined that cybersecurity practices related to nuclear weapons was poor.[162] The Executive Order seeks to raise cybersecurity standards across federal agencies and leverage the federal government's contracting and acquisition process to improve cybersecurity levels across multiple industries. The Executive Order provides timelines for agencies to report on compliance with the directives in the Order. The following is a discussion of the main provisions of the Executive Order.

The Executive Order has several main components, including: 1) Policy; 2) Removing Barriers to Sharing Threat Information; 3) Modernizing Federal Cybersecurity; 4) Enhancing Software Supply Chain Security; 5) Cyber Safety Review Board; 6) Standardizing the Federal Government's Playbook for Responding to Cybersecurity Vulnerabilities; 7) Improving Detection of Cybersecurity Vulnerabilities and Incidents on Federal Government Networks; 8) Improving the Federal Government's Investigative and Remediation Capabilities; and 9) National Security Systems. The first section on Policy provides that cooperation between the federal government and the private sector is critical to increase the level of cybersecurity protection across the digital infrastructure. The federal government's cybersecurity standards should "meet or exceed" the directives in the Executive Order. The second section is focused on ensuring that information concerning cyber incidents and threats are shared quickly with

---

[161] Importantly, poor cybersecurity may be present in the U.S. Judiciary. *See* Nate Raymond, "Federal judiciary 'vulnerable' to cyberattacks, U.S. lawmakers told," Reuters (May 12, 2022) ("Two federal judges on Thursday warned a U.S. Congressional panel that the judiciary's aging computer systems are "vulnerable" to cyberattacks, creating a risk that hackers could obtain confidential material or draft court decisions like the U.S. Supreme Court abortion opinion leaked earlier this month."), available at https://www.reuters.com/legal/government/federal-judiciary-vulnerable-cyberattacks-us-lawmakers-told-2022-05-12/.

[162] The Government Accounting Office found that government civilian agencies have poorly implemented ICT supply chain cybersecurity practices. GAO, Cybersecurity High-Risk Series: Challenges in Establishing a Comprehensive Cybersecurity Strategy and Performing Effective Oversight, GAO-23-106415 (January 19, 2023).
("Federal agencies face numerous information and communications technology (ICT) supply chain risks, which could lead to disrupted mission operations, theft of intellectual property, and harm to individuals. In December 2020, our review of 23 civilian agencies found that none had fully implemented all of the seven foundational practices for supply chain risk management and that 14 had not implemented any of the practices.").

CISA, FBI and "other elements of the Intelligence Community (IC)" by federal contractors through contractual obligations. The Executive Order itself sets forth those obligations, for example: service provides should be obligated to keep information regarding "cybersecurity event prevention, detection, response and investigation;" share that information, including threat and incident information, with relevant agencies; and work with federal cybersecurity agencies. Importantly, the sharing of information is to be "consistent with applicable privacy laws, regulations, and policies[.]"

Third, the Executive Order provides direction for federal agencies to modernize their cybersecurity practices. Importantly, section 3 notes that the Federal Government "must adopt security best practices; advance toward Zero Trust Architecture;[163] accelerate movement to secure cloud services . . .; centralize and streamline access to cybersecurity data to drive analytics for identifying and managing cybersecurity risk; and invest in both technology and personnel to match these modernization goals." The section also notes that civil liberties should be preserved. Fourth,

---

[163] The Executive Order defines Zero Trust Architecture:

> [T]he term "Zero Trust Architecture" means a security model, a set of system design principles, and a coordinated cybersecurity and system management strategy based on an acknowledgement that threats exist both inside and outside traditional network boundaries. The Zero Trust security model eliminates implicit trust in any one element, node, or service and instead requires continuous verification of the operational picture via real-time information from multiple sources to determine access and other system responses. In essence, a Zero Trust Architecture allows users full access but only to the bare minimum they need to perform their jobs. If a device is compromised, zero trust can ensure that the damage is contained. The Zero Trust Architecture security model assumes that a breach is inevitable or has likely already occurred, so it constantly limits access to only what is needed and looks for anomalous or malicious activity. Zero Trust Architecture embeds comprehensive security monitoring; granular risk-based access controls; and system security automation in a coordinated manner throughout all aspects of the infrastructure in order to focus on protecting data in real-time within a dynamic threat environment. This data-centric security model allows the concept of least-privileged access to be applied for every access decision, where the answers to the questions of who, what, when, where, and how are critical for appropriately allowing or denying access to resources based on the combination of sever. *Id.*

the Executive Order seeks to improve the software supply chain.[164] The Executive Order directs the Secretary of Commerce through NIST to identify or create best practices concerning securing the software supply chain. A reoccurring issue concerning software development is the very common usage of open-source software as part of a software solution which may be subject to vulnerabilities or include malware. Secure software by design is an attempt to encourage the development of secure software from the start.[165] A

---

[164] On April 27, 2023, the Department of Homeland Security, Cybersecurity and Infrastructure Security Agency, requested comments concerning the burdens associated with complying with NIST "guidance including standards, procedures, or criteria to strengthen the security of the software supply chain" and OMB requirements that "agencies only use software provided by software producers who can attest to complying with Federal Government-specified secure software development practices." Department of Homeland Security, Agency Information Collection Activities: Request for Comment on Secure Software Development Attestation Common Form, Vol. 88, No. 81, Federal Register 25670-25672 (April 27, 2023).

[165] NIST was directed by the Executive Order to solicit input from relevant parties concerning developing secure software development practices. NIST has released the Secure Software Development Framework to guide government contractors supplying software as well as to serve as a guide to industry generally. NIST, Secure Software Development Framework Webpage, available at https://csrc.nist.gov/Projects/ssdf (last visited, August 9, 2023). Government contractors must attest to compliance with requirements. The Secure Software Development Framework addresses the software lifecycle and is divided into practices:

- **Prepare the Organization (PO)**: Ensure that the organization's people, processes, and technology are prepared to perform secure software development at the organization level and, in some cases, for individual development groups or projects.
- **Protect the Software (PS)**: Protect all components of the software from tampering and unauthorized access.
- **Produce Well-Secured Software (PW)**: Produce well-secured software with minimal security vulnerabilities in its releases.
- **Respond to Vulnerabilities (RV)**: Identify residual vulnerabilities in software releases and respond appropriately to address those vulnerabilities and prevent similar vulnerabilities from occurring in the future. *Id.* (emphasis in original).

In Office of Management and Budget memorandum M-23-16, the OMB clarifies some of the requirements concerning attestation compliance:

> Attestations must be collected from the producer of the software end product used by an agency because the producer of that end product is best positioned to ensure its security. An attestation provided by that producer to an agency serves as an affirmative statement that the producer follows the secure software development minimum requirements, as

articulated in the common form. These minimum requirements include several best practices regarding how software producers should address and maintain the security of code. These naturally extend to and guide the utilization of third-party software components, for both open-source and proprietary, and reflect best practices for minimizing risk from such components, as articulated in NIST's SSDF. Best practices include: regularly logging, monitoring, and auditing trust relationships used for authorization and access among components within the develop and build environments; taking consistent and reasonable steps to document and minimize use of software products that create undue risk; maintaining provenance data for internal and third-party code; and maintaining trusted source code supply chains. . . .

M-22-18 provides that, if a software producer cannot attest to one or more practices identified in the attestation form, an agency may still use the software if the producer identifies the practices to which they cannot attest, documents practices they have in place to mitigate associated risks, and submits a satisfactory Plan of Action and Milestones (POA&M). That alternative to attestation creates a means for agencies to work with software producers who do not yet meet the minimum requirements identified in the common form, but plan to do so.

This memorandum makes an adjustment to M-22-18's alternative to attestation. First, the producer of a given software application must identify the practices to which they cannot attest, document practices they have in place to mitigate associated risks, and submit a POA&M to an agency. If the agency finds the documentation satisfactory, it may continue using the software, but must concurrently seek an extension of the deadline for attestation from OMB. . . .

The agency must discontinue use of the software if the agency finds the software producer's documentation unsatisfactory or if the agency is unable to confirm that the producer has identified the practices to which it cannot attest; documented practices they have in place to mitigate associated risk; and submitted a POA&M to the agency. Additionally, if the agency fails to submit an extension request, the POA&M is not considered valid, and the agency must discontinue use of the software. Office of Management and Budget, M-23-16 (June 9, 2023), available at https://www.whitehouse.gov/wp-content/uploads/2023/06/M-23-16-Update-to-M-22-18-Enhancing-Software-Security.pdf.

software bill of materials or SBOM[166] is necessary to understand where the parts of a software solution originate.[167] This can facilitate updating, affixing responsibility, and the identification of vulnerabilities, for example. This section also directs the investigation of pilot programs concerning "consumer product labeling programs" to educate consumers regarding the cybersecurity status of Internet of Things devices and other software development practices. The Federal Communications Commission is responsible for the voluntary labeling program.[168]

---

[166] The Executive Order defines the Software Bill of Materials:

> [T]he term "Software Bill of Materials" or "SBOM" means a formal record containing the details and supply chain relationships of various components used in building software. Software developers and vendors often create products by assembling existing open source and commercial software components. The SBOM enumerates these components in a product. It is analogous to a list of ingredients on food packaging. An SBOM is useful to those who develop or manufacture software, those who select or purchase software, and those who operate software. Developers often use available open source and third-party software components to create a product; an SBOM allows the builder to make sure those components are up to date and to respond quickly to new vulnerabilities. Buyers can use an SBOM to perform vulnerability or license analysis, both of which can be used to evaluate risk in a product. Those who operate software can use SBOMs to quickly and easily determine whether they are at potential risk of a newly discovered vulnerability. A widely used, machine-readable SBOM format allows for greater benefits through automation and tool integration. The SBOMs gain greater value when collectively stored in a repository that can be easily queried by other applications and systems. Understanding the supply chain of software, obtaining an SBOM, and using it to analyze known vulnerabilities are crucial in managing risk. *Id.*

[167] One firm reports that, "92% of large enterprises now maintain an SBOM or plan to implement in the next year, as Log4j and threat landscape prompt evolution in cybersecurity strategies." See Biden's Cybersecurity Executive Order Fuels Seismic Changes in Software Development Practices, Sonatype Research Reveals, Sonatype (August 3, 2023).

[168] On February 4, 2022, the NIST issued a White Paper, titled, "Recommended Criteria for Cybersecurity Labeling for Consumer Internet of Things (IoT) Products." *Id.* (February 4, 2022), available at Recommended Criteria for Cybersecurity Labeling for Consumer Internet of Things (IoT) Products (nist.gov). The abstract of the White Paper states:

> Executive Order (EO) 14028, "Improving the Nation's Cybersecurity," tasks the National Institute of Standards and

The labeling program may include a safe harbor for companies that comply and are certified. A safe harbor may protect the company from liability once it is certified.

The Executive Order further initiates the creation of a Cyber Safety Review Board that would review non-military "significant" cyber incidents involving the Federal Civilian Executive Branch. This Review Board would act in a similar way to the National Transportation Safety Board. The Executive Order also attempts to standardize incident response and improve detection of vulnerabilities and incidents across federal agencies. Again, sharing of information with CISA and across agencies is critical to an effective response and mitigation of harm from cyber incidents. The Executive Order also provides for ensuring that information relating to incidents is collected and maintained. Finally, the Secretary of Defense is mandated to adopt equivalent or better cybersecurity practices than those in the order.[169]

Technology (NIST), in coordination with the Federal Trade Commission (FTC) and other agencies, to initiate pilot programs for cybersecurity labeling. NIST is, among other actions, directed "… to identify IoT cybersecurity criteria for a consumer labeling program…" This document seeks to fulfill this directive by recommending consumer IoT product label criteria, label design and consumer education considerations, and conformity assessment considerations for use by a scheme owner to inform a consumer Internet of Things (IoT) product labeling program. *See* Recommended Criteria for Cybersecurity Labeling for Consumer Internet of Things (IoT) Products | CSRC (nist.gov)

[169] The Department of Defense has been working to implement through rulemaking the Cybersecurity Maturity Model Certification 2.0 program which would allow DOD certification of cybersecurity practices of defense contractors concerning nonclassified information. See Department of Defense, About CMMC (Dec. 3, 2021), available at https://dodcio.defense.gov/CMMC/about/; Billy Mitchell, CMMC Final Rulemaking Process Kicks Off with Submission to OMB for Review, DefenseScoop (July 25, 2023). The DOD states: "The CMMC 2.0 program has three key features: Tiered Model: CMMC requires that companies entrusted with national security information implement standards at progressively advanced levels, depending on the type and sensitivity of the information. The program also sets forward the process for requiring protection of information this is flowed down to subcontractors. Assessment Requirement: CMMC assessments allow the Department to verify the implementation of clear cybersecurity standards. Implementation through Congracts: Once CMMC is fully implemented, certain DOD contractors that handles sensitive unclassified DOD information will be required to achieve a particular CMMC level as a

7.3 National Cybersecurity Strategy

The White House released the National Cybersecurity Strategy on March 2023, which replaces the prior 2018 strategy. The new strategy is viewed as a move to a more heavy-handed form of government regulation than prior efforts that were mostly voluntary and involved incentives.[170] The 2023 National Cybersecurity Strategy includes introductory information and a discussion of five pillars supporting the strategy. The introductory information sets for the general context for the strategy as well as its ultimate goal. The strategy recognizes the centrality of the Internet and cybersecurity for the protection of our democracy, democratic institutions, economy and personal lives. The strategy attempts to refocus cybersecurity efforts away from a burden on individuals and small organizations. Importantly, President Biden's opening letter to the strategy states: "We must ensure the Internet remains open, free, global, interoperable, reliable, and secure—anchored in universal values that respect human rights and fundamental freedoms." The Introduction frames the strategy: "Technologies have promoted democracy, free speech, innovation, and equality[, but have also] have been misused to enable transnational repression and digital authoritarianism; steal data and intellectual property; distribute disinformation; disrupt critical infrastructure; proliferate online harassment, exploitation, and abuse, enable criminals and foster violent extremism; and threaten peace and stability." And, the Introduction sets forth the intended outcome of the strategy: "Our goal is a defensible, resilient digital ecosystem where it is costlier to attack systems than defend them, where sensitive private information is secure and protected, and where neither incidents nor errors cascade into catastrophic, systemic consequences."

The five pillars supporting the strategy include: 1) Defend Critical Infrastructure; 2) Disrupt and Dismantle Threat Actors; 3) Shape Market Forces to Drive Security and Resilience; 4) Invest in a Resilient Future; and 5) Forge International Partnerships to Pursue Shared Goals. The pillars are built and expand on enhanced cooperation amongst the community impacted by cybersecurity issues. The success of the pillars is dependent on two shifts: 1) the

---

condition of contract award." *Id.* The program generally includes compliance with NIST 800-171 and 800-172. *Id.*

[170] Gibson Dunn, The Biden Administration Signals New Director for Cybersecurity (April 18, 2023) ("[T]he administration has definitely taken the position that it does not think that companies have done enough.").

burden to protect against cybersecurity vulnerabilities and incidents should be on the owners and operators of the cyberspace instead of end users; and 2) realign incentives to support long term cyberspace resilience and defensibility. The next part will describe each pillar along with each pillar's respective strategic objective.

The first pillar is Defend Critical Infrastructure. There are five strategic objectives for the first pillar: 1) establish cybersecurity requirements to support national security and public safety; 2) scale public-private collaboration; 3) integrate federal cybersecurity centers; 4) update federal incident response plans and processes; 5) modernize federal defenses. For the first strategic objective concerning establishing cybersecurity requirements, the strategy recognizes that each industry has a different cybersecurity risk profile and may need specific regulations. This part of the strategy document recognizes that a one-size fits all approach to cybersecurity is likely unproductive in the long term. The strategy notes that gaps in regulations must also be filled to ensure that the necessary incentives exist for private actors to take measures to achieve adequate cybersecurity that protects "national security and public safety, in addition to the security and safety of individuals, regulated entities, and their employees, customers, operations and data."[171] The strategy notes the need for regulation concerning cloud service providers. The second strategic objective addresses scaling public-private collaboration through not only human to human sharing of information, but also technical sharing of information through existing networks such as CISA, Sector Risk Management Agencies and industry.[172] The third strategic objective to integrate federal cybersecurity centers is directed to utilizing the centers as "collaborative nodes" across "homeland defense, law enforcement, intelligence, diplomatic, economic and military missions."[173] The fourth strategic objective seeks to improve incident response. It notes that the Cyber Incident Reporting for Critical Infrastructure Act of 2022 "require[s] covered

---

[171] *Id.* at 8.

[172] Information Sharing and Analysis Centers (ISACs) have been formed in over 20 various industry sectors considered critical infrastructure such as healthcare, transportation, defense and energy. See Robert A. Norton & Marcus Sachs, Cybersecurity and Food Defense: Establishing an ISAC for the Food and Agriculture Sector, Food & Safety Magazine (April 10, 2023). For example, there is a Financial Services ISAC which shares financial cybersecurity information. Id. In 2023, an ISAC was formed for the food and agriculture industry. Tim Starks, The Food and Agriculture Industry Gets New Center to Share Cybersecurity Information, Washington Post (May 24, 2023).

[173] *Id.* at 11.

entities in critical infrastructure sectors to report covered incidents to CISA within hours."[174] The fifth strategic objective seeks to modernize federal defenses through adopting zero trust architecture, for example.

The second pillar is disrupt and dismantle threat actors. Enhanced cooperation between the government and industry will "improve intelligence sharing, execute disruption campaigns at scale, deny adversaries use of U.S.-based infrastructure, and thwart global ransomware campaigns."[175] There are five strategic objectives: 1) integrate federal disruption activities; 2) enhance public-private operational collaboration to disrupt adversaries; 3) increase the speed and scale of intelligence sharing and victim notification; 4) prevent abuse of U.S.-based infrastructure; and 5) counter cybercrime, defeat ransomware. The first strategy is directed toward increasing collaboration between government, industry and foreign partners to disrupt adversaries. The Department of Defense is tasked with building on its Defense Forward approach to create a new integrated strategy to disrupt "malicious activity at scale."[176] The second strategy is to enhance public-private operational collaboration to disrupt adversaries through encouraging the private sector to work through nonprofit centers and the government to provide "threat specific collaboration."[177] The third strategy is to increase the speed and scale of intelligence sharing and victim notification. The fourth strategy is to prevent abuse of U.S.-based infrastructure through increased collaboration between the government and private cloud services and infrastructure providers. The fifth strategy is to counter cybercrime, defeat ransomware through "1) leveraging international cooperation to disrupt the ransomware ecosystem and isolate those countries that provide safe havens for criminals; 2) investigating ransomware crimes using law enforcement and other authorities to disrupt ransomware infrastructure and actors; 3) bolstering critical infrastructure resilience to withstand ransomware attacks; and 4) addressing the abuse of virtual currency to launder ransomware payments."

The third pillar is to shape market forces to drive security and resilience. This pillar has six strategic outcomes: 1) hold the

---

[174] *Id.*

[175] *Id.* at 14.

[176] *Id.* at 15. The DOD has proposed revisions to rules concerning the sharing of cyber threat information with all contractors in the Defense Industrial Base Cybersecurity activities. *See* 88 FR 27832 (May 3, 2023).

[177] *Id.* at 15.

stewards of our data accountable; 2) drive the development of secure IoT devices; 3) shift liability for insecure software products and services; 4) use federal grants and other incentives to build in security; 5) leverage federal procurement to improve accountability; and 6) explore a federal cyber insurance backstop. For the first strategy concerning holding the stewards of our data accountable, the strategy asserts the administration's support for legislation and other methods to "impose robust, clear limits on the ability to collect, use, transfer, and maintain personal data and provide strong protections for sensitive data like geolocation and health information."[178] The second strategy is to drive development of secure IoT devices such as through a security labeling program. The third strategy is to shift liability for insecure software products and services. This strategy sets for the problem:

> Markets impose inadequate costs on – and often reward— those entities that introduce vulnerable products or services into our digital ecosystem. Too many vendors ignore best practices for secure development, ship products with insecure default configurations or known vulnerabilities, and integrate third-party software of unvetted or unknown provenance. Software makers are able to leverage their market position to fully disclaim liability by contract, further reducing their incentive to follow secure-by-design principles or perform pre-release testing. Poor software security greatly increases systemic risk across the digital ecosystem and leave American citizens bearing the ultimate cost.[179]

The administration expresses the desire for legislation that will increase liability on software manufacturers, including a more robust standard of care for software development. The strategy further supports SBOMS, cross-sector vulnerability disclosure, for example. The fourth strategy is to leverage federal grants to incentivize secure software development, including through the complete lifecycle of the product or service, particularly for critical infrastructure. The fifth strategy is to leverage federal procurement to improve accountability. The strategy notes the DOJ's Civil Cyber-Fraud Initiative and civil actions under the False Claims Act to enforce contractual cybersecurity requirements against contractors of the federal government. The sixth strategy is to explore a federal cyber insurance backdrop for the private cyber insurance market.

---

[178] *Id.* at 20.
[179] *Id.* at 20.

The fourth pillar is to invest in a resilient future. There are six strategic objectives: 1) secure the technical foundation of the internet; 2) reinvigorate federal research and development for cybersecurity; 3) prepare for our post-quantum future; 4) secure our clean energy future; 5) support development of a digital identity ecosystem; and 6) develop a national strategy to strengthen our cyber workforce. The first strategy is to secure the technical foundation of the Internet through addressing vulnerabilities as the Internet is further developed and to support non-governmental standards developing organizations "to secure emerging technologies, enable interoperability, foster global market competition, and protect our national security and economic advantage."[180] The strategy further recognizes opposition to autocratic government control of the Internet. The second strategy is to reinvigorate federal research and development for cybersecurity.[181] The third strategy is to prepare for a post-quantum future by creating "interoperable quantum resistant cryptography."[182] The sixth strategy is to secure our clean energy future. The fifth strategy is to support development of a digital identity ecosystem that provides "strong, verifiable digital identity solutions that promote security, accessibility and interoperability, financial and social inclusion, consumer privacy, and economic growth."[183] The final strategy is to develop a national strategy to strengthen our cyber workforce to address the gap in the number of qualified employees and jobs in the field.

---

[180] *Id.* at 24.

[181] The Resilient Investment Planning and Development Working Group drafted a White Paper on Research, Development, and Innovation for Enhancing Resilience of Cyber-Physical Critical Infrastructure: Needs and Strategic Actions which, in part, focuses on federal R&D groups such as "federal departments, agencies, national laboratories, and federally-funded research centers" and provides a non-exclusive list of research, development and innovation needs in three areas: "1) Resilience of critical services that depend on cyber-physical infrastructure systems; 2) Societal dimensions of cyber-physical infrastructure resilience including considerations of equity, capacity and economics; and 3) Applied and user-engaged research methods to address cyber-physical infrastructure resilience challenges at local and regional scales." Resilient Investment Planning and Development Working Group, White Paper: Research, Development, and Innovation for Enhancing Resilience of Cyber-Physical Critical Infrastructure: Needs and Strategic Actions (March 2023). The White Paper notes that industrial control systems for critical infrastructure such as water and manufacturing provide access points for compromise as they are digital and there is a lack of a comprehensive understanding of systems are interacting and related to the supply chain. *Id.* at 4.

[182] *Id.* at 25.

[183] *Id.* at 26.

The fifth pillar is to forge international partnerships to pursue shared goals. The fifth pillar has five strategic objectives: 1) build coalitions to counter threats to our digital ecosystem; 2) strengthen international partner capacity; 3) expand U.S. ability to assist allies and partners; 4) build coalitions to reinforce global norms of responsible state behavior; and 5) secure global supply chains for information, communications, and operational technology products and services. For the first strategy on building coalitions, the strategy sets a goal of expanding efforts to use coalitions to "advance common cybersecurity interests by sharing cyber threat information, exchanging model cybersecurity practices, comparing sector-specific expertise, driving secure-by-design principles, and coordinating policy and incident response activities."[184] The strategy also expresses the concern about the origin of cyber attacks on U.S. infrastructure and systems by foreign actors. The second objective is to strengthen international partner capacity through leveraging U.S. expertise for the benefit of allies. The third objective is to expand U.S. ability to assist allies and partners through the creation of policies to assess when to do so. The fourth strategic goal is to build coalitions to reinforce global norms of responsible state behavior through "hold[ing] irresponsible states accountable when they fail to uphold their commitments."[185] The final strategy objective is to secure global supply chains for information, communications, and operational technology products and services through, in part, ensuring that important "inputs, components, and systems [are] developed at home or in close coordination with allies and partners who share our vision of an open, free, global, interoperable, reliable, and secure Internet."[186] Notably, "[t]he Department of State will further accelerate these efforts through the new International Technology Security and Innovation Fund to support the creation of secure and diverse supply chains for semiconductors and telecommunications."[187]

---

[184] *Id.* at 30. The Cybersecurity and Infrastructure Agency issued a Press Release which includes representations concerning allies with respect to the LockBit Ransomware. See Cybersecurity & Infrastructure Agency, U.S. and International Partners Release Comprehensive Cyber Advisory on LockBit Ransomware (June 14, 2023) (listing comments from Australia, Canada, United Kingdom, Germany, France, and New Zealand concerning LockBit Ransomware.).

[185] *Id.* at 32.

[186] *Id.* at 32.

[187] *Id.* at 33.

7.4 Cyber Incident Reporting for Critical Infrastructure Act of 2022

On March 15, 2022, President Biden signed the Cyber Incident Reporting for Critical Infrastructure Act of 2022 [Reporting Act of 2022].[188] The Reporting Act of 2022 requires cybersecurity incident reporting for critical infrastructure. The National Cybersecurity and Communications Integration Center [NCCIC] of the Department of Homeland Security is primarily responsible for receiving and analyzing incident reports, including those related to ransomware. NCCIC is also responsible for sharing information to relevant entities. The Act also provides for rule-making, but also specifies certain information that must be part of the eventual rules. The Reporting Act of 2022 has several main provisions, including: Section 2242. Required Reporting of Certain Cyber Incidents; Section 2243. Voluntary Reporting of Other Cyber Incidents; Section 2244. Noncompliance with Required Reporting; Section 2245. Information Shared with or Provided to the Federal Government; Section 2246. Cyber Incident Reporting Council; Section 104 Federal Sharing of Incident Reports; Section 105. Ransomware Vulnerability Warning Pilot Program; and Section 106. Ransomware Threat Mitigation Activities.

The key parts include Section 2242. Required Reporting of Certain Cyber Incidents which is codified at 6 U.S.C. 681(b). Section 2242 requires reporting of covered cyber incidents within 72 hours after the entity reasonably believes the incident has occurred. Moreover, if a covered entity makes a ransomware payment, that payment must be disclosed within 24 hours after it was made. These requirements apply unless the entity has an agreement with the agency providing otherwise that satisfies the law. The final rules must specify types of covered entities as well as substantial cybersecurity incidents that trigger application of the law. For example, an applicable incident shall include substantial compromises of confidentiality, integrity and availability of networks or systems, or "serious impact on the safety and resiliency of operational systems and processes."[189] Additionally, "a disruption of business or industrial operations" is included in a covered incident.[190] Importantly, supply chain or third-party cloud service compromise shall be disclosed as a covered

---

[188] Cyber Incident Reporting for Critical Infrastructure Act of 2022, codified as amended at 6 U.S.C. §§681-681g.
[189] *Id.*
[190] *Id.*

incident. The definition of a substantial covered incident will also consider the following factors: "the sophistication or novelty of the tactics used" and "the type, volume, and sensitivity of the data at issue;" number of impacted individuals; and "potential impacts on industrial control systems."[191] A substantial covered incident does not include good faith intrusions at the request of the operator or threats of entry based on extortion. The description of a covered incident in a report includes information such as what happened and the attacks impact on the relevant network or systems, identify of the perpetrator, description of exploited vulnerabilities and other information concerning how the attack occurred, identification of the entity and, if applicable, categories of information impacted. Similar information is required for a ransomware report including information specific to the ransomware payment. Section 2242 also requires supplemental reporting and provides information concerning the required substance of all reporting.

Section 2243. Voluntary Reporting of Other Cyber Incidents allows the submission of reports that are not required under Section 2242, and importantly, the protections provided for submission of required reports are also provided to voluntary reports. Section 2243. Noncompliance with Required Reporting includes the ability of the Attorney General to bring a civil action to enforce a subpoena to obtain information concerning an unreported incident or ransomware payment after a failure of a covered entity to respond or inadequately respond to a request. Section 2245. Information Shared with or Provided to the Federal Government specifically delineates the purposes to which the information provided in incident reports can be used by the federal government.[192] That provision further provides protections for the information submitted for voluntary and involuntary reports as "commercial, financial and proprietary information" when designated by the entity and exempt from disclosure under the Freedom of Information Act.[193] Moreover, submitting information does not waive any legal or trade secret protection. The submitted information is also, "not . . . subject to a rule of any Federal agency or department or any judicial doctrine regarding ex parte communications with a decision-making official." Importantly, Section 2245 also provides an exemption from liability related to the submission of an incident report.[194]

---

[191] *Id.*

[192] *Id.*

[193] *Id.*

[194] That provision specifically states, in relevant part:

(c) LIABILITY PROTECTIONS.—

Section 104 authorizes the sharing of incident reports among federal agencies. Section 105. Ransomware Vulnerability Warning Pilot Program allows the creation of a warning program regarding ransomware designed "to leverage existing authorities and technology to specifically develop processes and procedures for, and to dedicate resources to, identifying information systems that contain security vulnerabilities associated with common ransomware attacks, and to notify the owners of those vulnerable systems of their security vulnerability." Section 106. Ransomware Threat Mitigation Activities authorizes the creation of a "Joint Ransomware Task Force to coordinate an ongoing nationwide campaign against ransomware attacks, and identify and pursue opportunities for international cooperation."

7.5 Additional Sectoral Federal Cybersecurity Regulation

The federal government has been creating cybersecurity regulation and guidance at a blistering pace.[195] As previously discussed, certain industry sectors have had cybersecurity regulations in place for quite some time. For example, industry sectors such as healthcare and finance that collect sensitive personal health and financial information have relatively robust

---

> (1) IN GENERAL.—No cause of action shall lie or be maintained in any court by any person or entity and any such action shall be promptly dismissed for the submission of a report pursuant to section 2242(a) that is submitted in conformance with this subtitle and the rule promulgated under section 2242(b), except that this subsection shall not apply with regard to an action by the Federal Government pursuant to section 2244(c)(2).
> (2) SCOPE.—The liability protections provided in this subsection shall only apply to or affect litigation that is solely based on the submission of a covered cyber incident report or ransom payment report to the Agency. *Id.*

[195] An example includes the Cybersecurity and Infrastructure Agency's Binding Operational Directive 23-02 released on June 13, 2023 which requires federal agencies to reduce attack surface by adopting zero trust architecture for internet facing devices. *See* Cybersecurity & Infrastructure Agency, Binding Operational Directive 23-02 (June 13, 2023). CISA also releases guidance such as the Guide to Securing Remote Access Software. See Cybersecurity & Infrastructure Agency, Guide to Securing Remote Access Software (June 6, 2023) (making numerous recommendations for securing remote access software such as compliance with NIST cybersecurity risk framework, use SBOMs and adopt zero trust architecture in most circumstances.).

cybersecurity regulatory schemes. Recently, the federal government has been addressing cybersecurity across various industries by updating regulations or creating new regulations. In some areas, the federal government is in the process of devising new regulations, such as satellite communications. Some directions are voluntary and others are mandatory. This section will review some cybersecurity mandatory and voluntary requirements __.

7.5.[A] Department of Labor, Employee Benefits Administration

The Department of Labor, Employee Benefits Administration has released a cybersecurity Best Practices document for ERISA retirement plan beneficiaries. The Best Practices document requires a relatively robust cybersecurity program. The document does not include a significant amount of detail, but provides the general requirements for a cybersecurity program. A "formal, well-documented cybersecurity program" is required.[196] The cybersecurity program requires, at a minimum, identifying threats, addressing those threats, recovering from threats and restoring operations. In addition to the program, annual risk assessments, third party audits of security controls, encryption of data in storage and transit, and cybersecurity training are required. There must be clearly assigned roles and responsibility for information security. Strong access controls are required. Moreover, cloud services must be subject to security review and independent audit. A secure system development life cycle program must be implemented.

7.5[B] Cybersecurity in Medical Devices

The Food and Drug Administration primarily regulates medical devices. U.S.C. section 360n-2 of Title 21 concerns premarket approval requirements by the Food and Drug Administration for cybersecurity for medical devices that are defined "cyber devices." A "cyber device" is a device that: "(1) includes software validated, installed, or authorized by the sponsor as a device or in a device; (2) has the ability to connect to the internet; and (3) contains any such technological characteristics validated, installed, or authorized by the sponsor that could be vulnerable to cybersecurity threats."[197] A cyber device must meet several cybersecurity requirements. First, the sponsor must submit a plan for monitoring, identifying and addressing post-market

---

[196] *Id.* at 1.

[197] 21 U.S.C. § 360n-2.

vulnerabilities. Second, the sponsor must have reasonable processes in place to demonstrate the device is cybersecure and to address post-market issues including patching regular and out of cycle vulnerabilities. Third, the sponsor must provide a software bill of materials that includes: "commercial, open-source, and off-the-shelf software components."[198] Finally, the sponsor must follow any cybersecurity requirements that are additionally set forth by the Secretary. There is an exemption to the cybersecurity requirements as specified by the Secretary.

7.5[C] FOOD AND AGRICULTURE[199]

The food and agriculture industry is primarily regulated by the Department of Agriculture and the Food and Drug Administration. The FDA provides some general advice concerning cybersecurity on its website.[200] Notably, several congresspeople

---

[198] *Id.*

[199] Related to food and agriculture is water safety. The Environmental Protection Agency provides resources concerning cybersecurity for the water sector at https://www.epa.gov/waterreslience/. The EPA has released a memorandum titled, "Guidance on Evaluating Cybersecurity During Public Water System Sanitary Surveys." Environmental Protection Agency, Guidance for Evaluating Cybersecurity During Public Water System Sanitary Surveys (March 2023). The memorandum provides instruction on how to include cybersecurity within a PWs sanitary survey, including a checklist with items such as "detect and block repeated unsuccessful login attempts[;] change default passwords[; require multi-factor authentication; r]equire approval before new software is installed or deployed[; c]ollect security logs[; u]se effective encryption[; h]ave a named role/position/title that is responsible and accountable for planning, resourcing, and execution of cybersecurity activities at PWS[; p]atch or otherwise mitigate known vulnerabilities within the recommended time frame[; i]nclude cybersecurity as an evaluation criterion for the procurement of OT assets and services[; h]ave a written cybersecurity incident response (IR) plan for critical threat scenarios[; maintain b]ackup systems necessary for operations[; s]egment OT and IT networks and deny connections to the OT network by default unless explicitly allowed[; k]eep a list of threats and adversary tactics, techniques, and procedures[; and u]se email security controls to reduce common email-based threats . . .." *Id.* at A-6. The appendices include significant additional information concerning the checklist. *Id.* at B-1 -B-63. Notably, the Eight Circuit has stayed the implementation of the cybersecurity interpretative rule. See American Water Works Association, Court Pauses Cybersecurity Rule for AWWA, NRWA Water Utility Members Following Legal Challenge (July 12, 2023), available at https://www.awwa.org/AWWA-Articles/court-pauses-cybersecurity-rule-for-awwa-nrwa-water-utility-members-following-legal-challenge1.

[200] https://www.fda.gov/food/food-defense-initiatives/food-and-agriculture-sector-and-other-related-activities.

have introduced bills in 2023 concerning agriculture and cybersecurity. For example, Congresspersons Pfluger, Veasey, Curtis and Matsui introduced H.R. 1219 titled, "Food and Agriculture Industry Cybersecurity Support Act."[201] The Act is primarily directed at creating a publicly available website concerning cybersecurity resources for food and agricultural industry participants. The "Food and Agriculture Industry " is defined as, "equipment and systems utilized in the food and agriculture supply chain, such as computer vision algorithms for precision agriculture, grain silos, and related food and agriculture storage infrastructure; food and agriculture goods processors, growers, and distributors; and information technology systems of businesses engaged in farming, ranching, planting, harvesting, food and agriculture product storage, food or animal genetic modification, the design or production of agrochemicals, or the design or production of food and agriculture tools."[202] The Act also requires the creation of a list of public and private cybersecurity best practices. The list should address the following:

(i) Risk-based cybersecurity-informed engineering, including continuous monitoring and resiliency. (ii) Planning for retention or recovery of positive control of systems in the food and agriculture industry in the event of a cybersecurity incident. (iii) Protection against unauthorized access to critical functions of the food and agriculture industry. (iv) Cybersecurity against threats to products of the food and agriculture industry throughout the lifetimes of such products. (v) How businesses in the food and agriculture industry should respond to ransomware attacks, including details on the legal obligations of such businesses in the even of such an attack, including reporting requirements and Federal resources for support. (vi) Any other recommendations to ensure the confidentiality, availability, and integrity of data residing on or in transit through systems in the food and agriculture industry.[203]

7.5[D] TRANSPORTATION[204]

The Department of Transportation primarily regulates rail, highway and air traffic. However, the Transportation Security

---

[201] House Report 1219 (February 27, 2023).

[202] Id. at Section 2(c)(4)(A-C).

[203] *Id.* at § 2(a)(2).

[204] The Coast Guard has proposed regulations concerning adopting cybersecurity requirements for the Maritime Transportation System, such as for ports and navigable waterways. CISA has also issued a Marine Transportation System Resilience Assessment Guide. See CISA, CISA Releases the Marine

Administration of the Department of Homeland Security has recently issued numerous cybersecurity requirements for rail and air traffic. In October of 2022, the Transportation Security Administration issued a security directive to owners and operators of freight and passenger railways concerning resilience.[205] The security directive requires the owners and operators to submit a TSA approved cybersecurity plan. The security directive contains details concerning the parts of the cybersecurity plan which include: establishing network segmentation of Operational Technology in case Information Technology is compromised to the railways system continues to operate; have network security controls and continuous monitoring in place to prevent unauthorized access to Critical Cyber System Operations and to detect anomalies in those operations; have a risk based patching system in place; and establish an assessment program and submit an annual report concerning "proactive[]" review of cybersecurity measures and deal with vulnerabilities. The security directive includes additional detail concerning specific cybersecurity measures. The cybersecurity information provided to the TSA is also considered sensitive security information and must be protected as described in 49 U.S.C. section 1520.[206] The Transportation Security Administration has issued similar cybersecurity requirements for airport and aircraft operators.[207] The Transportation Security Administration has issued an Advanced Notice of Proposed Rulemaking concerning "Enhancing

---

Transportation System Reliance Assessment Guide (March 15, 2023). The Cyberspace Solarium Commission has released a report titled, Full Steam Ahead: Enhancing Maritime Cybersecurity (March 28, 2023), available at https://cybersolarium.org/csc-2-0-reports/full-steam-ahead-enhancing-maritime-cybersecurity/.

[205] Department of Homeland Security, Transportation Security Administration, Security Directive (October 24, 2022), available at https://www.tsa.gov/sites/default/files/sd-1580-82-2022-01.pdf.

[206] The TSA has additional cybersecurity information concerning surface transportation at https://www.tsa.gov/for-industry/surface-transportation-cybersecurity-toolkit. The Federal Transit Administration also has cybersecurity resources for transit authorities at https://www.transit.dot.gov/regulations-and-programs/safety/cybersecurity-resources-transit-agencies.

[207] The TSA has issued similar cybersecurity requirements for pipelines and pipeline operators as railroad operators/owners and airport and aircraft operators. Transportation Security Administration, TSA Revises and Reissues Cybersecurity Requirements for Pipeline Owners and Operators (July 21, 2022), available at https://www.tsa.gov/news/press/releases/2022/07/21/tsa-revises-and-reissues-cybersecurity-requirements-pipeline-owners

Surface Cyber Risk Management" to solicit commentary concerning improving cybersecurity for surface transportation.[208]

The Department of Transportation, Federal Aviation Administration regulates aircrafts.[209] For example, the Federal Aviation Administration has an Aircraft Network Security Program requirement [ANSP].[210] The ANSP requirement was adopted to address the internet connectivity risks associated with aircraft, including issues associated with connected avionics components.[211] Notably, the Flight Standards Information Management System states that preexisting regulations fail to specifically address electronic risks associated with connected aircraft.[212] The ANSP requires a security system that protects the aircraft systems from attack or compromise, including providing risk mitigation strategies and that threats are identified and dealt with. Additionally, the operator of aircraft must provide cybersecurity information and implementation practices for initial certification of aircraft as well as existing aircraft that are connected.

---

[208] Transportation Security Administration, Vol. 87, No. 229 FR 73527 (November 30, 2022).

[209] The Federal Aviation Administration also holds a yearly cybersecurity awareness symposium with additional resources at https://www.faa.gov/air_traffic/technology/cas. The Department of Transportation also regulates other areas such as automobiles. The Department of Transportation issued a document titled, "Cybersecurity Best Practices for the Safety of Modern Vehicles" for public comment. *See* DEP'T OF TRANSPORTATION, *Cybersecurity Best Practices for the Safety of Modern Vehicles* (January 12, 2021), available at Regulations | US Department of Transportation. The TSA has also issued other cybersecurity directives concerning railroad and surface transportation. *See* DEP'T OF HOMELAND SECURITY, *Surface Transportation Cybersecurity Toolkit*, available at Surface Transportation Cybersecurity Toolkit | Transportation Security Administration (tsa.gov) (last visited May 18, 2022). The Department of Homeland Security has also issued a roadmap for dealing with the threat of quantum computing in the cybersecurity space. *See* DEP'T OF HOMELAND SECURITY, *Post-Quantum Cryptography*, available at Post-Quantum Cryptography | Homeland Security (dhs.gov) (last visited October 12, 2021).

[210] *See* Flight Standards Information Management System, Vol. 3 *General Technical Administration*, Chapter 61 *Aircraft Network Security Program* (June 5, 2019), available at FSIMS Document Viewer (faa.gov).

[211] *Id.*

[212] *Id.*

7.5[E] ENERGY[213]

This section discusses some cybersecurity requirements issued or approved by the Federal Energy Regulatory Commission and the Nuclear Regulatory Commission. The Federal Energy Regulatory Commission has approved numerous cybersecurity standards to safeguard the electrical grid.[214] FERC recently approved a proposal to increase the level of cybersecurity protection for "supply chain risk management for assets containing low impact Bulk Electric System ("BES") Cyber Systems."[215] The accepted proposal states, in part:

> Proposed Requirement R2 of CIP-003-9 requires Responsible Entities to implement cyber security plans for low impact BES Cyber Systems that address the following areas: (1) cyber security awareness; (2) physical security; (3) electronic access; (4) Cyber Security Incident response; (5) Transient Cyber Asset and Removable Media malicious code risk mitigation; and (6) vendor electronic remote access security controls. The revisions in proposed Reliability Standard CIP-003-9 improve upon Commission approved CIP-003-8 by adding new requirements focused on supply chain risk management for low impact BES Cyber Systems. Proposed Requirement R1, Part 1.2.6 requires Responsible Entities to include the topic of "vendor electronic remote access security controls" in their cyber security policies. Proposed Requirement R2, Attachment 1, Section 6 requires Responsible Entities with assets containing low impact BES Cyber Systems that have established vendor electronic remote access to have methods for determining and disabling that vendor electronic remote access as well as one or more methods for detecting malicious communications for only that vendor electronic remote access. The proposed requirements enhance reliability by requiring controls that grant Responsible Entities additional visibility into threats posed by supply chain

---

[213] The Federal Energy Regulatory Commission (FERC) "revis[ed] its regulations to provide incentive-based rate treatments for the transmission of electric energy in interstate commerce and the sale of electric energy at wholesale in interstate commerce by utilities for the purpose of benefiting consumers by encouraging investments by utilities in advanced cybersecurity technology and participation by utilities in cybersecurity threat information sharing programs, as directed by the Infrastructure Investment and Jobs Act of 2021 . . .." 88 FR 28348 (May 3, 2023).

[214] These cybersecurity standards are part of the Reliability Standards and are available at https://www.nerc.com/pa/Stand/Pages/USRelStand.aspx.

[215] FERC, Order Approving Reliability Standard CIP-003-9, 182 FERC 61, 155 (March 16, 2023).

risks to low impact BES Cyber Systems. The proposed requirements also address the risks identified in NERC assessments (Exhibit E) by requiring controls around vendor electronic remote access, a potential vector of attack into BES Cyber Systems.[216]

FERC has directed the North American Electric Reliability Corporation to "develop and submit for Commission approval new or modified Reliability Standards that require internal network security monitoring within a trusted Critical Infrastructure Protection networked environment for high and medium impact Bulk Electric System Cyber Systems."[217] FERC notes that, "In the context of an insider threat, an employee with elevated administrative credentials could identify and collect data, add additional accounts, delete logs, or even exfiltrate data without being detected."[218]

The Nuclear Regulatory Commission has issued regulations concerning the submission of a cybersecurity plan and creation of a program for nuclear power plant operators in 10 C.F.R. § 73.54 relating to digital computer and communications systems.[219] The program is designed to protect: "(i) Safety-related and important-to-safety functions; (ii) Security functions; (iii) Emergency preparedness functions, including offsite communications; and (iv) Support systems and equipment which, if compromised, would

---

[216] North American Electric Reliability Corporation, PETITION OF THE NORTH AMERICAN ELECTRIC RELIABILITY CORPORATION FOR APPROVAL OF PROPOSED RELIABILITY STANDARD CIP-003-9 (December 6, 2022), available at https://www.nerc.com/FilingsOrders/us/NERC%20Filings%20to%20FERC%20DL/Petition_for_Approval_CIP-003-9_filing.pdf.

[217] Department of Energy, Federal Energy Regulatory Commission, Vol. 87, No. 18 FR (January 27, 2022); see also FERC Strengthens Reliability Standards for Monitoring Electric Grid Cyber Systems (January 19, 2023) ("FERC today acted to strengthen the cybersecurity of the grid by directing the North American Electric Reliability Corporation (NERC) to develop and submit Reliability Standards requiring internal network security monitoring (INSM) for high-impact bulk electric system cyber systems and medium-impact systems with high-speed internet connections.
Today's final rule also directs NERC to study the risks posed by the lack of INSM. It also directs NERC to study the feasibility of implementing INSM at bulk electric cyber systems that would not be addressed by the new or modified standard."). This is designed to fill a gap in current Critical Infrastructure Protection Reliability Standards. *Id.*

[218] *Id.*

[219] 10 C.F.R. § 73.54.

adversely impact safety, security, or emergency preparedness functions."[220] The operator must: "(1) Analyze digital computer and communication systems and networks and identify those assets that must be protected against cyber attacks to satisfy paragraph (a) of this section, (2) Establish, implement, and maintain a cyber security program for the protection of the assets identified in paragraph (b)(1) of this section; and (3) Incorporate the cyber security program as a component of the physical protection program."[221] Additionally, the program should, "(1) Implement security controls to protect the assets identified by paragraph (b)(1) of this section from cyber attacks; (2) Apply and maintain defense-in-depth protective strategies to ensure the capability to detect, respond to, and recover from cyber attacks (3) Mitigate the adverse affects of cyber attacks; and (4) Ensure that the functions of protected assets identified by paragraph (b)(1) of this section are not adversely impacted due to cyber attacks."[222] The program must also provide training and awareness concerning cybersecurity issues, provide required notifications concerning incidents, and manage cybersecurity risks. The cybersecurity plan must address response and recovery, including: "(i) Maintain the capability for timely detection and response to cyber attacks; (ii) Mitigate the consequences of cyber attacks; (iii) Correct exploited vulnerabilities; and (iv) Restore affected systems, networks, and/or equipment affected by cyber attacks."[223]

7.5[F] COMMUNICATIONS

The Federal Communications Commission has acted in numerous ways to address cybersecurity issues in the telecommunications space. For example, the FCC has released a planning tool used to specifically help small business with developing effective cybersecurity plans called, "Cyberplanner." A user can enter various terms in the Cyberplanner such as Network Security, Website Security, and Privacy and Data Security.[224] In response to those terms, the Cyberplanner will provide specific inquiries and guidance concerning cybersecurity. The Federal Communications Commission has also released a best practices

---

[220] *Id.*

[221] *Id.*

[222] *Id.*

[223] *Id.* For additional information concerning NRC cybersecurity requirements, please see https://www.nrc.gov/security/cybersecurity.html.

[224] *See* FEDERAL COMMUNICATIONS COMMISSION, Cyberplanner, available at Cyberplanner | Federal Communications Commission (fcc.gov) (last visited October 1, 2021).

guide.[225] Moreover, the Federal Communications Commission has a Communications, Security, Reliability, and Interoperability Council (CSRIC). The CSRIC "make[s] recommendations to the Commission to promote the security, reliability, and resiliency of the Nation's communications systems." The Council consists of working groups who are tasked with specific inquires. In 2021, working groups were convened on numerous topics some of which included: Managing Security Risk in the Transition to 5G; Managing Security Risk in Emerging 5G Implementations; and Security Vulnerabilities during the IP Transition. CSRIC also provides best practices documents[226] and reports.[227]

The FCC has also engaged in investigating vulnerabilities in various telecommunications technologies impacting the Internet.[228] The FCC is also responsible for the cybersecurity software labeling program for internet of things devices.[229] The

---

[225] *See* FEDERAL COMMUNICATIONS COMMISSION, *Ten Cybersecurity Tips for Small Businesses*, available at DOC-306595A1.pdf (last visited October 1, 2021).

[226] FEDERAL COMMUNICATIONS COMMISSION, *CSRIC Best Practices*, available at CSRIC Best Practices | Data | Federal Communications Commission (fcc.gov) (last visited October 4, 2021).

[227] FEDERAL COMMUNICATIONS COMMISSION, *CSRIC Reports*, available at Communications Security, Reliability, and Interoperability Reports | Federal Communications Commission (fcc.gov) (last visited October 4, 2021).

[228] See Hogan Lovells, The Federal Communications Commission (again) sets its sights on cybersecurity, Lexology (October 31, 2022), available at https://www.lexology.com/library/detail.aspx?g=45c6a0fa-6de0-4f55-987b-c368952f844f ("The FCC launched a broad-reaching inquiry into the vulnerabilities threatening the security and integrity of the Border Gateway Protocol (BGP), which is central to the Internet's global routing system, their impact on the transmission of data from email, e-commerce, and bank transactions to interconnected Voice-over Internet Protocol (VoIP) and 9-1-1 calls, and how best to address them. . . . Most recently, on October 27, 2022, the FCC adopted a Notice of Proposed Rulemaking regarding strengthening the nation's Emergency Alert System (EAS) and Wireless Emergency Alerts (WEA) programs against security threats.").

[229] *See* White House, Biden-Harris Administration Announces Cybersecurity Labeling Program for Smart Devices to Protect American Consumers (July 18, 2023), available at https://www.whitehouse.gov/briefing-room/statements-releases/2023/07/18/biden-harris-administration-announces-cybersecurity-labeling-program-for-smart-devices-to-protect-american-consumers/ ("The new "U.S. Cyber Trust Mark" program proposed by Federal Communications Commission (FCC) Chairwoman Jessica Rosenworcel would raise the bar for cybersecurity across common devices, including smart refrigerators, smart microwaves, smart televisions, smart climate control systems, smart fitness trackers, and more."). The Press Release further states:

Several major electronics, appliance, and consumer product manufacturers, retailers, and trade associations have made voluntary commitments to increase cybersecurity for the products they sell. Manufacturers and retailers announcing support and commitments today to further the program include Amazon, Best Buy, Google, LG Electronics U.S.A., Logitech, and Samsung Electronics. Under the proposed new program, consumers would see a newly created "U.S. Cyber Trust Mark" in the form of a distinct shield logo applied to products meeting established cybersecurity criteria. The goal of the program is to provide tools for consumers to make informed decisions about the relative security of products they choose to bring into their homes.

Acting under its authorities to regulate wireless communication devices, the FCC is expected to seek public comment on rolling out the proposed voluntary cybersecurity labeling program, which is expected to be up and running in 2024. As proposed, the program would leverage stakeholder-led efforts to certify and label products, based on specific cybersecurity criteria published by the National Institute of Standards and Technology (NIST) that, for example, requires unique and strong default passwords, data protection, software updates, and incident detection capabilities.

Today, the FCC is applying to register a national trademark with the U.S. Patent and Trademark Office that would be applied to products meeting the established cybersecurity criteria. The Administration—including the Cybersecurity and Infrastructure Security Agency—would support the FCC in educating consumers to look for the new label when making purchasing decisions, and encouraging major U.S. retailers to prioritize labeled products when placing them on the shelf and online.

To further enhance transparency and competition:

- The FCC intends the use a QR code linking to a national registry of certified devices to provide consumers with specific and comparable security information about these smart products. Working with other regulators and the U.S. Department of Justice, the Commission plans to establish oversight and enforcement safeguards to maintain trust and confidence in the program.
- NIST will also immediately undertake an effort to define cybersecurity requirements for consumer-grade routers—a higher-risk type of product that, if compromised, can be used to eavesdrop, steal passwords, and attack other devices and high value networks. NIST will complete this

FCC also administers a data breach notification rule for telecommunication carriers.[230] The rule is titled, "Notification of customer proprietary network information security breaches."[231] The rule requires disclosure of the breach to law enforcement within seven days of reasonable determination of the breach and before customer notification.

---

work by the end of 2023, to permit the Commission to consider use of these requirements to expand the labeling program to cover consumer grade routers.

- The U.S. Department of Energy today also announced a collaborative initiative with National Labs and industry partners to research and develop cybersecurity labeling requirements for smart meters and power inverters, both essential components of the clean, smart grid of the future.
- Internationally, the U.S. Department of State is committed to supporting the FCC to engage allies and partners toward harmonizing standards and pursuing mutual recognition of similar labeling efforts. *Id.*

[230] 47 CFR § 64.2011. The FCC has proposed amendments to this rule. *See* FCC, Data Breach Reporting Requirements, 88 FR 3953-01 (January 23, 2023) ("In this document, the Federal Communications Commission (Commission) begins the process to update and strengthen its data breach rule to provide greater protections to the public. We propose to expand the Commission's definition of "breach" to include inadvertent disclosures of customer information and seek comment on adopting a harm-based trigger for breach notifications. We also propose to require carriers to notify the Commission, in addition to the Secret Service and FBI, as soon as practicable after discovery of a breach. We also propose to eliminate the mandatory waiting period before notifying customers and instead require carriers to notify customers of CPNI breaches without unreasonable delay after discovery of a breach unless requested by law enforcement. We also propose to make changes to our TRS data breach reporting rule consistent with those we propose to our CPNI breach reporting rule.").

[231] *Id.*

7.5[G] SATELLITE

The Trump Administration released the Space Policy Directive 5 concerning cybersecurity. The Directive paints in broad strokes both the need the policy as well as the requirements. The requirements section states:

> Sec. 4. Principles. (a) Space systems and their supporting infrastructure, including software, should be developed and operated using risk-based, cybersecurity-informed engineering. Space systems should be developed to continuously monitor, anticipate, and adapt to mitigate evolving malicious cyber activities that could manipulate, deny, degrade, disrupt, destroy, surveil, or eavesdrop on space system operations. Space system configurations should be resourced and actively managed to achieve and maintain an effective and resilient cyber survivability posture throughout the space system lifecycle.
>
> (b) Space system owners and operators should develop and implement cybersecurity plans for their space systems that incorporate capabilities to ensure operators or automated control center systems can retain or recover positive control of space vehicles. These plans should also ensure the ability to verify the integrity, confidentiality, and availability of critical functions and the missions, services, and data they enable and provide. At a minimum, space system owners and operators should consider, based on risk assessment and tolerance, incorporating in their plans:
>
> (i) Protection against unauthorized access to critical space vehicle functions. This should include safeguarding command, control, and telemetry links using effective and validated authentication or encryption measures designed to remain secure against existing and anticipated threats during the entire mission lifetime;
>
> (ii) Physical protection measures designed to reduce the vulnerabilities of a space vehicle's command, control, and telemetry receiver systems;

(iii) Protection against communications jamming and spoofing, such as signal strength monitoring programs, secured transmitters and receivers, authentication, or effective, validated, and tested encryption measures designed to provide security against existing and anticipated threats during the entire mission lifetime;

(iv) Protection of ground systems, operational technology, and information processing systems through the adoption of deliberate cybersecurity best practices. This adoption should include practices aligned with the National Institute of Standards and Technology's Cybersecurity Framework to reduce the risk of malware infection and malicious access to systems, including from insider threats. Such practices include logical or physical segregation; regular patching; physical security; restrictions on the utilization of portable media; the use of antivirus software; and promoting staff awareness and training inclusive of insider threat mitigation precautions;

(v) Adoption of appropriate cybersecurity hygiene practices, physical security for automated information systems, and intrusion detection methodologies for system elements such as information systems, antennas, terminals, receivers, routers, associated local and wide area networks, and power supplies; and

(vi) Management of supply chain risks that affect cybersecurity of space systems through tracking manufactured products; requiring sourcing from trusted suppliers; identifying counterfeit, fraudulent, and malicious equipment; and assessing other available risk mitigation measures.

(c) Implementation of these principles, through rules, regulations, and guidance, should enhance space system cybersecurity, including through the consideration and adoption, where appropriate, of cybersecurity best practices and norms of behavior.

(d) Space system owners and operators should collaborate to promote the development of best practices, to the extent permitted by applicable law. They should also share threat, warning, and incident information within the space industry, using venues such as Information Sharing and Analysis Centers to the greatest extent possible, consistent with applicable law.

(e) Security measures should be designed to be effective while permitting space system owners and operators to manage appropriate risk tolerances and minimize undue burden, consistent with specific mission requirements, United States national security and national critical functions, space vehicle size, mission duration, maneuverability, and any applicable orbital regimes.[232]

The National Institutes of Standards has released a report concerning applying the cybersecurity framework to satellite command and control.[233] In May of 2023, Senator Peters and Cornyn introduced the Satellite Cybersecurity Act which would:

require CISA to consolidate voluntary satellite cybersecurity recommendations – including guidance specifically for small businesses – to help companies understand how to best secure their systems. Additionally, the bill requires CISA to develop a publicly available, online resource to ensure companies can easily access satellite-specific cybersecurity resources and recommendations to secure their networks. The legislation will also require the Government Accountability Office to perform a study on how the federal government supports commercial satellite industry cybersecurity. It will ensure a better understanding of how network vulnerabilities in commercial satellites could impact critical infrastructure.

[232] White House, Memorandum on Space Policy Directive-5—Cybersecurity Principles for Space Systems (September 4, 2020), available at https://trumpwhitehouse.archives.gov/presidential-actions/memorandum-space-policy-directive-5-cybersecurity-principles-space-systems/

[233] NIST, Satellite Ground Segment: Applying the Cybersecurity Framework to Satellite Command and Control (December 2022).

Finally, the bill also requires the National Cyber Director and the National Space Council to develop a strategy to increase coordination across the federal government to address cybersecurity threats to these systems.[234]

[234] U.S. Senate, Homeland Security and Governmental Affairs Committee, Peters & Cornyn Reintroduce Bipartisan Bill to Protect Commercial Satellites from Cybersecurity Threats (May 23, 2023), available at https://www.hsgac.senate.gov/media/dems/peters-reintroduces-bipartisan-bill-to-protect-commercial-satellites-from-cybersecurity-threats/.

CHAPTER EIGHT. State Cybersecurity Laws

8.1 Introduction

As discussed in the preceding chapters, the United States does not have one overarching cybersecurity law but instead relies on a collection of privacy and cybersecurity laws that each cover a specific area. For example, the Health Insurance Portability and Accountability Act (HIPAA) focuses on an individual's protected health information and the medical industry. In contrast, the Gramm–Leach–Bliley Act (GLBA), also known as the Financial Services Modernization Act of 1999, focuses on the financial industry. All fifty states, the District of Columbia, and three territories: Puerto Rick, Guam and the U.S. Virgin Islands, have data breach notification laws. Some states have also promulgated cybersecurity laws concerning standards for the security of data, networks and computers.

In 2023, several state privacy laws went into effect and even more states promulgated new privacy acts that will go into effect after 2023. These new state privacy acts have proliferated with the failure of Congress to pass a national privacy act. The common theme across these state privacy acts is providing data subject rights for consumers and cybersecurity requirements to protect consumer data. In contrast to state data breach notification laws that require reporting on covered information after a data breach, the new state privacy acts do not turn on a breach. These new acts provide several privacy rights to data subjects and demand physical, administrative, and technical security measures to protect the confidentiality, integrity, and availability of consumer data. The data covered by the new privacy acts is also much broader than the covered information for state data breach notification laws. This Chapter will review the new state privacy acts from a cybersecurity perspective, and some select data breach notification laws and more specific cybersecurity laws promulgated by the states.

8.2 State Privacy Laws

The new state privacy laws are focused on providing data subject privacy rights such as:

1. Right to opt-out of sale/sharing of data
2. Right to delete
3. Right to access
4. Right to correct
5. Right to limit

The following includes a description of the state privacy laws with cybersecurity components for California, Colorado, Connecticut, Virginia and Washington state. California continues to lead the nation in protecting the consumer and has recently promulgated the California Consumer Privacy Act (CCPA). This law along with the European General Data Protection (GDPR) have changed the way companies do business. The CCPA is primarily a privacy law that gives individual customers rights to control how their data is collected, used, and disposed of. But the CCPA also gives a private right of action to hold companies accountable regarding reasonable cybersecurity measures. The California Privacy Rights Act, which was passed by the California voters on November 3, 2020, maintains the cybersecurity portion of the CCPA with some slight modifications and creates a new privacy agency.

The section 1798.150 of the California Privacy Rights Act amending the California Consumer Privacy Act creates a private civil cause of action, which can be brought individually or as a class, for failure to "implement and maintain reasonable security procedures and practices appropriate to the nature of the information to protect the personal information." The failure is based on a breach of a duty to implement and maintain reasonable security measures. The statute specifically provides that "unauthorized access and exfiltration, theft, or disclosure" of consumer "nonencrypted and non redacted personal information or whose email address in combination with a password or security question and answer that would permit access to the account" that "is subject to unauthorized access and exfiltration, theft, or disclosure" because of the breach is subject to liability. That liability includes the right to "recover damages in an amount not less than one hundred dollars ($100) and not greater than seven hundred and fifty ($750) per consumer per incident or actual damages, whichever is greater," injunctive or declaratory relief, or "[a]ny other relief the court deems proper." The court is directed to consider any relevant facts in determining the amount of statutory damages. The statute does specify a non-exclusive list of some specific circumstances to consider: "the nature and seriousness of the misconduct, the number of violations, the persistence of the misconduct, the length of time over which the misconduct occurred, the willfulness of the defendant's misconduct, and the defendant's assets, liabilities, and net worth."

The consumer may bring the cause of action as long as they provide, "a business 30 days' written notice identifying the specific provisions of this title the consumer alleges have been or are being violated." The business has the ability to cure the problem within the 30 days. The business must actually cure the problem and provide, "the consumer an express written statement that the violations have been cured and that no further violations shall occur." If a proper cure if taken by the business, then "no action for individual statutory damages or class-wide statutory damages may be initiated against the business." Notably, section 1798.81.5 concerns the implementation and maintenance of reasonable security measures, as discussed *infra*; however, compliance with that section, apparently after the violation, is not a cure of the relevant breach. The notice requirement does not apply if actual pecuniary damages are sought without statutory damages. The statute specifically provides that a consumer may bring an action against a business that violates the written statement provided by the business under the statute and can obtain statutory damages for damages accrued after the date of the written statement. The statute expressly provides that, "[n]othing in this title shall be interpreted to serve as the basis for a private right of action under any other law. This shall not be construed to relieve any party from any duties or obligations imposed under other law or the United States or California Constitution."

Additionally, a separate section of the California Civil Code, 1798.100, concerning general duties of companies that collect personal information has a provision that states: "(e) A business that collects a consumer's personal information shall implement reasonable security procedures and practices appropriate to the nature of the personal information to protect the personal information from unauthorized or illegal access, destruction, use, modification, or disclosure in accordance with Section 1798.81.5." Section 1798.81.5 provides that reasonable security measures must be implemented by the "business that owns, licenses or maintains personal information about a California resident" or "disclose[s] personal information about a California resident pursuant to a contract with a nonaffiliated third party. . .." Notably, there are exemptions to the application of 1798.100 such as entities regulated by HIPAA and certain financial institutions. Section 1798.81.5 also provides, in part, that the section does not apply to: "(5) A business that is regulated by state or federal law providing greater protection to personal information than that provided by this section in regard to the subjects addressed by this section. . . . This paragraph does not relieve a business from a duty to comply with any other requirements of other state and federal law regarding the protection and privacy of personal information." Please also note that compliance with section 1798.81.5 does not cure a breach under section 1798.150.

The California Privacy Rights Act and California Consumer Privacy Act contemplate the issuance of implementing regulations. Section 1798.185 requires regulations concerning annual cybersecurity audits and the submission of risk assessments to the California Privacy Protection Agency for "businesses whose processing of consumers' personal information presents a significant risk to consumers' privacy or security." Notably, the cybersecurity audit shall consider factors "in determining when processing may result in significant risk to the security of personal information" which "include[s] the size and complexity of the business and the nature and scope of the processing activities." The risk assessment must be provided on a "regular basis" and consider "whether the processing involves sensitive personal information, identifying and weighing the benefits resulting from the processing to the business, the consumer, other stakeholders, and the public, against the potential risks to the rights of the consumer associated with that processing, with the goal of restricting or prohibiting the processing if the risks to privacy of the consumer outweigh the benefits resulting from processing to the consumer, the business, other stakeholders, and the public." Finally, the section states that, "[n]othing in this section shall require a business to divulge trade secrets."

Colorado provides in C.R.S. 6-1-1308 Duties of Controllers a duty of care that requires controllers of personal data to "take reasonable measures of secure personal data during both storage and use from unauthorized acquisition." The section specifically states that those "data security practices must be appropriate to the volume, scope, and nature of the personal data processed and the nature of the business."

Connecticut in Public Act No. 22-15 titled "An Act Concerning Personal Data Privacy and Online Monitoring" provides, in section 6, that controllers comply with a data minimization requirement and "establish, implement and maintain reasonable administrative, technical and physical data security practices to protect the confidentiality, integrity and accessibility of personal data appropriate to the volume and nature of the personal data at issue." Additionally, processors of data for the controller, in section 7, must follow the directions of the controller and help the controller by, "(1) Taking into account the nature of processing and the information available to the processor, by appropriate technical and organizational measures, insofar as is reasonably practicable, to fulfill the controller's obligation to respond to consumer rights requests; (2) taking into account the nature of processing and the information available to the processor, by assisting the controller in meeting the controller's obligations in relation to the security of processing the personal data and in relation to the notification of a breach of security, as defined in section 36a-701b of the general statutes, of the system of the processor, in order to meet the controller's obligations; and (3) providing necessary information to enable the controller to conduct and document data protection assessments."

Virginia, in section 59.1-578 titled, Data controller responsibilities; transparency, requires that the data controller exercise data minimization practices and "[e]stablish, implement, and maintain reasonable administrative, technical, and physical data security practices to protect the confidentiality, integrity, and accessibility of personal data." The practices "shall be appropriate to the volume and nature of the personal data at issue."

The State of Washington recently passed the, "My Health My Data Act, Title 19 RCW chapter 44.28." This act requires regulated entities and small businesses to engage in data minimization requirements. For example, the act states in subsection (a): "Restrict access to consumer health data by the employees, processors, and contractors of such regulated entity or small business to only those employees, processors, and contractors for which access is necessary to further the purposes for which the consumer provided consent or where necessary to provide a product or service that the consumer to whom such consumer health data relates has requested from such regulated entity or small business." Additionally, the act requires those regulated entities and small businesses to "[e]stablish, implement, and maintain administrative, technical, and physical data security practices that, at a minimum, satisfy reasonable standard of care within the regulated entity's or the small business's industry to protect the confidentiality, integrity, and accessibility of consumer health data appropriate to the volume and nature of the consumer health data at issue." Importantly, small businesses must comply "beginning June 2024." Notably, the statute specifically requires the familiar "administrative, technical, and physical" measures to protect data. Moreover, the statute sets forth the base level requirement of reasonable standard of care. However, that is limited to the regulated entity or small business's industry. The cybersecurity triad is also noted as well as flexibility concerning volume and nature of the health data.

8.3 State Breach Notification Laws

All 50 states, with California being the first, have adopted privacy data breach notification laws that mandate the timing and content of the data breach notification to those who may have been affected by the data breach. Many states have followed the California model for data breach notification. Normally, a data breach notification will be sent to customers in all 50 states plus the US territories. For the most part, the data breach notification contains an explanation of what happened, unless the state mandates that information not be revealed due to an ongoing investigation. The data breach notification will also likely contain an outsourced call-center number where the customer can receive more information, and identity theft programs that the company may be offering. The law also normally mandates whether and how soon the state Attorney General should be notified and how soon the data breach notification should be mailed after the discovery of the data breach. The law may also have a threshold number of customers to require notification. The majority of the states' data breach notification laws are similar, so it becomes a matter of knowing the states that are not similar to make sure notification violations do not occur. Also note that in some states, encryption of the breached data may negate the need for breach notification.

8.3[A] National Conference of State Legislatures on Security Breach Notification Laws

The National Conference of State Legislatures maintains a database of state privacy laws, which includes breach notification. As states are constantly modifying their privacy laws, the following table is a good starting point for an attorney to keep track of current breach notification laws. Notably, there are 50 states with security breach notification laws. Moreover, Puerto Rico, the Virgin Islands, District of Columbia and Guam have security breach notification laws. The database of state privacy laws includes the state name along with the citation and link to the relevant law. The following is an excerpt of the database with some states removed.

Security Breach Notification Laws[235]

4/15/2021 . . .

State	Citation
California	Cal. Civ. Code §§ 1798.29, 1798.82
Florida	Fla. Stat. §§ 501.171, 282.0041, 282.318(2)(i)
Illinois	815 ILCS §§ 530/1 to 530/25, 815 ILCS 530/55 (2020 S.B. 1624)
New York	N.Y. Gen. Bus. Law § 899-AA
Texas	Tex. Bus. & Com. Code §§ 521.002, 521.053
Washington	Wash. Rev. Code §§ 19.255.010, 42.56.590

8.3[B] Example Private Cause of Actions Cases Brought Under State Breach Notification Laws

The following materials include some private right of action cases that demonstrate confusion by the courts concerning how to deal with cybersecurity deficiencies and demonstrate the need for state cybersecurity laws that provide a right of action to adequately

235 *Security Breach Notification Laws*, NAT'L CONF. OF STATE LEG., https://www.ncsl.org/research/telecommunications-and-information-technology/security-breach-notification-laws.aspx (last updated April 15, 2021).

protect its citizens from data breaches. Indeed, citizens and their data are not protected by poorly conceived or drafted cybersecurity laws, or a failure to enact cybersecurity laws.

The selected cases include excerpts from decisions from Georgia, Oregon, Delaware and Pennsylvania. The Georgia, Oregon and Delaware cases reject a private negligence right of action for various reasons. The Pennsylvania case includes an appellate court decision rejecting a private negligence right of action; however, the Supreme Court of Pennsylvania overruled that decision.

McConnell et al. v. George Department of Labor, 814 S.E.2d 790 (Ga. 2018).

McConnell argued that a common law duty exists to safeguard and protect the personal information of another and that OCGA §§ 10-1-393.8 and 10-1-910 help establish the duty of care to be exercised by those who collect or hold personal information. In OCGA §§ 10-1-910, the General Assembly set out legislative findings underlying the Georgia Personal Identity Protection Act, OCGA §§ 10-1-910 through 10-1-915 (the "GPIPA"), enacted in 2005. In the GPIPA, the General Assembly found, inter alia, that "[t]he privacy and financial security of individuals is increasingly at risk, due to the ever more widespread collection of personal information by both the private and public sectors[,]" that "[i]dentity theft is one of the fastest growing crimes committed in this state[,]" and that "[i]dentity theft is costly to the marketplace and to consumers[.]" OCGA § 10-1-910 (1), (6). Because "[v]ictims of identity theft must act quickly to minimize the damage[,] ... expeditious notification of unauthorized acquisition and possible misuse of a persons personal information is imperative." OCGA § 10-1-910 (7). In line with these findings, the GPIPA requires that affected persons be given certain notice of a data breach and the right and ability to place a security freeze on their credit report.

McConnell argued that in codifying these findings the General Assembly demonstrated its intent to protect citizens from the adverse effects of disclosure of personal information and created a general duty to preserve and protect personal information. Notably, however, despite the General Assembly's aspirational recognition of the harm caused by identity theft, the GPIPA does not proscribe any conduct in storing data or protecting data security. Rather the GPIPA proscribes particular conduct, that is, notification and the placement of a security freeze, only after a (known or suspected) data security breach has occurred. Because the GPIPA does not impose any standard of conduct in implementing and maintaining data security practices, the court concluded that it cannot serve as the source of a general duty to safeguard personal information. Wells Fargo Bank, N.A. v. Jenkins, 293 Ga. 162, 165, 744 S.E.2d 686 (2013). The court also concluded that OCGA § 10-1-393.8, which is part of the Fair Business Practices Act of 1975 (the "FBPA"), cannot serve as the source of a general duty to safeguard and protect the personal information of another.

Laurie Paul v. Providence Health System-Oregon, 351 Or. 587 (Or. 2012).

The issue in this case is whether a healthcare provider can be liable in damages when the provider's negligence permitted the theft of its patients' personal information, but the information was never used or viewed by the thief or any other person. Plaintiffs claimed economic and noneconomic damages for financial injury and emotional distress that they allegedly suffered when, through defendant's alleged negligence, computer disks and tapes containing personal information from an estimated 365,000 patients (including plaintiffs) were stolen from the car of one of defendant's employees. The trial court and Court of Appeals held that plaintiffs had failed to state claims for negligence or for violation of the Unlawful Trade Practices Act (UTPA), ORS 646.605 to 646.652. We conclude that, in the absence of allegations that the stolen information was used in any way or even was viewed by a third party, plaintiffs have not suffered an injury that would provide a basis for a negligence claim or an action under the UTPA. We therefore affirm, although our analysis differs in some respects from that of the Court of Appeals. . . .

Affy Tapple LLC v. Shopvisible, LLC and Aptos Inc., 2019 WL 1324500 (Del. Super. Ct. Mar. 7, 2019).

One of the causes of action was for gross negligence. Delaware imposes a statutory duty on businesses to protect personal information. The protection includes the implementation and maintenance "of reasonable procedures and practices to prevent the unauthorized acquisition, use, modification, disclosure, or destruction of personal information collected or maintained in the regular course of business." The statute does not create a private right of action and only the Delaware AG is responsible for enforcement.

Dittman v. UPMC Commonwealth Court of Pennsylvania, 2015 WL 13779479 (May 28, 2015).

In data protection negligence cases, the courts are also nervous about usurping the legislature in the area of data protection and will likely grapple with the reasonableness standard implemented by legislatures without guidance. In the above-listed case, the cause of action is negligence based on a "duty to exercise reasonable care to protect and secure its employees' personal and financial information within its possession or control from being compromised, stolen, lost, misused, and/or disclosed to unauthorized parties." The only duty imposed by the General Assembly is "notification of a data breach" and "[i]t is not for the courts to alter the direction of the General Assembly because public policy is a matter for the Legislature." Accordingly, the negligence claim was dismissed.

Dittman et al. v. UPMC et al., 196 A.3d 1036 (Pa. 2018).

This decision is the appeal of the prior case to the Supreme Court of Pennsylvania. The Supreme Court held that defendants did "owe a duty to Employees to use reasonable care to safeguard their sensitive personal data in collecting and storing it on an internet-accessible computer system." The court also held that "under Pennsylvania's economic loss doctrine, recovery for purely pecuniary damages is permissible under a negligence theory provided that the plaintiff can establish the defendants breach of a legal duty arising under common law that is independent of any duty assumed pursuant to contract."

The court found that "employees have sufficiently alleged that UPMCs affirmative conduct created the risk of a data breach. Thus, we agree with Employees that, in collecting and storing Employees' data on its computer systems, UPMC owed Employees a duty to exercise reasonable care to protect them against an unreasonable risk of harm arising out of that act." Accordingly, the court vacated the "judgement of the Superior Court, reverse[d] the order of the trial court, and remand[ed] the matter to the trial court for further proceedings consistent with this opinion."

8.4 Data Security Laws

As data breaches have become more common, state AGs have come to realize that they lacked power to address some of the root causes of some of the data breaches. The AGs did not have the authority to pursue companies that lacked proper cybersecurity and had to rely on teaming with the FTC to go after the bad actors. Many state legislatures have fixed that problem by promulgating data security laws that give the AG a channel to go after bad actors without the help of a federal agency.

8.4[A] SPECIFIC DATA SECURITY LAWS

As previously noted, some states have enacted data security laws or data breach notification laws with data security elements. The following materials summarize some of data security related laws from Alabama, Massachusetts, Colorado and California.

Alabama Data Breach Notification Act of 2018

Alabama was one of the last two states to adopt a data breach notification law. Because they were late to the table in promulgating a notification law, they were able to add cybersecurity measures in addition to just breach notification requirements.

Massachusetts Regulations Concerning Cybersecurity

Massachusetts was one of the earlier adopters of a cybersecurity law. The Massachusetts law is interesting because the law is fairly narrow in that it provides specific security measures on how to comply with the law for entities controlling personal data.[236] The Massachusetts law is 201 CMR 17.04 and titled," Computer System Security Requirements." The specific security measures, include, "at a minimum, and to the extent technically feasible[:]"

(1) Secure user authentication protocols including:

(a) control of user IDs and other identifiers;

(b) a reasonably secure method of assigning and selecting passwords, or use of unique identifier technologies, such as biometrics or token devices;

---

[236] 201 MASS. CODE REGS. 17 (2009).

(c) control of data security passwords to ensure that such passwords are kept in a location and/or format that does not compromise the security of the data they protect;

(d) restricting access to active users and active user accounts only; and

(e) blocking access to user identification after multiple unsuccessful attempts to gain access or the limitation placed on access for the particular system;

(2) Secure access control measures that:

(a) restrict access to records and files containing personal information to those who need such information to perform their job duties; and

(b) assign unique identifications plus passwords, which are not vendor supplied default passwords, to each person with computer access, that are reasonably designed to maintain the integrity of the security of the access controls;

(3) Encryption of all transmitted records and files containing personal information that will travel across public networks, and encryption of all data containing personal information to be transmitted wirelessly.

(4) Reasonable monitoring of systems, for unauthorized use of or access to personal information;

(5) Encryption of all personal information stored on laptops or other portable devices;

(6) For files containing personal information on a system that is connected to the Internet, there must be reasonably up-to-date firewall protection and operating system security patches, reasonably designed to maintain the integrity of the personal information.

(7) Reasonably up-to-date versions of system security agent software which must include malware protection and reasonably up-to-date patches and virus definitions, or a version of such software that can still be supported with up-to-date patches and virus definitions, and is set to receive the most current security updates on a regular basis.

(8) Education and training of employees on the proper use of the computer security system and the importance of personal information security.

Colorado Cybersecurity Law

Other states, such as Colorado, which promulgated its law years later, took a broader approach because it did not want to be boxed in by a narrow law. The Colorado law is at C.R.S.A. § 6-1-713.5 and the relevant section is titled, "Protection of personal identifying information—definition." This law adopts the reasonable security measures standard for personally identifiable information. The statute adopts flexibility through interpreting what is a reasonable security measure based on "the nature of the personal identifying information and the nature and size of the business and its operations." The law protects against "unauthorized access, use, modification, disclosure, or destruction" of that data as a result of failure to implement and maintain reasonable security processes and procedures.

The statute further provides specific requirements for third party providers, which are defined as "an entity that has been contracted to maintain, store, or process personal identifying information on behalf of a covered entity." Those requirements for third party providers, include:

> (2) Unless a covered entity agrees to provide its own security protection for the information it discloses to a third-party service provider, the covered entity shall require that the third-party service provider implement and maintain reasonable security procedures and practices that are:
>
> (a) Appropriate to the nature of the personal identifying information disclosed to the third-party service provider; and
>
> (b) Reasonably designed to help protect the personal identifying information from unauthorized access, use, modification, disclosure, or destruction.
>
> (3) For the purposes of subsection (2) of this section, a disclosure of personal identifying information does not include disclosure of

> information to a third party under circumstances where the covered entity retains primary responsibility for implementing and maintaining reasonable security procedures and practices appropriate to the nature of the personal identifying information and the covered entity implements and maintains technical controls that are reasonably designed to:
>
> (a) Help protect the personal identifying information from unauthorized access, use, modification, disclosure, or destruction; or
>
> (b) Effectively eliminate the third party's ability to access the personal identifying information, notwithstanding the third party's physical possession of the personal identifying information.

The Colorado statute also notes that compliance with "laws, rules, regulations, guidances, or guidelines" provided by a relevant state or federal regulator is suitable for compliance with the Colorado statute.

CHAPTER NINE. Additional Private Causes of Action for Cybersecurity Breaches

9.1 Introduction

This chapter provides an overview of potential causes of action that may be brought based on a data breach. This chapter also reviews common issues raised in data breach actions, such as standing and class action requirements.[237] A data breach may result in the assertion of causes of action ranging from negligence, breach of contract, misrepresentation, unjust enrichment, general unfair trade practices, breach of warranty, breach of fiduciary duty and other statutory-based claims.[238] Furthermore, the majority of these claims are based on state law which makes the choice of forum and law important.

9.2 Standing

Standing is a constitutional and prudential requirement as to whether an allegedly injured party can bring a cause of action. The U.S. Constitution requires that courts decide actual "cases and controversies." Courts require an "injury in fact" and not speculative harms. An injury in fact is "'(a) concrete and particularized, and (b) actual or imminent, not conjectural or hypothetical.'"[239] Standing requires an injury that is imminent and not just possible. Moreover, the U.S. Supreme Court clarified that standing not only requires a particularized injury, but one that is concrete.[240] A concrete injury must exist. While the risk of real harm may satisfy the concreteness requirement, the degree of risk should be considered by the court. Moreover, courts require causation—the harm must be fairly traceable to the defendant's conduct—and that the injury is redressable by the court's decision.

---

[237] The doctrine of sovereign immunity is addressed in Chapter Ten in the Computer Fraud and Abuse Act section, *infra.*

[238] In Chapter 4 U.S. Securities and Exchange Commission Cybersecurity, *supra*, there is a discussion of a case concerning a securities action related to cybersecurity.

[239] *Reilly v. Ceridian Corp.*, 664 F.3d 38 (3d. Cir. 2011).

[240] *Spokeo v. Robins*, 136 S.Ct. 1540 (2016).

Standing is a fundamental requirement for bringing a cause of action based on a data breach. Numerous courts have considered standing in the context of data breaches, and circuits are split regarding the allegations and evidence necessary to confer it.[241] The degree of evidentiary support may depend on the stage of the lawsuit.

Basically, standing has become an important issue depending on the nature of the harm suffered by the victims of the data breach. Moreover, timing and causation are critical. For example, the court is more likely to find standing if the victims of the data breach have suffered some concrete financial harm from having their data stolen as opposed to only an increased risk of identity theft. Courts are also less likely to find standing has been satisfied if the victims of the data breach have not suffered some financial harm and claim some emotional distress from the breach. However, some courts may discount financial harm that only includes efforts to prevent identify theft unless there is a substantial risk of harm. Courts may consider the type of data taken, and whether the data was somehow misused.[242] Additionally, the court is also unlikely to find standing fulfilled if there is a relatively high degree of uncertainty with respect to what a hacker may have done with the data without some financial harm. Relatedly, imminent injury—or injury that is "certainly

---

[241] *Tsao v. Captiva MVP Restaurant Partners*, 986 F.3d 1332, 1340 (11th Cir. 2021) ("On the one hand, the Sixth, Seventh, Ninth, and D.C. Circuits have all recognized—at the pleading stage—that a plaintiff can establish injury-in-fact based on the increased risk of identity theft. On the other hand, the Second, Third, Fourth, and Eighth Circuits have declined to find standing on that theory.").

[242] In *McMorris v. Carlos Lopez & Assoc.*, __ F.3d __, 2021 WL 1603808, *5 (2nd Cir. April 21, 2021), the Second Circuit provided:

> We therefore hold that courts confronted with allegations that plaintiffs are at an increased risk of identity theft or fraud based on an unauthorized data disclosure should consider the following non-exhaustive factors in determining whether those plaintiffs have adequately alleged an Article III injury in fact: (1) whether the plaintiffs' data has been exposed as the result of a targeted attempt to obtain that data; (2) whether any portion of the dataset has already been misused, even if the plaintiffs themselves have not yet experienced identity theft or fraud; and (3) whether the type of data that has been exposed is sensitive such that there is a high risk of identity theft or fraud.

impending"--is likely not satisfied by possibility that injury may occur in the future without more, particularly if the description of plaintiff's potential injury starts with the word "if." For example, in *Reilly v. Ceridian Corp.*, a case involving a hacker who may have accessed the following information: "first name, last name, social security numbers and, in several cases, birth date and/or bank account that is used for direct deposit," the Third Circuit found that:

> [A]llegations of hypothetical, future injury [such as increased risk of identity theft, incurred costs of credit monitoring, and emotional distress] are insufficient to establish standing. Appellants' contentions rely on speculation that the hacker: (1) read, copied, and understood their personal information; (2) intends to commit future criminal acts by misusing the information; and (3) is able to use such information to the detriment of Appellants by making unauthorized transactions in Appellants' names. Unless and until these conjectures come true, Appellants have not suffered any injury; there has been no misuse of information, and thus, no harm.[243]

In *Reilly*, the Third Circuit noted that the defendant Ceridian offered free credit monitoring and identify theft protection to allegedly injured parties, and that voluntarily undertaking monitoring costs without an actual injury does not confer standing. The Third Circuit also distinguished prior cases finding standing in data breach scenarios by pointing to the fact that in those cases there was some evidence of intention and malice, such as a physical theft of a laptop and an attempt to open a bank account. Moreover, the Third Circuit noted that in the present case there was only the breach of a firewall. The Third Circuit also distinguished cases involving medical-devices and environmental harm as involving an injury that has taken place and a change in the status quo. The Third Circuit also distinguished medical-device and toxic tort cases based on the fact that those cases involve human health and "[c]ourts resist strictly applying the 'actual injury' test when the future harm involves humans suffering or premature death."

[243] *Reilly v. Ceridian Corp.*, 664 F.3d 38 (3d. Cir. 2011).

Notably, the loss or alteration of medical information alone may be sufficient to confer standing given the difference in the nature of the potential harm.

In *In re Office of Personnel Management Data Security Litigation Breach*,[244] the DC Circuit found that a group of plaintiffs had adequately alleged "a concrete, particularized, and imminent injury in fact" of a constitutionally protected privacy interest in personal information based on the government's continued failure to protect their personal information. The DC Circuit also found that a different group of plaintiffs also adequately alleged standing based on the risk of future identity theft. The DC Circuit noted that, "[s]ocial security numbers and addresses cannot so readily be swapped out for new ones. And, of course, our birth dates and fingerprints are with use forever." The DC Circuit pointed to the fact some of the plaintiffs had already experienced some forms of identity theft, such as opening accounts for lines of credit. The DC Circuit also distinguished the *Reilly* case based on allegations that their information was intentionally targeted and there was misuse of that information. The DC Circuit further found that causation was satisfied—fairly traceable to the government's failure to act--by allegations that the government failed to adequately address warning about the insufficiency of its security and that the loss of data was a result of the failure to act. Moreover, a government contractor's failure to secure log-in credentials was also found to be a substantial factor to demonstrate causation.

Both of those cases were issued prior to the 2021 U.S. Supreme Court decision in *TransUnion*. In that case, the U.S. Supreme Court discussed in detail the requirement of standing in the context of mistakes made on a credit report governed by the Fair Credit Reporting Act that identified consumers as potential terrorists and serious criminals under the U.S. Department of Treasury's Office of Foreign Assets Control.[245] Importantly, this case makes it less likely that a statutory cause of action may satisfy the concrete injury requirement for standing.[246] Moreover, this

---

[244] *In re Office of Personnel Management Data Security Litigation Breach*, 928 F.3d 42 (D.C. Cir. 2019).

[245] *TransUnion v. Ramirez*, 141 S.Ct. 2190 (2021).

[246] This case follows *Spokeo v. Robins*, 136 S.Ct. 1540 (2016) which determined that a procedural violation of a statute may not satisfy standing. In *Spokeo v. Robins*, the U.S. Supreme Court emphasized that for allegations to confer

---

standing the injury must be "concrete" and not just particularized in considering a claim under the Fair Credit Reporting Act. The Supreme Court stated:

> "Concrete" is not, however, necessarily synonymous with "tangible." Although tangible injuries are perhaps easier to recognize, we have confirmed in many of our previous cases that intangible injuries can nevertheless be concrete. In determining whether an intangible harm constitutes injury in fact, both history and the judgment of Congress play important roles. Because the doctrine of standing derives from the case-or-controversy requirement, and because that requirement in turn is grounded in historical practice, it is instructive to consider whether an alleged intangible harm has a close relationship to a harm that has traditionally been regarded as providing a basis for a lawsuit in English or American courts. In addition, because Congress is well positioned to identify intangible harms that meet minimum Article III requirements, its judgment is also instructive and important. Thus, we said in *Lujan* that Congress may "elevat[e] to the status of legally cognizable injuries concrete, *de facto* injuries that were previously inadequate in law." Similarly, Justice Kennedy's concurrence in that case explained that "Congress has the power to define injuries and articulate chains of causation that will give rise to a case or controversy where none existed before."
>
> Congress' role in identifying and elevating intangible harms does not mean that a plaintiff automatically satisfies the injury-in-fact requirement whenever a statute grants a person a statutory right and purports to authorize that person to sue to vindicate that right. Article III standing requires a concrete injury even in the context of a statutory violation. For that reason, Robins could not, for example, allege a bare procedural violation, divorced from any concrete harm, and satisfy the injury-in-fact requirement of Article III.
>
> This does not mean, however, that the risk of real harm cannot satisfy the requirement of concreteness. For example, the law has long permitted recovery by certain tort victims even if their harms may be difficult to prove or measure. Just as the common law permitted suit in such instances, the violation of a procedural right granted by statute can be sufficient in some circumstances to constitute injury in fact. In other words, a plaintiff in such a case need not allege any *additional* harm beyond the one Congress has identified.
>
> In the context of this particular case, these general principles tell us two things: On the one hand, Congress plainly sought to curb the dissemination of false information by adopting procedures designed to decrease that risk. On the other hand, Robins cannot satisfy the demands of Article III by alleging a bare procedural violation. A violation of one of

case provides a helpful review of the U.S. Supreme Court's view of standing.

In analyzing the plaintiffs' claims, the Supreme Court noted that the allegations of the violations of the Fair Credit Act fell within two areas: "(i) to follow reasonable procedures to ensure the accuracy of credit files so that the files would not include OFAC alerts labeling the plaintiffs as potential terrorists; and (ii) to provide a consumer, upon request, with his or her complete credit file, including a summary of rights."[247] In addressing the first area, the court decided that the plaintiffs whose credit reports with a false OFAC alert sufficiently alleged a concrete harm that was reputational and had a "close relationship" to that traditional harm.[248] As the court previously noted, reputation harms have traditionally been recognized in the context of defamation.[249] The court distinguished those plaintiffs from the plaintiffs whose credit reports with false OFAC alerts were not disseminated to third parties.[250] The court decided that those plaintiffs had not suffered a concrete harm essentially because the reputational harm

---

> the FCRA's procedural requirements may result in no harm. For example, even if a consumer reporting agency fails to provide the required notice to a user of the agency's consumer information, that information regardless may be entirely accurate. In addition, not all inaccuracies cause harm or present any material risk of harm. An example that comes readily to mind is an incorrect zip code. It is difficult to imagine how the dissemination of an incorrect zip code, without more, could work any concrete harm.
>
> Because the Ninth Circuit failed to fully appreciate the distinction between concreteness and particularization, its standing analysis was incomplete. It did not address the question framed by our discussion, namely, whether the particular procedural violations alleged in this case entail a degree of risk sufficient to meet the concreteness requirement. We take no position as to whether the Ninth Circuit's ultimate conclusion—that Robins adequately alleged an injury in fact—was correct. *Id.* at 1549-1550.

In *A Post-Spokeo Taxonomy of Intangible Harms*, Jackson Erpenbach discusses case law recognizing privacy harms that would satisfy the two Spokeo factors. *See* Jackson Erpenbach, *A Post-Spokeo Taxonomy of Intangible Harms*, 118 MICH. L. REV. 471, 484-485 (2019).

[247] *Id.* at 2207.

[248] *Id.* at 2208-9.

[249] *Id.*

[250] *Id.* at 2209-12.

associated with defamation involves publication—here there was no publication.[251] Notably, this may be used against data breach plaintiffs—depending on the nature of the breached information—however, data breach information is often published.[252] The court basically concluded that, "In cases such as these where allegedly inaccurate or misleading information sits in a company database, the plaintiffs' harm is roughly the same, legally speaking, as if someone wrote a defamatory letter and then stored it in her desk drawer. A letter that is not sent does not harm anyone, no matter how insulting the letter is."[253]

The Supreme Court also rejected the plaintiffs' argument that a "risk of real harm" or "material risk of harm" is enough to satisfy standing in this context.[254] The court distinguished a prior case utilizing that language based because that case involved a request for injunctive relief—which is forward looking—as opposed to damages for a past act.[255] However, the court fails to discuss statutory penalties.[256] Moreover, this particular part of the opinion could jeopardize some data breach cases where there is evidence of a breach, but not whether there was a publication of information or what a third party may have done with the information.[257]

The Supreme Court also favorably discussed TransUnion's argument that the risk of future harm should eventually materialize into an existing harm and that whether that occurs should be considered by the court in a standing analysis:

> TransUnion advances a persuasive argument that in a suit for damages, the mere risk of future harm, standing alone, cannot qualify as a concrete harm—at least unless the exposure to the risk of future harm itself causes a *separate* concrete harm. TransUnion contends that if an individual is exposed to a risk of future harm, time will eventually reveal whether the risk materializes in the form of actual harm. If the risk of future harm materializes and the individual suffers a concrete harm, then the

---

[251] *Id.*
[252] *Id.*
[253] *Id.* at 2210.
[254] *Id.* at 2210-12.
[255] *Id.*
[256] *Id.*
[257] *Id.*

> harm itself, and not the pre-existing risk, will constitute a basis for the person's injury and for damages. If the risk of future harm does *not* materialize, then the individual cannot establish a concrete harm sufficient for standing, according to TransUnion.
>
> Consider an example. Suppose that a woman drives home from work a quarter mile ahead of a reckless driver who is dangerously swerving across lanes. The reckless driver has exposed the woman to a risk of future harm, but the risk does not materialize and the woman makes it home safely. As counsel for TransUnion stated, that would ordinarily be cause for celebration, not a lawsuit. But if the reckless driver crashes into the woman's car, the situation would be different, and (assuming a cause of action) the woman could sue the driver for damages.[258]

The problem with the hypothetical given by the court in the data breach context is that the risk of harm evaporates relatively quickly in the hypothetical; whereas, in the data breach context, the harm itself that materializes from the risk of harm may be difficult to detect and may materialize far into the future. Indeed, another way to analyze this issue is to consider that the risk is more significant for the harm to occur given the opportunistic behavior of third parties who may wish to capitalize on a person's data for whatever improper purpose.

In a 2022 post-Transunion decision, the Third Circuit in Clemens v. Execupharm stated:

> Following TransUnion's guidance, we hold that in the data breach context, where the asserted theory of injury is a substantial risk of identity theft or fraud, a plaintiff suing for damages can satisfy concreteness as long as he alleges that the exposure to that substantial risk caused additional, currently felt concrete harms. For example, if the plaintiff's knowledge of the substantial risk of identity theft causes him to presently experience emotional distress or spend money on mitigation measures like

[258] *Id.* at 2210-1.

> credit monitoring services, the plaintiff has alleged a concrete injury. . . .[259]

The standing requirement in the context of data breaches will continue to evolve as courts interpret the Transunion decision.

9.3 Other Common Law and Statutory Causes of Action

After a data breach, there are numerous causes of action that may be brought. This section does not describe in detail all of the potential causes of actions, but provides a general overview of common causes of action. Some of the potential causes of action, include negligence, breach of contract, misrepresentation, unjust enrichment, general unfair trade practices, breach of warranty, breach of fiduciary duty and other statutory-based claims. The success of these causes of action often depends on state law.

Two well-known data breach cases involved Target and Equifax. These two cases are excellent examples of the numerous potential causes of action that can be pled as a result of a data breach. The cases also highlight common problems and arguments raising these causes of action. This section also discusses other cases raising relevant issues concerning additional causes of action, including covering matters related to contract drafting.

In a 2014 decision, *In re Target Corporation Consumer Data Security Breach Litigation,*[260] a district court in Minnesota considered numerous causes of action brought by financial institutions against Target for a massive data breach involving around 100 million Target consumers' credit and debit card information. The causes of action included negligence, negligent omission, violation of Minnesota's Plastic Card Security Act and negligence per se based on the violation of the aforementioned Act. On the negligence claim, the district court noted that there are four elements for negligence: duty, breach, causation and injury. The district court found that a duty can exist under Minnesota law under two circumstances: 1) "when the defendant's own conduct creates a foreseeable risk of injury to a foreseeable plaintiff"; or 2)

---

[259] *Clemens v. Execupharm,* __ F.4th __ (3rd Cir. 2022).

[260] *In re Target Corporation Consumer Data Security Breach Litigation,* 64 F.Supp.3d 1304 (D. Minn. 2014).

"a defendant owes a duty to protect a plaintiff when action by someone other than the defendant creates a foreseeable risk of harm to the plaintiff and the defendant and plaintiff stand in a special relationship." The district court rejected Target's argument that the second circumstance applied and held that Target created a foreseeable risk of injury to the financial institutions by intentionally "disabling one of the security features that would have prevented the harm" and "failing to heed the warning signs as the hackers' attack began." The district court also pointed to the presence of the Minnesota Plastic Security Card Act as supporting the claim of a duty.

The district court dismissed the negligent omission claim based on a failure to allege reliance; however, the district court allowed the plaintiffs to amend its complaint to included allegations concerning reliance. The district court did find that Target properly pled duty and the alleged omissions. The plaintiffs alleged that Target "'failed to disclose material weaknesses in its data security systems and procedures' that it had an obligation to disclose" in the face of "Target h[olding] itself out as having secure data systems . . . and had taken affirmative steps to make its systems more vulnerable to attack."

The district court found the claim that the Minnesota Plastic Card Security Act was violated survived the motion to dismiss. The Minnesota Plastic Card Security Act essentially provides that a business accepting a credit or debit card for payment may not retain information regarding the card "subsequent to the authorization of the transaction or in the case of a PIN debit transaction, subsequent to 48 hours after authorization of the transaction." The district court rejected Target's argument that it did not cause the injury incurred by plaintiffs because "[p]laintiff's [sufficiently] allege that Target stored data for longer than the [Act] allows, and that the hackers were able to access some of this stored data, namely the CVV codes, without which the breach would not have been as serious." The negligence per se claim is validly claimed essentially based on the validity of the Minnesota Plastic Card Security Act alleged violation. Negligence per se is found when a party violates a statute that provides a duty and standard of care.

In a 2019 decision, *In re Equifax Customer Data Security Breach Litigation*,[261] the district court considered numerous causes of actions related to a massive data breach, including violations of the Fair Credit Reporting Act, negligence, negligence per se and state consumer act violations. The district court dismissed claims based on violations of the Fair Credit Reporting Act because defendant did not "furnish"—actively transmit—credit report information to a third party because it was stolen by hackers as required by the statute, and that the information stolen—"consumer's 'name, phone number, social security number, date of birth, driver's license, current address, and time spent at current address"—is not a credit report bearing on credit worthiness.

The district court then considered defendant's argument that plaintiffs failed to prove sufficient injury and proximate causation. The district court decided that the following allegations were sufficient to allege an injury: "tak[ing] measures to combat the risk of identify theft, by identity theft that has already occurred to some members of the class, by expending time and effort to monitor their credit and identity, and they all face a serious and imminent risk of fraud and identity theft due to the Data Breach." As discussed *supra* in the standing section, some courts are more reluctant to find injury from time and effort alone. Furthermore, the *Equifax* district court found proximate causation and rejected the defendant's argument that the harm may have been caused by another data breach. The district court found that the allegations that the harm was caused by the data breach was sufficient and that "the criminal acts of the hackers were reasonably foreseeable to the Defendants."

Defendant also argued that the economic loss doctrine—which "'generally provides that a contracting party who suffers purely economic loss must seek his remedy in contract and not in tort'"—does not apply because of the independent duty exception. Basically, since the defendant owed the plaintiffs an independent duty to safeguard their personal information, the economic loss doctrine does not apply.

---

[261] *In re Equifax Customer Data Security Breach Litigation*, 362 F.Supp.3d 1295 (2019).

The district court also held that a private cause of action for negligence per se could proceed based on an alleged violation of Section 5 of the FTC Act based on a failure to maintain reasonable and appropriate security measures. Courts do not always find that federal laws concerning privacy support a finding of negligence per se. For example, in *Weinberg v. Advanced Data Processing*, the district court held that violations of HIPAA cannot support a negligence per se claim under Florida law because HIPAA lacks an express private right of action. However, a court following that approach could use violation of a federal statute as evidence of breach of a standard to act reasonably in protecting confidential information. Additionally, the district court, in *Thymes v. Gillman Companies*, decided that the GLBA and Safeguards Rule did not provide a private right of action.[262] Again, the violations of federal statutes may serve as evidence of breach.

The *Equifax* district court also held that plaintiffs' cause of action for unjust enrichment was adequately pled for some plaintiffs, but not others. Unjust enrichment requires: "(1) a benefit has been conferred, (2) compensation has not been given for receipt of the benefit, and (3) the failure to so compensate would be unjust." Notably, the district court decided that plaintiffs who did not confer any information to Equifax did not confer a benefit and, thus, there could not be unjust enrichment. Apparently, some plaintiffs did provide information to Equifax and, thus, conferred a benefit to Equifax. The district court also rejected the express and implied contract claims. First, the district court noted that the plaintiffs failed to allege that they read, relied upon or were aware of the Privacy Policy on which they based their contract claims, and, thus mutual assent is lacking. Second, the district court rejected the argument that the Equifax Product Agreement and Terms of Use which arguably incorporated by reference the Privacy Policy provided any relief because it contained a term excluding any damages for use or reliance on information in the website. The implied contract claim failed because of a merger clause in the Equifax Product Agreement and Terms of Use and a lack of mutual assent. The district court then dismissed some claims based on numerous state data breach notification statutes. Importantly, the

---

[262] *Thymes v. Gillman Companies*, 2018 WL 1281852 (S.D. Tex. 2018). *But see In re Equifax Customer Data Security Breach Litigation*, 371 F.Supp.3d 1150 (N.D. Ga. 2019) (finding that GLBA could not serve as the basis of a negligence per se claim, but the Safeguards Rule does in a data breach situation).

district court made distinctions between statutes that expressly provided for a private cause of action, are ambiguous as to the provision of a private cause of action, or explicitly do not provide for one. The district court did not dismiss the actions under state data breach statutes that either provided for a cause of action or were ambiguous. The district court also considered other potential claims.

Some courts have been less willing to find a duty of care owed to the victims of data breaches. For example, the Georgia Supreme Court, in *Department of Labor v. McConnell*,[263] found that a general duty of care to protect against foreseeable risk of harm did not exist in a data breach matter. However, some courts have been more willing to find the existence of an express or implied contract in the data breach context; however, those cases are highly dependent on the specific facts and provisions present in the contracts. For example, the district court, in *In re Premera Blue Cross Customer Data Security Breach Litigation*,[264] found that a Privacy Notice was incorporated into health benefits contracts allowing the plaintiffs to proceed with their breach of express contract claims. Notably, the district court mentioned that the merger clause did not preclude the incorporation of the document based on the specific language of the merger clause. The district court also implied a term requiring the defendant to exercise reasonable security measures and to comply with the law, including HIPAA. Finally, the district court found that plaintiffs who were Premera policy holders had an implied in fact contract based on "policy booklets, Code of Conduct, and Privacy Notice" to reasonably protect confidential information.

From a counseling perspective, attorneys should protect their clients' interests by including carefully drafted merger clauses, warranty clauses, indemnification provisions, choice of law and forum clauses, binding arbitration clauses, clauses prohibiting oral modification and limitations of liability provisions. Notably, attorneys should ensure that clients have secured cybersecurity insurance and can verify that service providers, such as cloud services, have adopted reasonable and appropriate cybersecurity measures.

---

[263] Department of Labor v. McConnell, 305 Ga. 812 (2019).

[264] In re Premera Blue Cross Customer Data Security Breach Litigation, 2017 WL 539578 (D. Or. 2017).

9.4 Class Certification

Data breach lawsuits are often styled as class actions. In order for a class action to be brought, the class must be certified. Federal Rules of Civil Procedure, Rule 23, provides the general requirements for certification: Numerosity; Commonality; Fair and Adequate Representation; and Typicality. Specifically, Rule 23 provides, in relevant part:

> (a) Prerequisites. One or more members of a class may sue or be sued as representative parties on behalf of all members only if:
>
> (1) the class is so numerous that joinder of all members is impracticable;
>
> (2) there are questions of law or fact common to the class;
>
> (3) the claims or defenses of the representative parties are typical of the claims or defenses of the class; and
>
> (4) the representative parties will fairly and adequately protect the interests of the class.
>
> (b) Types of Class Actions. A class action may be maintained if Rule 23(a) is satisfied and if:
>
> (1) prosecuting separate actions by or against individual class members would create a risk of:
>
> (A) inconsistent or varying adjudications with respect to individual class members that would establish incompatible standards of conduct for the party opposing the class; or
>
> (B) adjudications with respect to individual class members that, as a practical matter, would be dispositive of the interests of the other members not parties to the individual adjudications or would substantially impair or impede their ability to protect their interests;

> (2) the party opposing the class has acted or refused to act on grounds that apply generally to the class, so that final injunctive relief or corresponding declaratory relief is appropriate respecting the class as a whole; or
>
> (3) the court finds that the questions of law or fact common to class members predominate over any questions affecting only individual members, and that a class action is superior to other available methods for fairly and efficiently adjudicating the controversy. The matters pertinent to these findings include:
>
> (A) the class members' interests in individually controlling the prosecution or defense of separate actions;
>
> (B) the extent and nature of any litigation concerning the controversy already begun by or against class members;
>
> (C) the desirability or undesirability of concentrating the litigation of the claims in the particular forum; and
>
> (D) the likely difficulties in managing a class action.

The Rule 23(a) requirement of numerosity does not include a strict numeric test and each case must be decided on its facts to determine satisfaction of numerosity. Moreover, an exact number of class members does not need to be proved, but a speculative showing is not enough to satisfy the standard. Plaintiffs must also demonstrate the impracticability of joinder. The Rule 23(a) requirement of commonality of questions and law to the class essentially requires common answers provided by the court to resolve questions presented in litigation. The Rule 23(a) requirement of typicality of the claims and defenses of the class representatives and class members ensures that the class representatives interests are aligned with those of the class as a whole. Thus, the benefit of the class representatives advocacy will inure to all members of the class. Finally, Rule 23(a) requires that the representative parties will adequately protect the class members interests. In order to satisfy this requirement, the class members and representatives must not have a potential conflict, and the representing attorneys must be skilled. Notably, at least one court has held that a "browsewrap" arbitration clause did not apply because of a lack of consent and that it was illusory, thus the class action could continue.

The following is a discussion of two cases reviewing the requirements for class certification in the data breach context. The district court, in *In re Hannaford Brothers Data Security Breach Litigation*,[265] found that the plaintiffs did not satisfy the predominance requirement of Rule 23(b)(3), which provides, in part: "the court finds that the questions of law or fact common to class members predominate over any questions affecting only individual members, and that a class action is superior to other available methods for fairly and efficiently adjudicating the controversy. . . ." The district court determined that data estimating around 12,000 class members was sufficient to satisfy numerosity. Moreover, the district court found that commonality was also satisfied based on the common claims of "whether Hannaford's conduct was negligent or a contractual breach and whether it caused a data security breach that resulted in theft of customers' data and reasonably prompted customers to take mitigation measures . . .." The district court also determined that the claims or defenses were typical even though there may be some differences between class members and representatives concerning the economic harm involved. Finally, the district court found that the class representatives did not appear to have conflicts with class members and the attorneys were qualified. Notably, the district court did not find Rule 23(b)(3) satisfied and stated that the requirement is to ensure "the promotion of economy and efficiency." On predominance of the common issues over individual issues, the district court noted that there were potential differences between the various plaintiffs' economic harm, such as their mitigation efforts and fees, and that the plaintiffs failed to produce an expert to testify as to a lump sum damage award. The latter reason resulted in a failure of the plaintiffs to satisfy their burden at class certification. On superiority of the class action to resolve the matter, the district court decided that a proposed refund program

[265] *In re Hannaford Brothers Data Security Breach Litigation*, 293 F.R.D. 21 (2013).

which would reimburse fees incurred in acquiring new credit cards was not an alternative adjudication method contemplated by the FRCP in resolving questions of superiority between a class action and individual lawsuits.

The second case is *In re Target Corporation Customer Data Security Breach Litigation*[266] and consists of two opinions. In the first opinion, the district court considered an attempt to decertify the class certification after settlement. The district court noted that the class must meet the requirements of FRCP 23 throughout the litigation. The district court specifically rejected arguments that the class representatives did not adequately represent the class because of the range of potential injuries to class members. Moreover, the district court rejected arguments that there were conflicts of interest between the class representatives and the class members, and the essential position of the challenger that the settlement itself was deficient. In the second opinion, the Eight Circuit affirmed the district court's re-certification of the class and approval of the settlement agreement.

[266] *In re Target Corporation Customer Data Security Breach Litigation*, 2017 WL 2178306 (May 17, 2017).

CHAPTER TEN. Cybersecurity Risk Assessment and National Institute of Standards and Technology Risk Management Framework

10.1 Introduction

This chapter covers risk assessment and the National Institute of Standards and Technology (NIST) Risk Management Framework. First, this chapter will review risk assessment to maintain reasonable security measures. Second, the NIST Risk Management Framework will be analyzed. This chapter also discusses the FBI and Secret Services role in investigating cybersecurity issues.

10.2 Risk Assessment

As we have seen in previous chapters, many agencies use a reasonable security measures standard to determine the liability for a company after a data breach or other cybersecurity mishap that affects the public or after the uncovering of a potential cybersecurity issue that does not result in a breach but that draws the attention of an enforcement agency. The reasonable security measures standard will be a moving target over time as technology advances and bad actors become even more efficient, effective, and intrusive. We also expect the courts to further define over time and cases, the reasonable security measures standard. How can companies ensure that they are maintaining a reasonable security measures standard? It all starts with a risk assessment.

10.2[A] Risk Analysis

This section concerns risk analysis impacting the lifeblood of many companies: data. The goal is to protect the data by maintaining confidentiality, integrity, and availability (CIA) of the data. The data must be protected at rest, in use and in transit. The Federal Information Security Management Act of 2002 ("FISMA") describes CIA as:

> CONFIDENTIALITY "Preserving authorized restrictions on information access and disclosure, including means for protecting personal privacy and proprietary information..." [44 U.S.C., Sec. 3542] A loss of confidentiality is the unauthorized disclosure of information.
>
> INTEGRITY "Guarding against improper information modification or destruction, and includes ensuring information non-repudiation and authenticity..." [44 U.S.C., Sec. 3542] A loss of integrity is the unauthorized modification or destruction of information.
>
> AVAILABILITY "Ensuring timely and reliable access to and use of information..." [44 U.S.C., SEC. 3542] A loss of availability is the disruption of access to or use of information or an information system.[267]

What is the risk in each of these categories in maintaining CIA? Risk can be measured by multiplying the threat times the vulnerability.

$$risk = threat * vulnerability$$

Reducing either the threat or the vulnerability will reduce the risk. Thus, to understand risk, we must be able to identify threats and vulnerabilities. Potential threats can include:

- Phishing
- Ransomware
- Cryptojacking
- Cyber-physical attacks
- State-sponsored attacks
- IoT attacks
- Smart medical devices and electronic medical records (EMRs)
- Third Parties (Vendor, Contractors, Partners)
- Connected cars and semi-autonomous vehicles
- Social Engineering

---

[267] STANDARDS FOR SECURITY CATEGORIZATION OF FEDERAL INFORMATION AND INFORMATION SYSTEMS, FED. INFO. PROCESSING STANDARDS PUBL'N 2 (2004), *available at* https://nvlpubs.nist.gov/nistpubs/FIPS/NIST.FIPS.199.pdf.

- Severe shortage of cybersecurity professionals[268]

Assessing Risk will cross many departments and should be led by upper management, including the legal department. The legal department must be involved to advise on risks associated with failing to meet laws, regulations and contracts. Only counsel will fully understand the risks of not meeting the reasonable security measures standard.

Sometimes risk can be measured (Quantitative Risk Analysis) but other times, it is left to a Qualitative Analysis.

> *Quantitative* assessments typically employ a set of methods, principles, or rules for assessing risk based on the use of numbers—where the meanings and proportionality of values are maintained inside and outside the context of the assessment. This type of assessment most effectively supports cost-benefit analyses of alternative risk responses or courses of action.[269]
>
> In contrast to quantitative assessments, qualitative assessments typically employ a set of methods, principles, or rules for assessing risk based on nonnumerical categories or levels (e.g., very low, low, moderate, high, very high).270
>
> Conducting risk assessments includes the following specific tasks:
>
> - Identify threat sources that are relevant to organizations;
> - Identify threat events that could be produced by those sources;
> - Identify vulnerabilities within organizations that could be exploited by threat sources through

---

[268] *See* Michelle Moore, *Top Cybersecurity Threats in 2020*, U. OF SAN DIEGO https://onlinedegrees.sandiego.edu/top-cyber-security-threats/ (last visited May 19, 2021).

[269] INFORMATION SECURITY, NAT'L INST. OF STANDARDS AND TECH. 14 (2012), *available at* https://nvlpubs.nist.gov/nistpubs/Legacy/SP/nistspecialpublication800-30r1.pdf.

[270] *Id.*

specific threat events and the predisposing conditions that could affect successful exploitation;

- Determine the likelihood that the identified threat sources would initiate specific threat events and the likelihood that the threat events would be successful;

- Determine the adverse impacts to organizational operations and assets, individuals, other organizations, and the Nation resulting from the exploitation of vulnerabilities by threat sources (through specific threat events); and

- Determine information security risks as a combination of likelihood of threat exploitation of vulnerabilities and the impact of such exploitation, including any uncertainties associated with the risk determinations.[271]

Counsel must keep in mind that in the event of litigation, the risk analysis may likely be discoverable. It is likely that most of the risk analysis team members will not be thinking of future litigation. But the risk analysis documentation could pose problems in court. For example, if the risk analysis identifies a significant risk and it is not addressed in the company's security measures, a company may have issues with making a case that it took reasonable security measures. Another issue could be identifying the "extent of loss if realized." For example, if a company identified the amount of loss in a data breach, it may be hard for the company to argue against that amount in court. For this reason, the authors recommend against putting any sort of precise damage figure on certain assets, particularly, personally identifiable information (PII) data records because this figure could be used against the company in court.

Now that the risks have been identified and analyzed, the company's next step is to determine what action should or should not be taken for each of the identified risks. The following are the possible responses:

---

[271] *Id.* at 29.

- Mitigate
- Assign to an outside party such as an insurance company
- Accept as part of the risk of doing business
- Ignore

For the last response - Ignore - no security measures are taken. The reasoning for this response must be well documented because it does not provide a security measure. If a security measure is not applied, it may be hard to argue and meet the threshold defense of providing reasonable security measures without convincing documentation as to why no action was taken. The cost/benefit analysis is extremely helpful in deciding a risk response, but could give a misleading answer if potential future legal action is not adequately priced in.

Data is often at the core of risk analysis with the objective being maintaining the confidentiality, integrity, and availability of the data. But there are many assets (physical, administrative, technology) that go into the protection of data such as:

- Maintaining the facility that houses the data
- Providing the proper environment for housing the machines that contain the data
- Managing access to the facility and machines
- Protecting the machines, operating system and software that provide access to the data
- Protecting the network that transports the data
- Maintaining backups of the data
- Maintaining business continuity and disaster recovery plans

A simple example of a risk analysis using the quantitative method could be as follows: What is the risk that a company's facility located in the Midwest could be affected by an earthquake? This would be a physical risk. To calculate using a quantitative approach, we must know the probability for an earthquake to occur in the Midwest region. Let's say the probability is .01 times in a year. And let's guess that the damage caused by an earthquake to the facility would be $50,000. Taking $50,000 time .01 gives us a $500 risk per year. Now, please assume the facility is in northern California on the fault line and the probability of an earthquake in a year is .5 or one earthquake every two years. We can also assume that the damage might be higher based on a more severe earthquake, so we may guess it might be $200,000 for one earthquake. Taking $200,000 times .5 for one year equals a $100,000 risk per year.

Of course, the facility is only one company asset. This exercise must be conducted for all significant company assets and all potential risks. For example, what would happen to all assets if a power outage occurred? That would answer the question as to whether a second source of power is needed such as a diesel generator. Or what happens when a hacker takes essential systems down for multiple days?

The next section examines the NIST Risk Management Framework that can be used as a guide for forming a company's security policies and procedures.

10.3 National Institute of Standards and Technology (NIST) Risk Management Framework

There are several cybersecurity frameworks available. A few examples include ISO:27001:2013, NIST CSF v.1.1, and CIS Critical Security Controls. Notably, some frameworks require a third party certification, such as ISO:27001:2013, but not NIST CSF v.1.1, which can be self-attested. The NIST CSF v. 1.1, sometimes referred to as the NIST Risk Management Framework is widely recognized as a useful tool for analyzing and managing risk in the context of cybersecurity issues. The Framework provides cybersecurity professionals and counsel an analytical framework to address potential issues as those problems arise.

10.3[A] Overview of the NIST Risk Management Framework

Congress created NIST on March 3, 1901. After enacting the Computer Fraud and Abuse Act (CFAA) in 1986, Congress reviewed computer security in the federal government systems. That led to Congress promulgating the Computer Security Act (CSA) of 1987. The CSA mandated baseline security requirements for all federal agencies:

> Section 2 (b) SPECIFIC PURPOSES.-The purposes of this Act are--
>
> (1) by amending the Act of March 3, 1901, to assign to the National Bureau of Standards responsibility

> for developing standards and guidelines for Federal computer systems, including responsibility for developing standards and guidelines needed to assure the cost-effective security and privacy of sensitive information in Federal computer systems, drawing on the technical advice and assistance (including work products) of the National Security Agency, where appropriate;
>
> (2) to provide for promulgation of such standards and guidelines by amending section 111(d) of the Federal Property and Administrative Services Act of 1949;
>
> (3) to require establishment of security plans by all operators of Federal computer systems that contain sensitive information; and
>
> (4) to require mandatory periodic training for all persons involved in management, use, or operation of Federal computer systems that contain sensitive information.[272]

The Federal Information Security Management Act (FISMA) of 2002 resulted in the FISMA Implementation Project.

> To produce security standards and guidelines for FISMA, the National Institute of Standards and Technology (NIST) established the FISMA Implementation Project in 2003. The project aims to support the implementation of and compliance with FISMA standards. Per FISMA, an effective information security program should include, among other things,
>
> - periodic assessments of risk, including the harm that could result from the unauthorized access, use, disclosure, disruption, modification, or destruction of information and information systems that support the operations and assets of the organization

[272] Computer Security Act of 1987, 15 U.S.C. §§ 271, 278g-3, 278h.

- policies and procedures that are based on risk assessments, cost-effectively reduce information security risks to an acceptable level, and ensure that information security is addressed throughout the life cycle of each organizational information system

- security awareness training to inform personnel of information security risks

- periodic testing and evaluation of the effectiveness of information security policies, procedures, practices, and security controls

- a process for planning, implementing, evaluating, and documenting remedial actions to address any deficiencies

- procedures for detecting, reporting, and responding to security incidents

- plans and procedures to ensure continuity of operations for information systems that support the operations and assets of the organization[273]

FISMA was amended in 2014 by the Federal Information Security Modernization Act.

The Federal Information Security Modernization Act of 2014 amends the Federal Information Security Management Act of 2002 (FISMA) providing several modifications that modernize Federal security practices to address evolving security concerns. These changes result in less overall reporting, strengthens the use of continuous monitoring in systems, increased focus on the agencies for compliance, and reporting that is more focused on the issues caused by security incidents.

FISMA, along with the Paperwork Reduction Act of 1995 and the Information Technology Management Reform Act of 1996 (Clinger-Cohen Act), explicitly emphasizes a risk-based policy for cost-effective security. In support of and reinforcing this legislation, the Office of Management and Budget (OMB) through Circular A-

---

[273] *NIST FISMA Guidance*, OFFICE OF INSPECTOR GENERAL, https://oig.federalreserve.gov/fisma.htm (last visited May 19, 2021).

130, "Managing Federal Information as a Strategic Resource," requires executive agencies within the federal government to:

- Plan for security
- Ensure that appropriate officials are assigned security responsibility
- Periodically review the security controls in their systems
- Authorize system processing prior to operations and, periodically, thereafter[274]

This chapter contains references to two NIST risk management frameworks, one for cybersecurity covering federal computer systems as mandated by FISMA (2002) that can also be applied by private companies and one for critical infrastructure cybersecurity as directed by 2013 Executive Order 13636. Both fundamentally rely on the same risk management principles outlined in the NIST Special Publications discussed later.

The NIST Framework for Improving Critical Infrastructure Cybersecurity was encouraged by Executive Order 13636 in February 2013, was updated to version 1.1 in 2018 and is further described below.[275]

Executive Order 13636 defines "Critical Infrastructure" as:

> Sec. 2. Critical Infrastructure. As used in this order, the term critical infrastructure means systems and assets, whether physical or virtual, so vital to the United States that the incapacity or destruction of such systems and assets would have a debilitating impact on security, national economic security, national public health or safety, or any combination of those matters.

---

[274] *FISMA Implementation Project, FISMA Background*, NAT'L INST. OF STANDARDS AND TECH. https://csrc.nist.gov/Projects/risk-management/detailed-overview (last updated May 7, 2021).

[275] FRAMEWORK FOR IMPROVING CRITICAL INFRASTRUCTURE CYBERSECURITY, NAT'L. INST. OF STANDARDS AND TECH. (2018), *available at* https://nvlpubs.nist.gov/nistpubs/CSWP/NIST.CSWP.04162018.pdf.

The Executive Order also directed NIST to lead the development of a framework for critical infrastructure.[276] Following through on its guidance from the Executive Order, NIST created a Cybersecurity Framework concerning Critical Infrastructure for adoption by government and private organizations.[277]

Thus, the Framework can not only be used by government, but also for any organization in different industries. There is the ability to customize the Framework to account for variability in need and industry.[278] The Risk Based Framework provides objectives or outcomes.[279] The Framework is also considered a "living" document that can be modified over time because of changes to technology as well as regulation.[280] One way to think about the Framework is to consider it as a way to thoughtfully consider cybersecurity issues and importantly to demonstrate that one is "compliant" with their own cybersecurity policy.[281]

10.4 The NIST Risk Management Framework: Selected Information

This section provides materials from the NIST concerning the Risk Management Framework. The Risk Management Framework document is supplemented by many guidance documents provided by the NIST. Appendix B of the Risk Management Framework provides a helpful Glossary of terms.

10.4[a] NIST 800 SERIES OF SPECIAL PUBLICATIONS

The NIST publishes the 800 series of Special Publications for guidance in providing computer security for the federal government.[282] These Special Publications were a result of the

[276] Exec. Order No. 13636 (2013).
[277] *Cybersecurity Framework Version 1.1. Overview*, NAT'L INST. OF STANDARDS AND TECH. (May 1, 2018), https://www.nist.gov/video/cybersecurity-framework-version-11-overview.
[278] *Id.*
[279] *Id.*
[280] *Id.*
[281] *Id.*
[282] *See Computer Security Resource Center*, NAT'L INST. OF STANDARDS AND TECH. https://csrc.nist.gov/publications/sp800 (last visited May 19, 2021) (listing the series of special publications for guidance in a searchable list).

Federal Information Security Management Act (FISMA) of 2002 that resulted in the FISMA Implementation Project.

Even though FISMA and the resulting FISMA Implementation Project were directed at federal government information systems and not corporate America, companies have used the NIST Special Publications for cybersecurity guidance for managing risk.

Other risk management frameworks have been developed by notable organizations such as: Operationally Critical Threat, Asset and Vulnerability Evaluation (OCTAVE)[283]; Factor Analysis Information Risk (FAIR)[284]; and Intel's Threat Agent Risk Assessment (TARA).[285]

Attorneys and security engineers alike, both share an aversion to risk. Risk is always at the forefront of any business action or transaction. In the cybersecurity world, risk is defined as "A measure of the extent to which an entity is threatened by a potential circumstance or event, and typically a function of: (i) the adverse impacts that would arise if the circumstance or event occurs; and (ii) the likelihood of occurrence."[286]

The cybersecurity professional, through the use of controls and/or countermeasures, seeks to reduce or eliminate vulnerabilities, or where the vulnerabilities cannot be reduced or eliminated, then to reduce the effect of possible threats through the management of Organizational risk.

As in-house counsel, you may have the chief information security officer (CISO) reporting to the legal department or even directly to the CEO, such is the importance of the CISO mission. Other parts of the organization that may be involved in risk

---

[283] *See CTAVE FORTE: Establish a More Adaptable and Robust Risk Program*, CARNEGIE MELLON UNIVERSITY: SOFTWARE ENGINEERING INSTITUTE (June 2020), *available at* https://resources.sei.cmu.edu/library/asset-view.cfm?assetid=643959.

[284] *See What is the FAIR Institute*, FAIR INSTITUTE, https://www.fairinstitute.org (last visited May 19, 2021).

[285] *See* JACKSON WYNN, ET AL., THREAT ASSESSMENT & REMEDIATION ANALYSIS (TARA), MITRE (Oct. 2011), *available at* https://www.mitre.org/sites/default/files/pdf/11_4982.pdf

[286] GUIDE FOR CONDUCTING RISK ASSESSMENTS, NAT'L INST. OF STANDARDS AND TECH. B-9 (2012), Section 2.3 *Key Risk Concepts*, *available at* https://nvlpubs.nist.gov/nistpubs/Legacy/SP/nistspecialpublication800-30r1.pdf.

management of information systems include engineering, application development, and operations. The application development team focus is on developing an application on time and ready for market distribution or in-house use. The development team is often under stress to deliver on time. Implementing security measures in the application can be viewed as a nuisance that is keeping the team from meeting its goals. The CISO is not part of the development team but has a vested interest in making sure that security is properly implemented in the application. And the legal department has a huge interest in making sure that the implemented application security measures will meet legal requirements. Your job as counsel may depend on being able to communicate effectively with all of these departments. What makes counsel's task even tougher is that each department may speak its own language just as counsel has its own language of motions, injunctions, summary judgement, complaints, for example, that an engineer may not grasp. The next few paragraphs are an attempt at giving counsel a foundation in understanding application/software development.

Software development can happen in house or be outsourced to an entity anywhere in the world. Or if a commercial application that exists that meets a company's requirements it can be purchased. This is called Commercial Off The Shelf (COTS) software. COTS can usually be configured or modified by the purchaser to provide an even closer requirements fit. It bears mentioning that adding security to an application may require a balancing act of not having the security take over the functionality or user-friendliness of the final product. As one might expect, the security/risk team should be involved as soon as possible in the process of either acquiring COTS or the System Development Life Cycle (SDLC).

There is no one-size-fits-all approach to the System Development Life Cycle and several methods exist. One method that is long in the tooth is the waterfall model. It can be envisioned as the results from the first step falling into the second step and then the results from the third step falling into the fourth step and so forth, with the steps being:

- Collection of system requirements
- Collection of software requirements
- Preliminary design
- Detailed design

- Coding and debugging of the code through unit testing of each module
- Testing of complete code
- Placing code into operations
- Maintaining the code through bug fixes and feature enhancements.

The waterfall approach can be a long process depending on the size of the system and can take years to complete. Each step may have a walkthrough of the results before passing it onto the next step. If issues are found, it remains in the same step, the issue is resolved, and another walkthrough takes place. A walkthrough is normally a team sitting around a conference table reviewing pages and pages of results. The advantage of waterfall development is that there is abundant documentation to follow and review. The disadvantage is that by the time the product is delivered, the requirements may have changed over time and the user is unhappy because the system no longer meets their current requirements.

Rapid Application Prototyping (RAD) was introduced to remedy some of the waterfall shortcomings. The goal of RAD was to produce a quick and dirty prototype based on the user's requirements that could be shown to the user for immediate feedback. This is an iterative process. It may start with just mocked up screenshots being shown to the user for feedback. Eventually after enough iterations, a final product is produced for the user group that is not a surprise to the users because the users have been intimately involved in the process from the start.

Another model that has become popular today is the Agile Software Development. The core tenants of Agile are:

> "Individual and interactions over processes and tools; Working software over comprehensive documentation; Customer collaboration over contract negotiation; Responding to change over following a plan. That is, while there is value in the items on the right, we value the items on the left more."[287]

---

[287] Kent Beck, et al., *Manifesto for Agile Software Development*, AGILE, http://agilemanifesto.org (last visited May 19, 2021).

Notice that in the above models, security is not a specific step or called out as a core tenant. This is probably because the code will function without security measures. There is likely a lot of legacy code in production today that was developed before the focus on cybersecurity. For example, the programming language COBOL is 60 years old and still prevalent in many systems today.[288] This is part of the challenge for the CISO and counsel. They must educate the development teams on the importance of reasonable security measures and the potential cost for not applying those measures. Often, when the importance of proper security measures is explained in engineering English along with the risk of not applying the measure, and not legalese, the development team is more likely to take the measures to heart. Afterall, engineers are just as risk adverse as attorneys.

The 800 series of Special Publications for guidance in providing computer security is a risk-based approach that can be used with a system development life cycle.[289] Following is a high-level view of the Risk Management Framework Steps:

As an overarching step, the prepare step includes "[e]ssential activities to prepare the organization to manage security and privacy risks."[290]

The categorize step categorizes "the system and the information processed, stored, and transmitted based on an impact analysis."[291]

The select step is selecting "the set of NIST SP 800-53 controls to protect the system based on risk assessment(s)."[292]

---

[288] *See* Charles R. Martin, *Brush up your COBOL: Why is a 60 year old language suddenly in demand?*, THE OVERFLOW (Apr. 20, 2020), https://stackoverflow.blog/2020/04/20/brush-up-your-cobol-why-is-a-60-year-old-language-suddenly-in-demand/.

[289] *See* Risk-Based Approach, *available at* https://csrc.nist.gov/projects/risk-management/rmf-overview.

[290] *FISMA Implementation Project: Risk Management Framework (RMF) Overview*, NAT'L INST. OF STANDARDS AND TECH., https://csrc.nist.gov/projects/risk-management/rmf-overview (last updated May 7, 2021).

[291] *Id.*

[292] *Id.*

The Implement step is implementing "the controls and document how controls are deployed." [293]

The assess step is "to determine if the controls are in place, operating as intended, and producing the desired results."[294]

In the authorize step a "[s]enior official makes a risk-based decision to authorize the system (to operate)."[295]

The monitor step is to "[c]ontinuously monitor control implementation and risk to the system."[296]

10.4[A][I] FEDERAL INFORMATION PROCESSING STANDARDS, NIST SPECIAL PUBLICATIONS AND NIST INTERAGENCY REPORTS

This section contains a closer look at each of the Federal Information Processing Standards (FIPS) Publications, NIST Special Publications and NIST Interagency Reports. Although these documents were originally created for protecting federal assets, they have been adopted as guidelines by non-government businesses. This is a lot of material. The goal here is not to make Counsel an expert on each of these documents, but instead to give Counsel enough knowledge that Counsel will be able to participate in a knowledgeable conversation with the security team.

FIPS 199: Standards for Security Categorization of Federal Information and Information Systems

FIPS 199 is focused on the standards used "to categorize all information and information systems . . . based on the objectives of providing appropriate levels of information security according to a range of risk levels."[297]

FIPS 199 looks at the potential impact on organizations and individuals if the CIA [44 U.S.C., Sec. 3542] for information and

---

293 *Id.*
294 *Id.*
295 *Id.*
296 *Id.*
297 STANDARDS FOR SECURITY CATEGORIZATION OF FEDERAL INFORMATION AND INFORMATION SYSTEMS, NAT'L INST. OF STANDARDS AND TECH. 1 (2004), *available at* https://nvlpubs.nist.gov/nistpubs/FIPS/NIST.FIPS.199.pdf.

information systems is breached.[298] The potential impact is divided into three categories, low, moderate, and high.[299]

Low potential impact is defined as "[t]he loss of confidentiality, integrity, or availability could be expected to have a **limited** adverse effect on organizational operations, organizational assets, or individuals."[300] Moderate potential impact is "[t]he loss of confidentiality, integrity, or availability could be expected to have a **serious** adverse effect on organizational operations, organizational assets, or individuals."[301] High potential impact is "[t]he loss of confidentiality, integrity, or availability could be expected to have a **severe or catastrophic** adverse effect on organizational operations, organizational assets, or individual."[302]

FIPS 199 provides examples to help in categorization. This categorization exercise could be very helpful to a company that is in the risk analysis phase.[303]

FIPS 200: Minimum Security Requirements for Federal Information and Information Systems

FIPS 200 "specifies minimum security requirements for federal information and information systems in seventeen security-related areas," and "must meet the minimum security requirements . . . through the use of security controls in accordance with NIST Special Publication 800-53."[304]

FIPS 200 relies on the categorization for information and systems from the potential impact analysis of FIPS 199, pages 1-2. Because the impact analysis categorizes CIA, and CIA categorizations may not receive the same categorization across all three components of CIA, there is an opportunity for three different impact scores. For example, Confidentiality could be categorized as

---

[298] *Id.* at 2.
[299] *Id.* at 2.
[300] *Id.* at 2.
[301] *Id.* at 2.
[302] *Id.* at 3.
[303] STANDARDS FOR SECURITY CATEGORIZATION OF FEDERAL INFORMATION AND INFORMATION SYSTEMS, NAT'L INST. OF STANDARDS AND TECH. 2–5 (2004), *available at* https://nvlpubs.nist.gov/nistpubs/FIPS/NIST.FIPS.199.pdf.
[304] MINIMUM SECURITY REQUIREMENTS FOR FEDERAL INFORMATION AND INFORMATION SYSTEMS, NAT'L. INST. OF STANDARDS AND TECH. iv (2006), *available at* https://nvlpubs.nist.gov/nistpubs/FIPS/NIST.FIPS.200.pdf.

high, Integrity as moderate, and Availability as low. In determining the minimum security requirement for a particular item, the highest impact score (high water mark) across CIA prevails.[305]

The minimum security requirements cover seventeen security-related areas with regard to protecting the confidentiality, integrity, and availability of federal information systems and the information processed, stored, and transmitted by those systems.[306]

The 17 minimum security specifications include:

- Access Control (AC)
- Awareness and Training (AT)
- Audit and Accountability (AU)
- Certification, Accreditation, and Security Assessments (CA)
- Configuration Management (CM)
- Contingency Planning (CP)
- Identification and Authentication (IA)
- Incident Response (IR)
- Maintenance (MA)
- Media Protection (MP)
- Physical and Environmental Protection (PE)
- Planning (PL)
- Personnel Security (PS)
- Risk Assessment (RA)
- System and Services Acquisition (SA)
- System and Communications Protection (SC)
- System and Information Integrity (SI)[307]

The minimum security requirements are met "by selecting the appropriate security controls and assurance requirements as described in NIST Special Publication 800-53, *Recommended Security Controls for Federal Information Systems.*"[308]

NIST Special Publication 800-53 addresses security controls based on whether the system is low-impact, moderate-impact, or high-impact.

---

[305] *Id.* at 2.
[306] *Id.*
[307] *Id.*
[308] *Id.*

The NIST 800 series of Special Publications is focused on Computer Security. Related series include Special Publications 1800 that covers Cybersecurity practice guides, and Special Publication 500 that covers Information technology.[309] Next, we list the relevant documents of the 800 series. The title provides insight into what is inside the document.

SP 800-18 Revision 1: Guide for Developing Security Plans for Federal Information Systems

> The purpose of the system security plan is to provide an overview of the security requirements of the system and describe the controls in place or planned for meeting those requirements.[310]

SP 800-30 Revision 1: Guide for Conducting Risk Assessments

> The purpose of Special Publication 800-30 is to provide guidance for conducting risk assessments of federal information systems and organizations, amplifying the guidance in Special Publication 800-39.[311]

SP 800-34 Revision 1: Contingency Planning Guide for Federal Information Systems

The importance of contingency planning cannot be understated, whether it be government systems and data or private business systems and data. Planning can make the difference between survival or ruin for a commercial enterprise.

This guide defines the following seven-step contingency planning process that an organization may apply to develop and maintain a viable contingency planning program for their

[309] *See Publications*, NAT'L INST. OF STANDARDS AND TECH., https://csrc.nist.gov/publications (last visited May 20, 2021).
[310] GUIDE FOR DEVELOPING SECURITY PLANS FOR FEDERAL INFORMATION SYSTEMS, NAT'L INST. OF STANDARDS AND TECH. (2006), *available at* https://nvlpubs.nist.gov/nistpubs/Legacy/SP/nistspecialpublication800-18r1.pdf.
[311] GUIDE FOR CONDUCTING RISK ASSESSMENTS, NAT'L INST. OF STANDARDS AND TECH. 2 (2012), *available at* https://nvlpubs.nist.gov/nistpubs/Legacy/SP/nistspecialpublication800-30r1.pdf.

information systems. These seven progressive steps are designed to be integrated into each stage of the system development life cycle.

1. **Develop the contingency planning policy statement.** A formal policy provides the authority and guidance necessary to develop an effective contingency plan.

2. **Conduct the business impact analysis (BIA).** The BIA helps identify and prioritize information systems and components critical to supporting the organization's mission/business processes. A template for developing the BIA is provided to assist the user.

3. **Identify preventive controls.** Measures taken to reduce the effects of system disruptions can increase system availability and reduce contingency life cycle costs.

4. **Create contingency strategies.** Thorough recovery strategies ensure that the system may be recovered quickly and effectively following a disruption.

5. **Develop an information system contingency plan.** The contingency plan should contain detailed guidance and procedures for restoring a damaged system unique to the system's security impact level and recovery requirements.

6. **Ensure plan testing, training, and exercises.** Testing validates recovery capabilities, whereas training prepares recovery personnel for plan activation and exercising the plan identifies planning gaps; combined, the activities improve plan effectiveness and overall organization preparedness.

7. **Ensure plan maintenance.** The plan should be a living document that is updated regularly to

> remain current with system enhancements and organizational changes.[312]

One of the most import steps is conducting the Business Impact Analysis.

Some key metrics in understanding business impact analysis are:

> Working directly with mission/business process owners, departmental staff, managers, and other stakeholders, estimate the downtime factors for consideration as a result of a disruptive event.
>
> - **Maximum Tolerable Downtime (MTD).** The MTD represents the total amount of time leaders/managers are willing to accept for a mission/business process outage or disruption and includes all impact considerations. Determining MTD is important because it could leave continuity planners with imprecise direction on (1) selection of an appropriate recovery method, and (2) the depth of detail which will be required when developing recovery procedures, including their scope and content.
>
> - **Recovery Time Objective (RTO).** RTO defines the maximum amount of time that a system resource can remain unavailable before there is an unacceptable impact on other system resources, supported mission/business processes, and the MTD. Determining the information system resource RTO is important for selecting appropriate technologies that are best suited for meeting the MTD.
>
> - **Recovery Point Objective (RPO).** The RPO represents the point in time, prior to a disruption or system outage, to which mission/business process data must be recovered (given the most

---

[312] CONTINGENCY PLANNING GUIDE FOR FEDERAL INFORMATION SYSTEMS, NAT'L INST. OF STANDARDS AND TECH. ES-1 (2010), *available at* https://nvlpubs.nist.gov/nistpubs/Legacy/SP/nistspecialpublication800-34r1.pdf.

recent backup copy of the data) after an outage.[313]

Because contingency planning covers many areas of the business, there are several plan types available, such as:

- Business Continuity Plan (BCP)
- Continuity of Operations Plan (COOP)
- Crisis Communication Plan
- Critical Infrastructure Protection (CIP) Plan
- Cyber Incident Response Plan
- Disaster Recovery Plan (DRP)
- Information System Contingency Plan (ISCP)
- Occupant Emergency Plan (OEP)[314]

The following table from NIST summarizes each of the above stated plans. MEF stands for Mission Essential Functions.

Plan	Purpose	Scope	Plan Relationship
Business Continuity Plan (BCP)	Provides procedures for sustaining mission/business operations while recovering from a significant disruption.	Addresses mission/business processes at a lower or expanded level from COOP MEFs.	Mission/business process focused plan that may be activated in coordination with a COOP plan to sustain non-MEFs.
Continuity of Operations (COOP) Plan	Provides procedures and guidance to sustain an organization's MEFs at an alternate site for up to 30 days; mandated by	Addresses MEFs at a facility; information systems are addressed based only on their support of the mission essential functions.	MEF focused plan that may also activate several business unit-level BCPs, ISCPs, or DRPs, as appropriate.

[313] *Id.* at B-3

[314] *Id.* at 9-10.

Plan	Purpose	Scope	Plan Relationship
	federal directives.		
Crisis Communications Plan	Provides procedures for disseminating internal and external communications; means to provide critical status information and control rumors.	Addresses communications with personnel and the public; not information system- focused.	Incident-based plan often activated with a COOP or BCP, but may be used alone during a public exposure event.
Critical Infrastructure Protection (CIP) Plan	Provides policies and procedures for protection of national critical infrastructure components, as defined in the National Infrastructure Protection Plan.	Addresses critical infrastructure components that are supported or operated by an agency or organization.	Risk management plan that supports COOP plans for organizations with critical infrastructure and key resource assets.
Cyber Incident Response Plan	Provides procedures for mitigating and correcting a cyber attack, such as a virus, worm, or Trojan horse.	Addresses mitigation and isolation of affected systems, cleanup, and minimizing loss of information.	Information system- focused plan that may activate an ISCP or DRP, depending on the extent of the attack.
Disaster Recovery Plan (DRP)	Provides procedures for relocating information systems operations to an	Activated after major system disruptions with long-term effects.	Information system- focused plan that activates one or more ISCPs for recovery of

Plan	Purpose	Scope	Plan Relationship
	alternate location.		individual systems.
Information System Contingency Plan (ISCP)	Provides procedures and capabilities for recovering an information system.	Addresses single information system recovery at the current or, if appropriate alternate location.	Information system- focused plan that may be activated independent from other plans or as part of a larger recovery effort coordinated with a DRP, COOP, and/or BCP .
Occupant Emergency Plan (OEP)	Provides coordinated procedures for minimizing loss of life or injury and protecting property damage in response to a physical threat.	Focuses on personnel and property particular to the specific facility; not mission/busines s process or information system-based.	Incident-based plan that is initiated immediately after an event, preceding a COOP or DRP activation.

Figure 4.[315]

Although we are focused on protecting cyber-related assets, we should never forget that protecting human life is the number one priority. Protecting systems is secondary to protecting human life.

SP 800-37 Revision 2: Risk Management Framework for Information Systems and Organizations, A System Life Cycle Approach for Security and Privacy

[315] *Id.* at 11.

SP 800-37 "describes the RMF and provides guidelines for managing security and privacy risks and applying the RMF to information systems and organizations."[316]

SP 800-39: Managing Information Security Risk, Organization, Mission, and Information System View

The risk management approach described in this publication is supported by a series of security standards and guidelines necessary for managing information security risk. In particular, the Special Publications developed by the Joint Task Force Transformation Initiative supporting the unified information security framework for the federal government include:

- Special Publication 800-37, *Guide for Applying the Risk Management Framework to Federal Information Systems: A Security Life Cycle Approach*;

- Special Publication 800-53, *Recommended Security Controls for Federal Information Systems and Organizations*;

- Special Publication 800-53A, *Guide for Assessing the Security Controls in Federal Information Systems and Organizations*; and

- Draft Special Publication 800-30, *Guide for Conducting Risk Assessments.*

In addition to the Joint Task Force publications listed above, the International Organization for Standardization (ISO) and the International Electrotechnical Commission (IEC) publish standards for risk management and information security including:

- ISO/IEC 31000, *Risk management – Principles and guidelines*;

[316] RISK MANAGEMENT FRAMEWORK FOR INFORMATION SYSTEMS AND ORGANIZATIONS: A SYSTEM LIFE CYCLE APPROACH FOR SECURITY AND PRIVACY, NAT'L INST. OF STANDARDS AND TECH. 3 (2018), *available at* https://nvlpubs.nist.gov/nistpubs/SpecialPublications/NIST.SP.800-37r2.pdf.

- ISO/IEC 31010, *Risk management – Risk assessment techniques*;
- ISO/IEC 27001, *Information technology – Security techniques – Information security management systems – Requirements*; and
- ISO/IEC 27005, *Information technology – Security techniques – Information security risk management systems.*

> NIST's mission includes harmonization of international and national standards where appropriate. The concepts and principles contained in this publication are intended to implement for federal information systems and organizations, an information security management system and a risk management process similar to those described in ISO/IEC standards. This reduces the burden on organizations that must conform to both ISO/IEC standards and NIST standards and guidance.[317]

SP-800-39 breaks risk management into three tiers, tier 1, tier 2, and tier 3. The following figure shows the relationship between the tiers:

[317] MANAGING INFORMATION SECURITY RISK: ORGANIZATION, MISSION, AND INFORMATION SYSTEM VIEW, NAT'L INST. OF STANDARDS AND TECH. 4 (2011), *available at* https://nvlpubs.nist.gov/nistpubs/Legacy/SP/nistspecialpublication800-39.pdf.

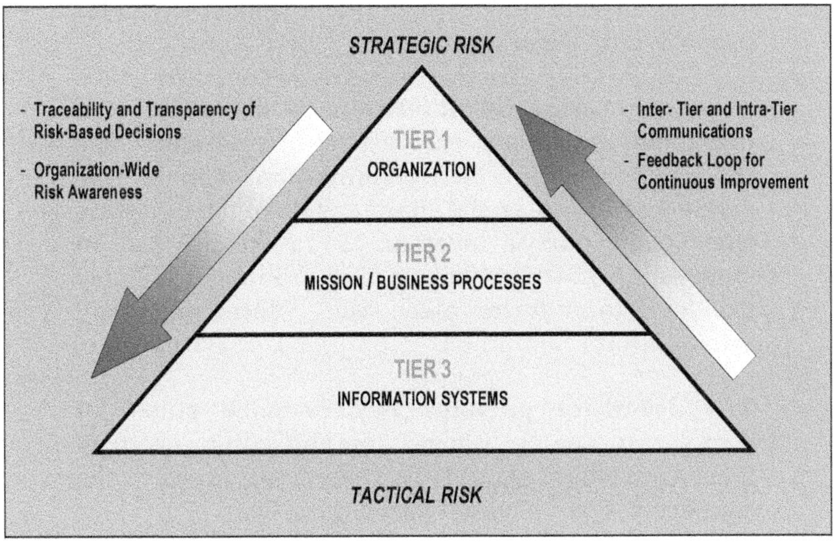

Figure 6.[318]

SP 800-47: Security Guide for Interconnecting Information Technology Systems

> This document presents a "life-cycle management" approach for interconnecting IT systems, with an emphasis on security. The four phases of the interconnection life cycle are addressed:
>
> + Planning the interconnection: the participating organizations perform preliminary activities; examine all relevant technical, security, and administrative issues; and form an agreement governing the management, operation, and use of the interconnection.
>
> + Establishing the interconnection: the organizations develop and execute a plan for establishing the interconnection, including implementing or configuring appropriate security controls.
>
> + Maintaining the interconnection: the organizations actively maintain the interconnection

[318] *Id.* at 9.

> after it is established to ensure that it operates properly and securely.
>
> + Disconnecting the interconnection: one or both organizations may choose to terminate the interconnection. The termination should be conducted in a planned manner to avoid disrupting the other party's system. In response to an emergency, however, one or both organizations may decide to terminate the interconnection immediately.
>
> The document provides recommended steps for completing each phase, emphasizing security measures that should be taken to protect the connected systems and shared data.[319]

SP 800-53 Revision 5: Security and Privacy Controls for Information Systems and Organizations

SP 800-53 is a significant document. This document is so large because it gives guidance on how to apply a tailored set of baseline security controls. As one might expect, applying the baseline security controls is not a small task. And this is a key document because one cannot have reasonable security measures without applying adequate security controls.

> It accomplishes this objective by providing a comprehensive and flexible catalog of security and privacy controls to meet current and future protection needs based on changing threats, vulnerabilities, requirements, and technologies. The publication also improves communication among organizations by providing a common lexicon that supports the discussion of security, privacy, and risk management concepts.[320]

---

[319] SECURITY GUIDE FOR INTERCONNECTING INFORMATION TECHNOLOGY SYSTEMS: RECOMMENDATIONS OF THE NATIONAL INSTITUTE OF STANDARDS AND TECHNOLOGY, NAT'L INST. OF STANDARDS AND TECH. ES-1 (2002), *available at* https://nvlpubs.nist.gov/nistpubs/Legacy/SP/nistspecialpublication800-47.pdf.

[320] SECURITY AND PRIVACY CONTROLS FOR INFORMATION SYSTEMS AND ORGANIZATIONS, NAT'L INST. OF STANDARDS AND TECH. (2020), *available at* https://nvlpubs.nist.gov/nistpubs/SpecialPublications/NIST.SP.800-53r5.pdf.

SP 800-53A Revision 4: Assessing Security and Privacy Controls in Federal Information Systems and Organizations, Building Effective Assessment Plans

SP 800-53A, "a companion guideline to Special Publication 800-53," was "written to facilitate security control assessments and privacy control assessments conducted within and effective risk management framework."[321]

Also, SP 800-53A "is designed to support Special Publication 800-37, *Guide for Applying the Risk Management Framework to Federal Information Systems: A Security Life Cycle Approach.*"[322]

As with SP 800-53, SP 80053A goes into great detail on how to assess. The figure below gives a condensed version.[323]

---

[321] ASSESSING SECURITY AND PRIVACY CONTROLS IN FEDERAL INFORMATION SYSTEMS AND ORGANIZATIONS: BUILDING EFFECTIVE ASSESSMENT PLANS, NAT'L INST. OF STANDARDS AND TECH. xi (2014), *available at* https://nvlpubs.nist.gov/nistpubs/SpecialPublications/NIST.SP.800-53Ar4.pdf.

[322] *Id.* at 4.

[323] *Id.* at 28.

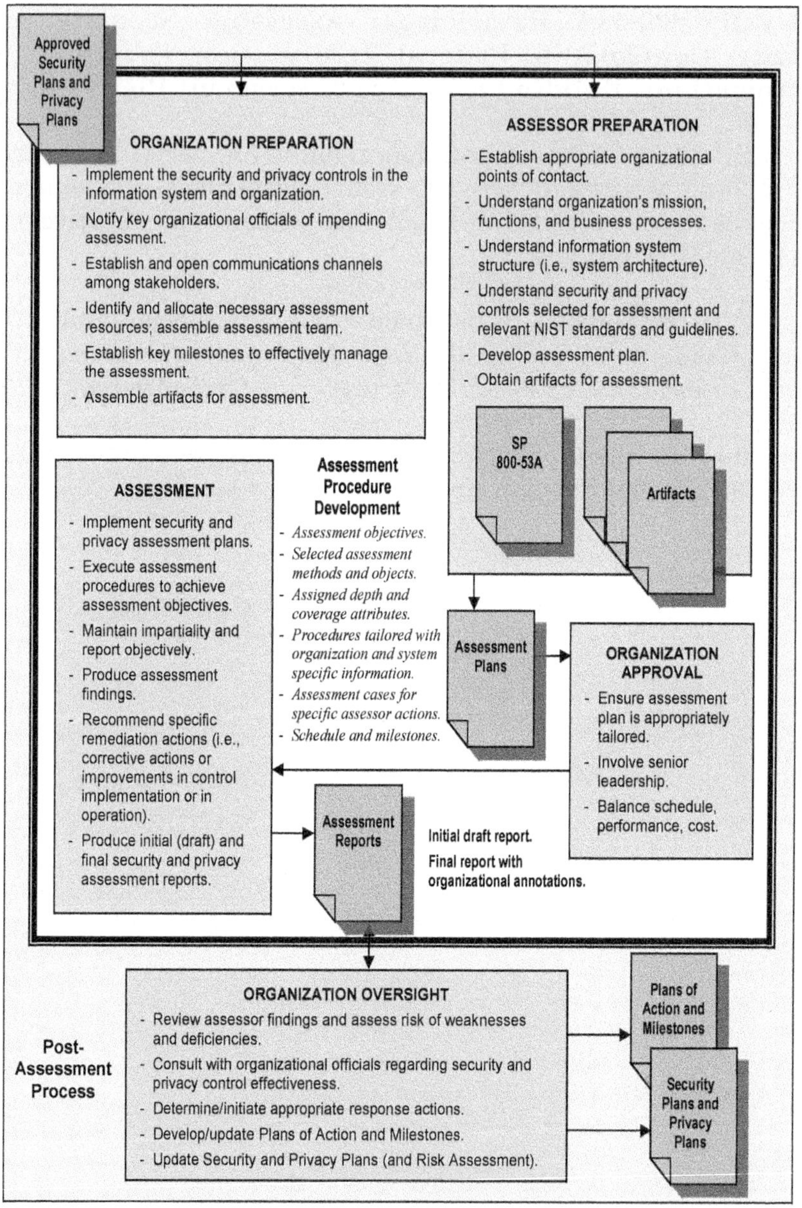

SP 800-59: Guideline for Identifying an Information System as a National Security System

This document provides guidelines developed in conjunction with the Department of Defense, including the National Security Agency, for identifying an information system as a national security system. The basis for these guidelines is the Federal Information Security Management Act of 2002 (FISMA, Title III, Public Law

107-347, December 17, 2002), which provides government-wide requirements for information security, superseding the Government Information Security Reform Act and the Computer Security Act.[324]

SP 800-60 Revision 1: Guide for Mapping Types of Information and Information Systems to Security Categories

The identification of information processed on an information system is essential to the proper selection of security controls and ensuring the confidentiality, integrity, and availability of the system and its information. The National Institute of Standards and Technology (NIST) Special Publication (SP) 800-60 has been developed to assist Federal government agencies to categorize information and information systems.[325]

SP 800-61 Revision 2: Computer Security Incident Handling Guide

The revised NIST guide provides step-by-step instructions for new, or well-established, incident response teams to create a proper policy and plan. NIST recommends that each plan should have a mission statement, strategies and goals, an organizational approach to incident response, metrics for measuring the response capability, and a built-in process for updating the plan as needed. The guide recommends reviewing each incident afterward to prepare for future attacks and to provide stronger protections of systems and data.

The guide provides recommendations for agencies to consider before adding coordination and information sharing to the incident response plan, including how to determine what information is shared with other organizations and consulting with

---

[324] GUIDELINE FOR IDENTIFYING AN INFORMATION SYSTEM AS A NATIONAL SECURITY SYSTEM, NAT'L INST. OF STANDARDS AND TECH. 1 (2003), *available at* https://nvlpubs.nist.gov/nistpubs/Legacy/SP/nistspecialpublication800-59.pdf.

[325] VOLUME I: GUIDE FOR MAPPING TYPES OF INFORMATION AND INFORMATION SYSTEMS TO SECURITY CATEGORIES, NAT'L INST. OF STANDARDS AND TECH. 1 (2008), *available at* https://nvlpubs.nist.gov/nistpubs/Legacy/SP/nistspecialpublication800-60v1r1.pdf.

legal departments.[326] Consider United States Cybersecurity Investigative Resources as Part of the Incident Response Plan[327]

When a cybersecurity incident occurs, there are several outside sources that can be called for assistance. Those contacts and under what circumstances to call should be contained in the incident response plan (IRP). Outside counsel could be one of those contacts. Local law enforcement, if they are equipped to handle cyber security incidents could be another. At a national and regional field-office level, the Secret Service and the Federal Bureau of Investigation (FBI) can be valuable resources for cybersecurity incidents, and also for keeping informed on potential incident risks. As a cybersecurity in-house counsel, it would be advisable to build relationships with all of these resources and to understand under which circumstances each of these resources can be of assistance.

The Secret Service

The Secret Service can be a good resource to turn to for assistance after a cybersecurity incident:

> The U.S. Secret Service has a long and storied history of safeguarding America's financial and payment systems from criminal exploitation. The agency was created in 1865 to combat the rise of counterfeit currency following the Civil War. As the U.S. financial system has evolved - from paper currency to plastic credit cards to, now, digital information - so too have our investigative responsibilities.
>
> Today, Secret Service agents, professionals, and specialists work in field offices around the world to fight the 21st century's financial crimes, which are increasingly conducted through cyberspace. These

---

[326] COMPUTER SECURITY INCIDENT HANDLING GUIDE: RECOMMENDATIONS OF THE NATIONAL INSTITUTE OF STANDARDS AND TECHNOLOGY, NAT'L INST. OF STANDARDS AND TECH. (2012), *available at* http://nvlpubs.nist.gov/nistpubs/SpecialPublications/NIST.SP.800-61r2.pdf.

[327] *Updated NIST Guide is a How-To for Dealing With Computer Security Incidents*, NAT'L INST. OF STANDARDS AND TECH., https://www.nist.gov/news-events/news/2012/08/updated-nist-guide-how-dealing-computer-security-incidents (last updated Jan. 8, 2018).

> investigations continue to address counterfeit, which still undermines confidence in the U.S. dollar, but it is credit card fraud, wire and bank fraud, computer network breaches, ransomware, and other cyber-enabled financial crimes, that have become the focus of much of the Secret Service investigative work.[328]

The FBI

As one might expect, the FBI has become heavily involved in a broad range of cybersecurity topics:

> Malicious cyber activity threatens the public's safety and our national and economic security. The FBI's goal is to change the behavior of criminals and nation-states who believe they can compromise U.S. networks, steal financial and intellectual property, and put critical infrastructure at risk without facing risk themselves. To do this, we use our unique mix of authorities, capabilities, and partnerships to impose consequences against our cyber adversaries.
>
> The FBI is the lead federal agency for investigating cyber attacks and intrusions. We collect and share intelligence and engage with victims while working to unmask those committing malicious cyber activities, wherever they are.[329]

The FBI is particularly focused on the following cybersecurity areas:

- **Business e-mail compromise (BEC)** scams exploit the fact that so many of us rely on e-mail to conduct business—both personal and professional—and it's one of the most financially damaging online crimes.
- **Identity theft** happens when someone steals your personal information, like your Social

---

[328] *The Investigative Mission*, U. S. SECRET SERVICE, https://www.secretservice.gov/investigation/#menu-collapse-press (last visited May 20, 2021).

[329] *The Cyber Threat*, FED. BUREAU OF INVESTIGATION, https://www.fbi.gov/investigate/cyber (last visited May 20, 2021).

Security number, and uses it to commit theft or fraud.

- **Ransomware** is a type of malicious software, or malware, that prevents you from accessing your computer files, systems, or networks and demands you pay a ransom for their return.
- **Spoofing and phishing** are schemes aimed at tricking you into providing sensitive information to scammers.
- **Online predators** are a growing threat to young people.[330]

How the FBI is combating the cybersecurity threat:

> Our adversaries look to exploit gaps in our intelligence and information security networks. The FBI is committed to working with our federal counterparts, our foreign partners, and the private sector to close those gaps.
>
> These partnerships allow us to defend networks, attribute malicious activity, sanction bad behavior, and take the fight to our adversaries overseas. The FBI fosters this team approach through unique hubs where government, industry, and academia form long-term trusted relationships to combine efforts against cyber threats.
>
> Within government, that hub is the National Cyber Investigative Joint Task Force (NCIJTF). The FBI leads this task force of more than 30 co-located agencies from the Intelligence Community and law enforcement. The NCIJTF is organized around mission centers based on key cyber threat areas and led by senior executives from partner agencies. Through these mission centers, operations and intelligence are integrated for maximum impact against U.S. adversaries.
>
> Only together can we achieve safety, security, and confidence in a digitally connected world.[331]

[330] *Id.*
[331] *Id.*

The FBI's efforts in the cybersecurity area are extensive:

> Whether through developing innovative investigative techniques, using cutting-edge analytic tools, or forging new partnerships in our communities, the FBI continues to adapt to meet the challenges posed by the evolving cyber threat.
>
> - The FBI has specially trained cyber squads in each of our 56 field offices, working hand-in-hand with interagency task force partners.
> - The rapid-response Cyber Action Team can deploy across the country within hours to respond to major incidents.
> - With cyber assistant legal attachés in embassies across the globe, the FBI works closely with our international counterparts to seek justice for victims of malicious cyber activity.
> - The Internet Crime Complaint Center (IC3) collects reports of Internet crime from the public. Using such complaints, the IC3's Recovery Asset Team has assisted in freezing hundreds of thousands of dollars for victims of cyber crime.
> - CyWatch is the FBI's 24/7 operations center and watch floor, providing around-the-clock support to track incidents and communicate with field offices across the country.[332]

To gather complaints, the FBI maintains an Internet Crime Complaint Center (IC3):

> The mission of the Internet Crime Complaint Center is to provide the public with a reliable and convenient reporting mechanism to submit information to the Federal Bureau of Investigation concerning suspected Internet-facilitated criminal activity and to develop effective alliances with law enforcement and industry partners. Information is analyzed and disseminated for investigative and

---

[332] *Id.*

> intelligence purposes to law enforcement and for public awareness.
>
> Since 2000, the IC3 has received complaints crossing the spectrum of cyber crime matters, to include online fraud in its many forms including Intellectual Property Rights (IPR) matters, Computer Intrusions (hacking), Economic Espionage (Theft of Trade Secrets), Online Extortion, International Money Laundering, Identity Theft, and a growing list of Internet facilitated crimes. It has become increasingly evident that, regardless of the label placed on a cyber crime matter, the potential for it to overlap with another referred matter is substantial. Therefore, the IC3, formerly known as the Internet Fraud Complaint Center (Internet Fraud Complaint Center), was renamed in October 2003 to better reflect the broad character of such matters having an Internet, or cyber, nexus referred to the IC3, and to minimize the need for one to distinguish "Internet Fraud" from other potentially overlapping cyber crimes.[333]

The IC3 websites provides a web page for filing a complaint. But counsel should develop a relationship with the regional FBI cybersecurity agent so that counsel will have direct access during an incident. The agent can also be a good resource for keeping informed of potential cybersecurity risks. Indeed, the FBI encourages direct contact after a corporation has an incident.

SP 800-128: Guide for Security-Focused Configuration Management of Information Systems

> Organizations apply configuration management (CM) for establishing baselines and for tracking, controlling, and managing many aspects of business development and operation (e.g., products, services, manufacturing, business processes, and information technology). Organizations with a robust and effective CM process need to consider information security implications with respect to the

[333] *Internet Crime Complaint Center (IC3)*, FED. BUREAU OF INVESTIGATION, https://www.ic3.gov/Home/About (last visited May 20, 2021).

> development and operation of systems including hardware, software, applications, and documentation. Effective CM of systems requires the integration of the management of secure configurations into the organizational CM process or processes. For this reason, this document assumes that information security is an integral part of an organization's overall CM process; however, the focus of this document is on implementation of the information security aspects of CM, and as such the term *security-focused configuration management* (SecCM) is used to emphasize the concentration on information security. Though both IT business application functions and security-focused practices are expected to be integrated as a single process, *SecCM* in this context is defined as the management and control of configurations for systems to enable security and facilitate the management of information security risk.[334]

Security-focused configuration management of systems involves a set of activities that can be organized into four major phases: Planning; Identifying and Implementing Configurations; Controlling Configuration Changes; and Monitoring.

[334] GUIDE FOR SECURITY-FOCUSED CONFIGURATION MANAGEMENT OF INFORMATION SYSTEMS, NAT'L INST. OF STANDARDS AND TECH. 1 (2011), *available at* https://nvlpubs.nist.gov/nistpubs/SpecialPublications/NIST.SP.800-128.pdf.

The four phases of SecCM are illustrated in NIST's Figure 2-1.[335]

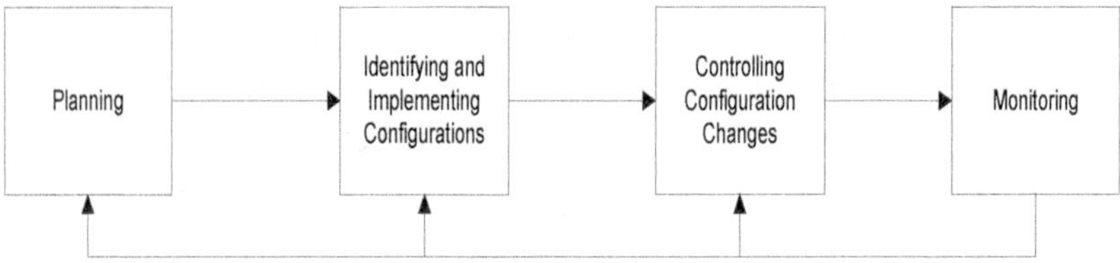

Figure 2-1 – Security-focused Configuration Management Phases

SP 800-137: Information Security Continuous Monitoring (ISCM) for Federal Information Systems and Organizations

> *Information security* continuous monitoring (ISCM) is defined as maintaining ongoing awareness of information security, vulnerabilities, and threats to support organizational risk management decisions. This publication specifically addresses assessment and analysis of security control effectiveness and of organizational security status in accordance with organizational risk tolerance. Security control effectiveness is measured by correctness of implementation and by how adequately the implemented controls meet organizational needs in accordance with current risk tolerance (i.e., is the control implemented in accordance with the security plan to address threats and is the security plan adequate). Organizational security status is determined using metrics established by the organization to best convey the security posture of an organization's information and information systems, along with organizational resilience given known threat information. This necessitates:
>
> - Maintaining situational awareness of all systems across the organization;
> - Maintaining an understanding of threats and threat activities;
> - Assessing all security controls;

[335] *Id.* at 7.

- Collecting, correlating, and analyzing security-related information;

- Providing actionable communication of security status across all tiers of the organization; and

- Active management of risk by organizational officials.[336]

SP 800-137A: Assessing Information Security Continuous Monitoring (ISCM) Programs: Developing an ISCM Program Assessment

This publication:

- Offers guidance on the development of an ISCM program assessment process for all organizational risk management levels, i.e., as defined in NIST SP 800-39, *Managing Information Security Risk: Organization, Mission, and Information System View;*

- Describes how an ISCM program assessment relates to important security concepts and processes, such as the NIST Risk Management Framework (RMF), organization-wide risk management levels, organizational governance, metrics applicable to ISCM, and ongoing authorization;

- Describes the properties of an effective ISCM program assessment;

- Presents a set of ISCM program assessment criteria, with references to the sources from which the criteria are derived, that can be adopted by an organization and used for ISCM program assessments or as a starting point for further development of an organization's assessment criteria; and

---

[336] INFORMATION SECURITY CONTINUOUS MONITORING (ISCM) FOR FEDERAL INFORMATION SYSTEMS AND ORGANIZATIONS, NAT'L INST. OF STANDARDS AND TECH. (2011), *available at* https://nvlpubs.nist.gov/nistpubs/Legacy/SP/nistspecialpublication800-137.pdf.

- Defines a way to conduct ISCM program assessments by using assessment procedures defined in the companion document containing the ISCM Program Assessment Element Catalog and designed to produce a repeatable assessment process.[337]

SP 800-160 Vol. 1: Systems Security Engineering: Considerations for a Multidisciplinary Approach in the Engineer of Trustworthy Secure Systems

After four years of research and development, NIST has published a groundbreaking new security guideline that addresses the longstanding problem of how to engineer trustworthy, secure systems—systems that can provide continuity of capabilities, functions, services, and operations during a wide range of disruptions, threats, and other hazards.[338]

SP 800-171 Revision 2: Protecting Controlled Unclassified Information in Nonfederal Systems and Organizations

The purpose of this publication is to provide federal agencies with recommended security requirements for protecting the *confidentiality* of CUI: (1) when the CUI is resident in a nonfederal system and organization; (2) when the nonfederal organization is *not* collecting or maintaining information on behalf of a federal agency or using or operating a system on behalf of an agency; and (3) where there are no specific safeguarding requirements for protecting the confidentiality of CUI prescribed by the authorizing law, regulation, or governmentwide policy for the CUI category listed in the CUI Registry. The requirements apply *only* to components of nonfederal systems that process, store, or transmit CUI, or that provide security

[337] ASSESSING INFORMATION SECURITY CONTINUOUS MONITORING (ISCM) PROGRAMS: DEVELOPING AN ISCM PROGRAM ASSESSMENT, NAT'L INST. OF STANDARDS AND TECH. v (2020), *available at* https://nvlpubs.nist.gov/nistpubs/SpecialPublications/NIST.SP.800-137A.pdf.

[338] Ron Ross, *Rethinking Cybersecurity from the Inside Out*, NAT'L INST. OF STANDARDS AND TECH. (Nov. 15, 2016), https://www.nist.gov/blogs/taking-measure/rethinking-cybersecurity-inside-out.

protection for such components. The requirements are intended for use by federal agencies in appropriate contractual vehicles or other agreements established between those agencies and nonfederal organizations. In CUI guidance and the CUI Federal Acquisition Regulation (FAR), the CUI Executive Agent will address determining compliance with security requirements.[339]

SP 800-144: Guidelines on Security and Privacy in Public Cloud Computing.

This publication provides helpful guidance concerning security and public cloud computing. For example, 1) "carefully plan the security and privacy aspects of cloud computing solutions before engaging them; 2) Understand the public cloud computing environment offered by the cloud provider; 3) Ensure that a cloud computing solution satisfies organizational security and privacy requirements; 4) Ensure that the client-side computing environment meets organizational security and privacy requirements for cloud computing; and 5) Maintain accountability over the privacy and security of data and applications implemented and deployed in public cloud computing environments.

SP 800-160 Vol. 1: Systems Security Engineering: Considerations for a Multidisciplinary Approach in the Engineer of Trustworthy Secure Systems.

This publication provides a starting point for ensuring secure systems at the design and engineering state of development.

---

[339] PROTECTING CONTROLLED UNCLASSIFIED INFORMATION IN NONFEDERAL SYSTEMS AND ORGANIZATIONS, NAT'L INST. OF STANDARDS AND TECH. 2 (2020), *available at* https://nvlpubs.nist.gov/nistpubs/SpecialPublications/NIST.SP.800-171r2.pdf.

CHAPTER ELEVEN. Laws Prohibiting and Addressing Hacking

11.1 Introduction

This chapter explores some laws related to prohibiting and addressing hacking. This chapter provides an introduction to numerous federal and state laws. The federal laws include the Computer Fraud and Abuse Act, Defend Trade Secrets Act, Economic Espionage Act, Stored Communications Act and the Digital Millennium Copyright Act's provisions on anti-circumvention. This chapter also sets forth an overview of two state anti-hacking laws, the Washington Cybercrime Act, and the California Comprehensive Computer Data Access and Fraud Act. A common set of facts could result in the violation of several of the aforementioned laws.

11.2 Federal Computer Fraud and Abuse Act

The federal Computer Fraud and Abuse Act [CFAA] was enacted in 1986 and has been amended multiple times. The CFAA is designed to address unauthorized access to computers and a violation may result in a criminal penalty, such as prison sentences and a fine.[340] The CFAA also allows for private civil actions in certain circumstances[341] with a statute of limitations of two years

---

[340] Criminal penalties may vary from a fine and a prison term depending on the violation of the particular subsection and number of violations of the CFAA. *Id.* at 1030(c).

[341] In order for the private cause of action to be triggered under subsection (g), the violation of subsection (a) or (b) must include one of the aggravating factors set forth in (c)(4)(A)(i) in subclauses (I), (II), (III), (IV) or (V). Subsection (c)(4)(A)(i)(I)-(V) provides: (I) loss to 1 or more persons during any 1-year period . . . aggregating at least $5,000 in value; (II) the modification or impairment, or potential modification or impairment, of the medical examination, diagnosis, treatment, or care of 1 or more individuals; (III) physical injury to any person; (IV) a threat to public health or safety; (V) damage affecting a computer used by or for an entity of the United States Government in furtherance of the administration of justice, national defense, or national security . . .."

from the act or discovery of damage. A violation of the civil cause of action may result in injunctive relief or damages. Moreover, the CFAA does not allow civil actions "for negligent design or manufacture of computer hardware, computer software, or firmware."

The CFAA has a relatively broad definition of computer and protected computer. The CFAA has seven sections in subsection (a) of 1030 in Title 18, which set forth the conditions for a violation. Some of the sections can be violated in more than one set of circumstances. For example, subsection (a)(5) includes three separate potential set of circumstances resulting in a different violation. Some of the subsections are directed to the unauthorized access or access exceeding authorization of U.S. government computers, in particular. However, several of the subsections are quite broad. For example, subsection (a)(2) states: whoever – intentionally accesses a computer without authorization or exceeds authorization access, and thereby obtains – (C) information from any protected computer.[342] Moreover, subsection (a)(5)(B) and (C) are also relatively broad. Subsection (B) of (a)(5) provides: "intentionally accesses a protected computer without authorization, and as a result of such conduct, recklessly causes damage." Subsection (C) of (a)(5) states: "intentionally accesses a protected computer without authorization and as a result of such conduct, causes damage and loss."

The other subsections cover additional potential violations. For example, (a)(1) covers unauthorized access or access that exceeds authority concerning national security or foreign relations. Subsection (a)(3) generally concerns unauthorized access to federal government computers.[343] Subsection (a)(4) relates to accessing

---

[342] Subsection (a)(2)(A) provides, in part: "intentionally accesses a computer without authorization or exceeds authorized access, and thereby obtains—(A) information contained in a financial record of a financial institution, or of a card issuer . . . or contained in a file of a consumer reporting agency on a consumer. . .." Subsection (a)(2)(B) provides, in part: "intentionally accesses a computer without authorization or exceed authorized access, and thereby obtains—(B) information from any department or agency of the United States. . .."

[343] Subsection (a)(3) provides: "intentionally, without authorization to access any nonpublic computer of a department or agency of the United States, accesses such a computer of that department or agency that is exclusively for the use of the Government of the United States or, in the case of a computer not exclusively for such use, is used by or for the Government of the United States

without authorization or in excess of authorization with intent to defraud.[344] Subsection (a)(5) has three subparts which concern causing damage or loss to a protected computer. Subsection (a)(5)(A) applies to "'knowingly' causes the transmission of a program, information, code, or command, and as a result of subject conduct, intentionally causes damage without authorization to a protected computer." As discussed *supra*, subsections (B) and (C) concern "intentionally access[ing] a protected computer without authorization", in (B) recklessly causing damage, and in (C) causing damage and loss. Subsection (a)(6) concerns trafficking in passwords or similar information used for unauthorized access to a computer.[345] Subsection (a)(7), as discussed *infra*, relates to communications concerning threats of extortion related to damage to a computer. The CFAA also provides that conspiracy or attempt to violate one of the prohibitions in subsection (a) is penalized.

Almost all of the prohibited conduct in subsection (a) involve "unauthorized access" or "access exceeding authorization." Subsection (a)(7) does not require any "unauthorized access" or "access exceeding authorization" in two circumstances: (a)(7)(A) provides "with intent to extort from any person any money or other thing of value, transmits in interstate or foreign commerce any communication containing any—(A) threat to cause damage to a protected computer" and (a)(7)(B) states "with intent to extort from any person any money or other thing of value, transmits in interstate or foreign commerce any communication containing any—(C) demand or request for money or other thing of value in relation to damage to a protected computer, where such damages was caused to facilitate the extortion. Those two provisions appear to be directed to situations similar to ransomware threats, but

---

and such conduct affects that use by or for the Government of the United States."

[344] Subsection (a)(4) provides: "knowingly and with intent to defraud, accesses a protected computer without authorization or exceeds authorized access, and by means of such conduct furthers the intended fraud and obtains anything of value, unless the object of the fraud and the thing obtained consists only of the use of the computer and the value of such use is not more than $5,000 in any 1-year period."

[345] Subsection (a)(6) provides: "knowingly and with intent to defraud traffics in any password or similar information through which a computer may be accessed without authorization, if—(A) such trafficking affects interstate or foreign commerce; (B) such computer is used by or for the Government of the United States."

appear to arise before data may be encrypted because they do not involve unauthorized access or access exceeding authorization. Subsection (a)(7)(B) applies when "with intent to extort from any person any money or other thing of value, transmits in interstate or foreign commerce any communication containing any—(B) threat to obtain information from a protected computer without authorization or in excess of authorization or to impair the confidentiality of information obtained from a protected computer without authorization or by exceeding authorized access." The first part of (a)(7)(B) appears to cover situations where a threat is being made to obtain information and access without authorization or exceeding authorized access has not occurred. The second part of (a)(7)(B) appears to cover situations where information has been obtained from a protected computer without authorization or in situations where authorized access has been exceeded.

Importantly, in 2022, the U.S. Department of Justice announced a change in charging policy under the CFAA. The DOJ has decided not to bring charges against defendants for allegedly violating the CFAA by conducting "good faith" security research—or "white hat hacker" activity. Notably, the policy change is not a "green light" to engage in hacker activity under the "security research" shield. The Press Release concerning the policy notes: "However, the new policy acknowledges that claiming to be conducting security research is not a free pass for those acting in bad faith. For example, discovering vulnerabilities in devices in order to extort their owners, even if claimed as "research," is not in good faith. The policy advises prosecutors to consult with the Criminal Division's Computer Crime and Intellectual Property Section (CCIPS) about specific applications of this factor."[346]

Another issue that may arise concerning the CFAA and other causes of action is sovereign immunity when actions are brought against governments implicating the Foreign Sovereign Immunity Act. Moreover, an additional issue concerns whether sovereign immunity applies to the agents or contractors of foreign governments. For example, a recent case, *WhatsApp v. NSO*,[347]

---

[346] Department of Justice, Department of Justice Announces New Policy for Charging Cases under the Computer Fraud and Abuse Act (May 19, 2022), available at https://www.justice.gov/opa/pr/department-justice-announces-new-policy-charging-cases-under-computer-fraud-and-abuse-act.

[347] 472 F.Supp.3d 649, (N.D. Cal. 2020).

involved WhatsApp and Facebook bringing numerous causes of action, including violation of the CFAA, against Israeli defendants who allegedly used malware to surveille phones and other devices of users of WhatsApp software. The defendants allegedly used their malware for the benefit of foreign governments. The defendants argued that the common law doctrine of foreign sovereign immunity or derivative foreign sovereign immunity barred the actions against them because they were contractors of foreign governments operating in the scope of their employment. The district court essentially found that the common law doctrine of foreign sovereign immunity did not apply to the defendants because the plaintiffs were not enforcing a rule of law against the foreign governments such that the foreign government would be responsible to pay for a judgment and that injunctive relief could be crafted to avoid the foreign sovereigns from taking affirmative action. Finally, the district court decided that the doctrine of derivative sovereign immunity does not extend to foreign contractors of foreign sovereigns.

In 2021, the Ninth Circuit affirmed the result of district court's opinion with different reasoning and found that foreign sovereign immunity did not apply to private companies.[348] The Court of Appeals noted that the Foreign Sovereign Immunity Act occupies the field of foreign sovereign immunity as applied to entities. The immunity provided to entities by this Act is only to those that fall under the Act's definition of a foreign state. The Court held that NSO did not meet the definition of a foreign state because it is not itself a sovereign. Further, NSO could not enjoy the immunity extended to its sovereigns because it is not an agency or instrumentality of a foreign state and is a private company without a majority foreign sovereign owner. NSO also argued that it could claim foreign sovereign immunity under common-law immunity doctrines that apply to foreign officials. The Court dismissed this argument because the Supreme Court has not expressed an intention to provide foreign official immunity to entities. Thus, NSO is not entitled to foreign sovereign immunity. The Court of Appeals affirmed the district court's denial of NSO's motion to dismiss.

---

[348] WhatsApp v. NSO Group Tech., 17 F.4th 930 (9th Cir. 2021).

11.2[A] UNAUTHORIZED ACCESS OR ACCESS EXCEEDING AUTHORIZATION

The questions of what constitutes unauthorized access or access exceeding authorization are some of the most litigated questions under the CFAA. "Unauthorized access" is not defined by the CFAA. "Access" is also not defined. "Exceeds authorized access" is defined by the CFAA: "to access a computer with authorization and to use such access to obtain or alter information in the computer that the accesser is not entitled so to obtain or alter."

Authorized access has been defined by courts as meaning "accessing a computer without permission." In *HiQ Labs v. Linkedin*, the Ninth Circuit clarified that "the CFAA contemplates the existence of three kinds of computer information: (1) information for which access is open to the general public and permission is not required, (2) information for which authorization is required and has been given, and (3) information for which authorization is required but has not been given (or, in the case of the prohibition on exceeding authorized access, has not been given for the part of the system accessed)."[349] In that case, HiQ Labs scraped user information that was publicly available on Linkedin's website. Linkedin then sent HiQ Labs a cease and desist letter. In deciding that HiQ Labs was entitled to a motion for preliminary injunction, the Ninth Circuit reasoned, in part, that, "[i]t appears that the CFAA's prohibition on accessing a computer 'without authorization" is violated when a person circumvents a computer's generally applicable rules regarding access permissions, such as username and password requirements, to gain access to a computer. It is likely that when a computer network generally permits public access to its data, a user's accessing that publicly available information will not constitute access without authorization under the CFAA."

In 2022, in *HiQ Labs v. Linkedin*, the Ninth Circuit, after the Supreme Court's decision in *Van Buren v. United States*[350], addressed the case again on remand from the Supreme Court. The Ninth Circuit held that *Van Buren* reinforced its earlier decision, so the Court affirmed the granting of the preliminary injunction. The

---

[349] *HiQ Labs v. Linkedin*, 938 F.3d 985 (9th Cir. 2019).

[350] *Van Buren v. United States*, __ U.S. __, 141 S. Ct. 1648 (2021).

Court decided that plaintiffs had established that the balance of hardships tipped in its favor. This is because HiQ likely needs to access Linkedin's data to maintain its data collection business and Linkedin's privacy arguments on behalf of its customers were relatively weak. The likelihood-of-success prong of the preliminary injunction analysis focused on whether HiQ had raised serious questions going to the merits. The Court found that there was a question as to whether once HiQ received LinkedIn's cease-and-desist letter, any further gathering and use of information from LinkedIn's site was "without authorization" within the meaning of the CFAA and thus a violation of the statute. The Court stated that the CFAA's prohibition on accessing a computer "without authorization" is violated when a person circumvents a computer's generally applicable rules regarding access permissions, such as username and password requirements, to gain access to a computer. This is analogous to "breaking and entering" which was referred to in the legislative history. *Van Buren* supports this interpretation because it essentially distinguishes between websites that require authorization to access data and those that are publicly available and do not require authorization to access data. The Court concluded that the concept of "without authorization" does not apply to public websites. The data HiQ sought to access was not owned by LinkedIn and does not require a person to input a username and password to access the information.

In a 2016 decision, the Ninth Circuit explained that authorization can be revoked resulting in further access as not "authorized access."[351] The Ninth Circuit stated that, "authorization is not pegged to website terms and conditions [and] that this definition has a simple corollary: once authorization has been affirmatively revoked, the user cannot sidestep the statute by going through the back door and accessing the computer through a third party. Unequivocal revocation of computer access closes both the front door and the back door."[352]

The U.S. Supreme Court, in *Van Buren v. United States*[353], recently considered the issue of the meaning of exceeds authorization under subsection (a)(2) and resolved a circuit split

[351] *United States v. Nosal*, 844 F.3d 1024 (9th Cir. 2016).
[352] *Id.*
[353] *Van Buren v. United States*, __ U.S. __, 141 S. Ct. 1648 (2021).

considering the definition of those terms.[354] In *Van Buren v. United States*, the Eleventh Circuit followed its precedent in *United States v. Rodriguez*[355] and held that a police officer violated the CFAA by accessing a computer database that exceeded authorization even though he had permission to use the database because he did so for an improper purpose. In *Van Buren*, the police officer searched the license plate number of a woman in the Georgia Crime Information Database, a database that he had access to, to determine if she was an undercover officer in exchange for money. The police officer later admitted to the FBI that he knew what he did was "wrong."

In that case, the Eleventh Circuit declined to follow the Ninth Circuit's definition of "exceeds authorized access." The Ninth Circuit sitting *en banc*, in *United States v. Nosal*, stated that there were two ways to interpret "exceeds authorized access:" first, "it could refer to someone who's authorized to access only certain data or files but accesses unauthorized data or files—what is colloquially known as hacking[;]" or section, "the language could refer to someone who has unrestricted physical access to a computer, but is limited in the use to which he can put the information." The Ninth Circuit essentially reasoned that the second broader interpretation would result in construing the CFAA as a general misappropriation statute that would criminalize wide swaths of conduct performed by people using the Internet and computers every day. According to the Ninth Circuit, this could not have been contemplated by Congress, and the statute should be confined to situations involving "hacking"—"circumvention of technological access barriers"—and "not misappropriation of trade secrets." This is particularly true given the rule of lenity concerning the construction of a criminal statute with two possible meanings—the narrower reading is preferred for "fair notice" to citizens and Congress as to what conduct is prohibited by a criminal statute. The Ninth Circuit was concerned about turning users of the Internet into criminals because of a website's terms of use or modifications of those terms of use. On June 3, 2021, primarily based on statutory interpretation, the U.S. Supreme Court reversed the Eleventh Circuit and held that a police officer who accessed information he

---

354 *Van Buren v. United States*, 940 F.3d 1192 (11th Cir. 2019).

355 *United States v. Rodriguez*, 628 F.3d 1258 (11th Cir. 2010).

was authorized to access for an improper purpose did not exceed his authorization.[356] The U.S. Supreme Court stated:

> This provision covers those who obtain information from particular areas in the computer—such as files, folders, or databases—to which their computer access does not extend. It does not cover those who, like Van Buren, have improper motives for obtaining information that is otherwise available to them.

11.2[B] DAMAGE OR LOSS

The meaning of "damage or loss" is also important, particularly because subsection (g) of the CFAA requires "damage or loss" to maintain a civil action. The CFAA defines "damage" as, "(e)(8) the term "damage" means any impairment to the integrity or availability of data, a program, a system, or information." The CFAA defines "loss" as, "(e)(11) the term "loss" means any reasonable cost to any victim, including the cost of responding to an offense, conducting a damage assessment, and restoring the data, program, system, or information to its condition prior to the offense, and any revenue lost, cost incurred, or other consequential damages incurred because of interruption of service."

In *Shurgard Storage Centers v. Safe Guard Self Storage*, the district court considered plaintiff Shurgard Storage Centers' CFAA claim involving a former employee who took trade secrets from plaintiff while employed by plaintiff and sent those trade secrets to defendant.[357] The defendant argued that the plaintiff failed to plead damage under the statute because a loss of information in itself is not damage. The district court decided that the collection and dissemination of confidential information constituted the impairment to the integrity of information, and thus, was "damage" even though that information was not "physically changed or erased." In *NetApp v. Nimble Storage*, the district court determined that merely copying information did not constitute damage under the CFAA.[358] The district court essentially declined to follow the *Shugard Storage Centers* decision and reasoned that copying did

---

[356] *Van Buren v. United States*, 593 U.S. __ (2021).
[357] *Shurgard Storage Centers v. Safe Guard Self Storage*, 119 F.Supp.2d 1121 (W.D. Wash. 2000).
[358] *NetApp v. Nimble Storage*, 2015 WL 400251 (N.D. Cal. 2015).

not impair the integrity of information as would impacting the "wholeness or soundness" of the information. The district court also rejected plaintiff's claims that damage included the lessening of the value of the information by eroding its exclusivity and "accessing and downloading information" alone.

11.3 State Anti-Hacking Laws: Washington and California

Numerous states have adopted similar laws to the CFAA. The following materials consider two examples. The first is the Washington state law, the "Washington Cybercrime Act." The second is the California state law, the "Comprehensive Computer Data Access and Fraud Act."

11.3[A] WASHINGTON STATE LAW

In 2016, the Washington legislature passed the "Washington Cybercrime Act." Please note that the Cybercrime Act is a much more modern attempt to address some of the issues the CFAA was designed to cover. An interesting question is whether the Washington Cybercrime Act significantly improves the CFAA. Importantly, the Washington legislature states that the intent of the statute is to "provide prosecutors the twenty-first century tools they need to combat twenty-first century crimes." The legislature specifically states its intent is not to regulate each technology as it emerges, but instead to provide a comprehensive law directed to multiple technologies. The legislature also notes the failure of traditional crimes to provide the necessary "clarity, certainty and predictability" to regulators and the "innovation community about the actions and activities that are prohibited." Further, the legislature expresses its intent to ensure that white hat hackers and whistleblowers continue to have the space function under the law. Another interesting question is whether the law will continue to effectively punish and deter activities that may be considered improper as technology evolves. The law also does not appear to contain a private right of action similar to the CFAA.

The Cybercrime Act essentially creates seven new crimes: 1) computer trespass in the first degree; 2) computer trespass in the second degree; 3) electronic data service interference; 4) spoofing; 5) electronic data tampering in the first degree; 6) electronic data tampering in the second degree; and 7) electronic data theft. The Cybercrime Act also includes 11 definitions, including for terms such as "access," "malware," "white hat security research," and "without authorization." Critically, the term "without authorization" is utilized in all seven crimes, and itself includes three defined terms within that definition. "Without authorization" is defined as:

> to knowingly circumvent technological access barriers to a data system in order to obtain information without the express or implied permission of the owner, where such technological access measures are specifically designed to exclude or prevent unauthorized individuals from obtaining such information, but does not include white hat security research or circumventing a technological measure that does not effectively control access to a computer. The term "without the express or implied permission" does not include access in violation of a duty, agreement or contractual obligation, such as an acceptable use policy or terms of services agreement, with an internet service provider, internet web site, or employer. The term "circumvent technological access barriers" may include unauthorized elevation of privileges, such as allowing a normal user to execute code as administrator, or allowing a remote person without any privileges to run code.

Please note that the definition of "without authorization" attempts to resolve some of the ambiguity present in the CFAA definition by expressly excluding the violation of "an acceptable use policy or terms of services agreement, with an internet provider, internet web site, or employer." The Cybercrime Act also relies on a term similar to that used in the Digital Millennium Copyright Act "circumvent technological access barriers," and terminology such as, "effectively control[ling] access to a computer." Courts may interpret those terms to have similar meaning as under the Digital Millennium Copyright Act. Moreover, the Cybercrime Act differs from the CFAA by clearly providing that "white hat security research" and technological circumvention measures which "do[] not effectively control access to a computer" are not covered by the

Cybercrime Act. "White hat security research" is defined as "accessing a data program, service, or system solely for the purpose of good faith testing, investigation, and/or correction of a security flaw or vulnerability, where such activity is carried out, and where the information derived from the activity is used, primarily to promote security or safety." Court decisions concerning the scope of white hat security activities are likely forthcoming, particularly decisions interpreting "good faith." Additionally, "access" is defined as, "gain entry to, instruct, communicate with, store data in, retrieve data from, or otherwise make use of any resources of electronic data, data network, or data system, including via electronic means." This would seem to include social engineering means to access a system without using technological means.

The first two crimes are computer trespass in the first degree and computer trespass in the second degree. Basically, both crimes involve a "person, [who] without authorization, intentionally gains access to a computer system or electronic database of another . . .." The two main differences between the first degree and the second degree involve additional requirements to constitute a first degree crime, and the first degree is a class C felony and the second degree is a gross misdemeanor. The first degree crime also requires either that: "(a) The access is made with the intent to commit another crime in violation of a state law not included in this chapter; or (b) The violation involves a computer or database maintained by a government agency." Thus, there is a significant difference in classification of the crime based on whether the computer is privately owned versus a government agency, unless access is made with intent to create another crime. Notably, the statute does not define "computer system" or "electronic database."

The third crime is electronic data service interference. This crime involves a person who without authorization maliciously "causes the transmission of data, data program, or other electronic command that intentionally interrupts or suspends access to or use of a data network or data service." Data, data program, data network and data service are defined terms under the Cybercrime Act. A "data network" is defined as "any system that provides digital communications between one or more data systems or other digital input/output devices including, but not limited to, display terminals, remote systems, mobile devices, and printers." The definition of a data network also includes a defined term, "data systems." "Data systems" is "an electronic device or collection of electronic devices, including support devices one or more of which contain data programs, input data, and output data, and that performs functions, including, but not limited to, logic, arithmetic, data storage and retrieval, communication, and control. . . . " A "data program" is "an ordered set of electronic data representing coded instructions or statements that when executed by a computer causes the device to process electronic data." "Data services" "include[] data processing, storage functions, internet services, email services, electronic gaming services, and other similar system, network or internet-based services." Electronic data service interference is a class C felony.

The fourth crime is "spoofing." Spoofing is when a person without authorization "knowingly initiates the transmission, display, or receipt of identifying information of another organization or person for the purpose of gaining unauthorized access to electronic data, a data system, or a data network . . .." Importantly, the statute also requires that the person have "the intent to commit another crime in violation of a state law not included in this chapter." An example of a violation of a state law not included in the chapter may be extortion for example. "Identifying information" is defined under the Act. This is a gross misdemeanor.

The fifth and sixth crimes include electronic data tampering in the first degree and electronic data tampering in the second degree. The main differences between the two crimes involve a purpose requirement for a first degree crime and the difference in classification of the crime. Both crimes require a person who acts "maliciously and without authorization: (a)(1) Alters data as it transmits between two data systems over an open or unsecure network; or Introduces any malware into any electronic data, data system, or data network. The first degree crime also requires the person to do so, "(b)(i) . . . for the purpose of devising or executing any scheme to defraud, deceive, extort, or commit any other crime in violation of a state law not included in this chapter, or of wrongfully controlling, gaining access to, or obtaining money property, or electronic data; or (ii) The electronic data, data system, or data network is maintained by a government agency." Electronic data tampering includes the defined terms "data systems," "data," "data network" and "malware." Notably, the definition of malware includes, but is not limited to, viruses and worms. The first degree crime is a class C felony, and the second degree crime is a gross misdemeanor.

The seventh crime is electronic data theft. This crime applies to a person who "intentionally, without authorization, and without reasonable grounds to believe that he or she has such authorization, obtains any electronic data with the intent to: (a) Devise or execute any scheme to defraud, deceive, extort, or commit any crime in violation of a state law no included in this chapter; or (b) wrongfully control, gain access to, or obtain money, property, or electronic data. Notably, this crime requires intentionality with respect to specific purposes. Moreover, the crime states that "reasonable grounds" supporting a belief of authorization will result in the person not violating the statute. Courts will have to define reasonable grounds. This crime is a class C felony.

11.3[B] California State Law

The California Comprehensive Computer Data Access and Fraud Act (CCDA) is loosely modeled after the federal CFAA. It was enacted in 1987 and has been amended multiple times. Importantly, the CCDA includes 14 separate provisions which create liability under the statute. The CCDA is a criminal statute with a civil cause of action. Thirteen of the provisions require knowing access without permission. Notably, "without permission" is not defined in the statute. Please compare that to Washington's Cybercrime Law which defines "without authorization." California courts have defined without permission under the CCDA as to not include violations of terms of use, but the circumvention of some technological or code-based barrier similar to some federal courts interpretation of "without authorization" under the CFAA.[359] "Access" is defined as a, "means to gain entry to, instruct, cause input to, cause output from, cause data processing with, or communicate with, the logical, arithmetical, or memory function resources of a computer, computer system, or computer network."

---

[359] *See, e.g.*, *Underhill v. Kornblum*, 2017 WL 2869734 (S.D. Cal. 2017).

Subsection	**"Knowing" and "Without Permission"**	**Actions**	**Subject**	**Additional Purpose or Result**
Subsection (c)(1)	Knowingly accesses and without permission	alters, damages, deletes, destroys, or otherwise uses	any data, computer, computer system, or computer network	in order to either (A) devise or execute any scheme or artifice to defraud, deceive, or extort, or (B) wrongfully control or obtain money, property, or data.
Subsection (c)(2)	Knowingly accesses and without permission	takes, copies, or makes use of **OR** takes or copies	any data from a computer, computer system, or computer network **OR** any supporting documentation, whether existing or residing internal or *external* to a	

			computer, computer system, or computer network.	
Subsection (c)(3)	Knowingly and without permission	uses or causes to be used	computer services	
Subsection (c)(4)	Knowingly accesses and without permission	adds, alters, damages, deletes, or destroys	any data, computer software, or computer programs which reside or exist internal or external to a computer, computer system, or computer network.	
Subsection (c)(5)	Knowingly accesses and without permission	disrupts or causes the disruption **OR** causes the denial	of computer services **OR** of computer services to an authorized user of a computer, computer system, or computer network.	
Subsection (c)(6)	Knowingly accesses and	provides or assists in	a computer, computer system, or	in violation

	without permission	providing a means of accessing	computer network	of this section.
Subsection (c)(7)	Knowingly accesses and without permission	accesses or causes to be accessed	any computer, computer system, or computer network.	
Subsection (c)(8)	Knowingly	introduces any computer contaminant into	any computer, computer system, or computer network.	
Subsection (c)(9)	Knowingly accesses and without permission	uses the internet domain name or profile of another individual, corporation, or entity in connection with the sending of one or more electronic mail messages or posts and thereby damages or causes damage to	a computer, computer data, computer system, or computer network.	

Subsection (c)(10)	Knowingly accesses and without permission	disrupts or causes the disruption **OR** denies or causes	of government computer services **OR** the denial of government computer services to an authorized user of a government computer, computer system, or computer network.	
Subsection (c)(11)	Knowingly accesses and without permission	adds, alters, damages, deletes, or destroys	any data, computer software, or computer programs which reside or exist internal or external to a public safety infrastructure computer system computer, computer system, or computer network.	
Subsection (c)(12)	Knowingly accesses and	disrupts or causes the disruption	public safety infrastructure computer system	

	without permission	**OR** denies or causes the denial	computer services **OR** of computer services to an authorized user of a public safety infrastructure computer system computer, computer system, or computer network.	
Subsection (c)(13)	Knowingly accesses and without permission	provides or assists in providing	a means of accessing a computer, computer system, or public safety infrastructure computer system computer, computer system, or computer network	in violation of this section.
Subsection (c)(14)	Knowingly	introduces	any computer contaminant into any public safety infrastructure computer system computer, computer	

			system, or computer network.	

The broadest subsections are likely (c)(7) and (c)(3). Subsection (c)(7) provides: "Knowingly accesses and without permission accesses or causes to be accessed any computer, computer system, or computer network." This appears to cover any intrusion or any purpose. Subsection (c)(3) is directed to use of computer services with knowing access and without permission. Moreover, (c)(6) covers anyone who "knowingly accesses and without permission" "provides or assists" in giving a "means of accessing" "a computer, computer system, or computer network." The CCDA provides for a range of penalties depending on which subdivision is violated and the number of sequential violations for some provisions. Notably, the CCDA also provides a private right of action for violation of any of the provisions of subdivision (c), and specifically allows for reasonable attorney's fees and punitive damages under certain circumstances. There is also a three year statute of limitations from the later of either the date of incident or discovery of damages.

Importantly, there is an exemption for acts by employees in the scope of their employment as well as an exemption from subsection (c)(3) for certain acts by employees outside the scope of their employment. Notably, in *Crisman v. City of Los Angeles*, the California Court of Appeal determined that a police officer's conduct fell within the former exemption even though he was utilizing police computers for searches not related to his employment.[360] The court stated:

> Together these cases show that an employer's disapproval of an employee's conduct does not cast the conduct outside the scope of employment. If the employer's disapproval were the measure, then virtually any misstep, mistake, or misconduct by an employee involving an employer's computer would, by respondents' reasoning, be criminal. For example, if an employer prohibited employees from logging onto the Internet to check their personal email,

---

[360] *Crisman v. City of Los Angeles*, 155 Cal.App.4th 29, 35-37 (2nd Dist. 2007).

> respondents' definition of scope of employment would make reading one's email on company time a crime even where the employee read the email on a computer regularly assigned to that employee.[361]

The CCDA allows for the forfeiture of computers, computer systems and computer networks used in violation of the provisions or computers used to store illegally obtained data.

11.4 Defend Trade Secrets Act and Economic Espionage Act

Causes of action for trade secret misappropriation may involve the same or similar set of facts as a CFAA claim or a state cybercrime statute. Trade secret misappropriation-type claims can be brought under state law or federal law. This section provides an overview of two federal laws: Defend Trade Secrets Act (DTSA) and the Economic Espionage Act. Importantly, the DTSA was based on the Uniform Trade Secrets Act. The Uniform Trade Secrets Act or a variation of it has been adopted in many states.

11.4[a] Defend Trade Secrets Act

The DTSA is a relatively new federal statute enacted in 2016. The DTSA provides a federal cause of action for trade secret misappropriation. Notably, while based on the Uniform Trade Secrets Act, there are differences. Trade secret misappropriation generally requires a trade secret as well as acts constituting misappropriation. A trade secret is usually defined as information that is subject to reasonable efforts to keep it secret and derives independent economic value from not being generally known and readily ascertainable. For example, a court has found that a failure to utilize reasonable efforts included not using available Zoom features to control access and making call-in information publicly available. In another case, *Espire Ads v. TAPP Influencer Corp.*, the court determined that reasonable efforts were exercised when information, including source code, was stored on a secure cloud server and passwords were used among other measures.[362] Trade secret misappropriation generally involves the acquisition or use of

---

[361] *Id.* at 37.

[362] Espire Ads v. TAPP Influencers Corp., __ F. Supp. 3d __ (S.D.N.Y. 2023).

a trade secret through improper means. For example, courts have found trade secret misappropriation based on a violation of a contract requiring secrecy or law. Trade secret misappropriation usually does not include discovering the trade secret independently or through reverse engineering. The DTSA includes provisions concerning *ex parte* seizure orders as well as procedural safeguards for seized materials, particularly digital materials. The following three cases discuss, first, whether a preliminary injunction should issue in a trade secret misappropriation claim, second, whether a trade secret misappropriation claim was properly pled under the DTSA, and third, whether scraping involves trade secret misappropriation under Florida's Uniform Trade Secret's law. The first case examines preliminary relief in a trade secret case. The second case explores whether certain information is a trade secret. The third case examines misappropriation.

In *Physicians Interactive v. Lathian Systems, Inc.*, plaintiff is the host of an interactive website for medical professionals called Physicians Interactive.[363] Defendant is Lathian Systems, Inc., is the host of a similar website. Plaintiff alleges that Lathian's information technology employee, Stephen Martinez, hacked its website and stole their confidential customer lists and computer software code. Physicians Interactive maintains an extensive confidential electronic database of the physicians and other medical professionals who use its service. This information is kept on its file server and is not accessible by the general public. Plaintiff alleges that Defendants launched three attacks on its file servers to steal the customer list, computer code, and confidential data from its website. After plaintiff determined the place and nature of these computer hacking attacks, it implemented a software patch to prevent any further attacks.

Physicians Interactive sued Lathian Systems, Inc., Stephen Martinez, and John Doe(s) 1-10 to account for other IT employees who may have been involved based on a private right of action under the Virginia Uniform Trade Secret Act, and other claims. Plaintiff also made a motion for preliminary injunction to enjoin Defendants from (1) accessing plaintiff's file servers; (2) obtaining confidential proprietary and trade secret information belonging to

[363] Physicians Interactive v. Lathian Systems, Inc., 2003 WL 23018270 (E.D. Va. 2003).

Plaintiff; (3) using or disclosing any information that Defendants acquired by their allegedly unauthorized and illegal intrusions into Plaintiff's website file servers; and (4) destroying or altering any evidence of such acts.

The Court applied the four-part test to determine if a preliminary injunction should issue: (1) the likelihood of irreparable harm to the plaintiff if the injunction is not granted; (2) the likelihood of harm to the defendant if the injunction is granted; (3) the likelihood of plaintiff's success on the merits; and (4) the public interest. The Court held that Physicians Interactive had established probable cause that the three hacking attacks alleged were directly linked to the defendants which demonstrated irreparable harm. The Court rejected an argument that patching a used vulnerability would negate irreparable harm because the patch may not be "foolproof" and continued attacks may occur. The Court pointed to the fact that if defendants attacked the plaintiffs again that plaintiff would incur costs, including time and money. The Court further found that defendants would not suffer irreparable harm if the injunction issued because they could still utilize the "authorized, and public functions" of plaintiff's website. And, the Court found that the injunctive relief will not result in harm to defendants' ability to compete. The Court additionally found that a likelihood of success on the merits existed for the Virginia Uniform Trade Secrets Act for misappropriation. The plaintiff sufficiently alleged that the customer lists were traditional trade secrets that would economically benefit competitors and were subject to reasonable efforts to keep them secret through significant electronic measures and patching. The Court found that use of a robot to hack a computer system was clearly an improper means to access a trade secret, and thus met the definition of trade secret misappropriation. Finally, the Court found the public interest satisfied because, "[t]his Court has an obligation to enjoin any alleged computer hackers from continuing to attack and steal plaintiff's proprietary information." However, the Court also found that plaintiff's proposed injunction request was vague, so it issued a more narrowly tailored form of injunctive relief in a separate order.

In *Iacovacci v. Brevet Holdings*, the district court denied a motion to dismiss a counterclaim under the DTSA.[364] In that case, the plaintiff brought causes of action related to his termination, including claims under the DTSA and Stored Communications Act. The defendant, Brevet Holdings, responded with counterclaims concerning trade secret misappropriation. In analyzing the trade secret misappropriation claims, the district court noted that reliance on state law trade secret cases in resolving DTSA claims is appropriate.

First, the court stated that the definition of a trade secret under the DTSA includes: "all forms and types of financial, business, scientific, technical, economic, or engineering information, including patterns, plans, compilations, program devices, formulas, designs, prototypes, methods, techniques, processes, procedures, programs, or codes,' so long as: (1) 'the owner thereof has taken reasonable efforts to keep such information secret'; and (2) 'the information derives independent economic value . . . from not being generally known to, and not being generally ascertainable through proper means by, another person who can obtain economic value from the disclosure of the information." In determining whether there was a trade secret, the court pointed to New York law providing factors that are "guideposts:" (1) the extent to which the information is known outside of [the] business; (2) the extent to which it is known by employees and others involved in [the] business; (3) the extent of measures taken by [the business] to guard the secrecy of the information; (4) the value of the information to [the business] and to [its] competitors; (5) the amount of effort or money expended by [the business] in developing the information; (6) the ease or difficulty with which the information could be property acquired or duplicated by others."

In finding a DTSA claim properly pled, the court pointed to allegations concerning specific potential trade secrets such as "non-public sourcing information for over 2,000 clients" and measures to protect those trade secrets including "a 'firewall' and 'log-in and password protect[ion].'" Moreover, the court stated that allegations that "they 'expended considerable resources, both financial and in personnel time, developing this non-public information,' which is an extremely valuable asset[] of the company' . . . are sufficient to

---

[364] *Iacovacci v. Brevet Holdings*, 437 F.Supp.3d 367 (S.D.N.Y. 2020).

defeat a motion to dismiss." Finally, the court found that Iacovacci stole the alleged trade secrets and "forwarded several documents in his personal email and disseminated them[, including] modifi[ng] other Brevet documents [and] execut[ing] business transactions using Defendants' trade secrets."

In *Compulife Software v. Newman*, the Eleventh Circuit considered a case involving scraping and misappropriation of trade secrets under Florida's Uniform Trade Secrets Law.[365] Compulife Software alleged that defendants used a hacker to "scrape" trade secrets consisting of insurance-quote data in two zip codes—43 million quotes. Scraping is the use of a bot "that can make many requests [from a server] automatically and much more rapidly than a human could . . . and then instantaneously record the returned information in an electronic database." A human could make the same requests, but at a much slower rate than a bot—thousands of hours versus four days. Compulife Software alleges that defendants then used the scraped information on defendants' websites.

The Eleventh Circuit upheld the magistrate judge's finding that the information was a trade secret. The next question concerned misappropriation. The Eleventh Circuit explained that, "[o]ne party can misappropriate another's trade secret by either acquisition, disclosure or use." The court focused on acquisition and use. Acquisition is when defendant "acquir[es] it and 'knows or has reason to know that the trade secret was acquired by improper means." The court explained that:

> A person misappropriates a secret by use if he uses it 'without express or implied consent' and either: 1. Used improper means to acquire knowledge of the trade secret; or 2. At the time of disclosure or use, knew or had reason to know that her or his knowledge of the trade secret was: a. Derived from or through a person who had utilized improper means to acquire it; b. Acquired under circumstances giving rise to a duty to maintain its secrecy or limit its use; or c. Derived from or through a person who owed a duty to the person seeking

---

365 *Compulife Software v. Neman*, 959 F.3d 1288 (11th Cir. 2020).

> relief to maintain its secrecy or limit its use; or 3. Before a material change of her or his position, knew or had reason to know that it was a trade secret and that knowledge of it had been acquired by accident or mistake.[366]

The Eleventh Circuit further explained that "improper means" "is defined to include 'theft, bribery, misrepresentation, breach or inducement of a breach of a duty to maintain secrecy, or espionage through electronic or other means'" and that, "'theft, wiretapping, or even aerial reconnaissance' can constitute improper means, but 'independent invention, accidental disclosure, or . . . reverse engineering' cannot." Additionally, the court noted that measures only have to be reasonable to protect the trade secret—even if ultimately inadequate to protect the trade secrets.

In analyzing misappropriation, the Eleventh Circuit rejected the magistrate judge's finding that defendants did not misappropriate the trade secrets and remanded. First, the Eleventh Circuit determined, in part, that the magistrate judge erred by requiring that misappropriation include violation of a duty external to the statute. The Eleventh Circuit noted that several categories of a violation of the use of another's trade secret did not include violation of a duty external to the statute, such as acquiring knowledge of a trade secret "'by accident or mistake' and still us[ing] it." Second, the Eleventh Circuit determined that the magistrate judge erred by finding that there was not misappropriation based on the fact that the scraped individual quotes were publicly available. The Eleventh Circuit reasoned that public availability of individual quotes may impact whether there is a trade secret in those individual quotes, but taking a protected portion of the collective quotes—a part of the database—could be misappropriation of the compilation. The Eleventh Circuit further noted that, "while manually accessing quotes from Compulife's database is unlikely to constitute improper means, using a bot to collect an otherwise infeasible amount of data may well be. . . ." The court also rejected the possibility that, "the trade-secret owner's 'failure to place a usage restriction on its website' did not automatically render the hacking proper." The court remands on

---

366 *Id.*

the question of whether scraping itself was "improper such that acquisition or use of the quotes could amount to misappropriation."

11.4[B] ECONOMIC ESPIONAGE ACT

The Economic Espionage Act [EEA] creates two main causes of action concerning criminal trade secret misappropriation. The EEA also creates a civil cause of action that can be brought by the U.S. Department of Justice, but not a private right of action.[367] The two main criminal prohibitions include, first, a trade secret misappropriation-type action related to espionage on behalf of a foreign government, instrumentality or agent, section 1831, and second, a trade secret misappropriation-type action that applies generally, section 1832. Both also include a provision directed to prohibit conspiracy. Notably, the definition of a "trade secret," "misappropriation" and "improper means" are similar to those defined in the DTSA and the Uniform Trade Secrets Act.[368] The EEA also applies to acts occurring outside the United States in limited circumstances.[369]

U.S.C. section 1831, in Title 18, has multiple requirements for a violation of the section. First, section 1831 requires that the person must intend or know "that the offense will benefit any foreign government, foreign instrumentality, or foreign agent." Second, the person must "knowingly" engage in one of three sets of actions: (1) "steals, or without authorization appropriates, takes, carries away, or conceals, or by fraud, artifice, or deception obtains a trade secret; (2) without authorization copies duplicates, sketches, draws, photographs, downloads, uploads, alters, destroys, photocopies, replicates, transmits, delivers, sends, mails, communicates, or conveys a trade secret; [and] (3) receives, buys, or possesses a trade secret, knowing the same to have been stolen or appropriated, obtained, or converted without authorization. Section 1831 can also be violated by "knowingly" attempting to violate subsections (1) to (3). Knowingly conspiring to violate subsections (1) to (3) can also be a violation of section 1831 "if one or more such persons do any act to effect the object of the conspiracy." The penalty for a violation is a fine of "not more than $5,000,000 or

---

[367] 18 U.S.C. § 1836.
[368] 18 U.S.C. § 1839.
[369] 18 U.S.C. § 1837.

imprisoned not more than 15 years, or both." Importantly, if an organization violates section 1831, the penalty is a fine "not more than the greater of $10,000,000 or 3 times the value of the stolen trade secret to the organization . . .." That fine also includes "expenses for research and design and other costs of reproducing the trade secret that the organization has thereby avoided."

U.S.C. section 1832, in Title 18, has multiple requirements. First, the person must have "intent to convert a trade secret, that is related to a product or service used in or intended for use in interstate or foreign commerce." Second, the conversion must be "to the economic benefit of anyone other than the owner" of the trade secret. Third, the person must intend or know that the offense will cause injury to the owner of the trade secret. Fourth, the person must "knowingly" commit one of the three prohibited actions which are similar to 1831(a)(1)-(3) described in the preceding paragraph. Section 1832 can also be violated by "knowingly" attempting to violate subsections (1) to (3). Knowingly conspiring to violate subsections (1) to (3) can also be a violation of section 1831 "if one or more such persons do any act to effect the object of the conspiracy." The penalty for a violation is a fine "or imprison[ment] not more than 10 years, or both." If an organization violates section 1832, the penalty is a fine "not more than the greater of $5,000,000 or 3 times the value of the stolen trade secret to the organization . . .." That fine also includes "expenses for research and design and other costs of reproducing the trade secret that the organization has thereby avoided."

The United States Department of Justice and the Department of Commerce are leading a cross agency task force called the, "Disruptive Technology Task Force."[370] The Task Force purpose is "to counter efforts by hostile nation-states to illicitly acquire sensitive U.S. technology to advance their authoritarian regimes and facilitate human rights abuses." In 2023, the Task Force announced its two cases involving trade secrets:

> Two of the other cases announced today charge former software engineers with stealing software

[370] Department of Justice, Justice Department Announces Five Cases as Part of Recently Launched Disruptive Technology Strike Force (May 16, 2023), available at https://www.justice.gov/opa/pr/justice-department-announces-five-cases-part-recently-launched-disruptive-technology-strike

> and hardware source code from U.S. tech companies in order to market it to Chinese competitors. In the Central District of California, a senior software engineer was arrested on May 5 for theft of trade secrets for allegedly stealing source code used in metrology software which is used in "smart" automotive manufacturing equipment. The defendant then allegedly marketed the stolen technology to multiple Chinese companies. In the Northern District of California, a citizen of the People's Republic of China (PRC) and former Apple engineer is accused of allegedly stealing thousands of documents containing the source code for software and hardware pertaining to Apple's autonomous vehicle technology. This defendant fled to China and is believed to be working for a PRC-based autonomous vehicle competitor.

In *U.S. v. Hanjuan Jin*, the district court resolved multiple issues as to whether a defendant violated 18 U.S.C. sections 1831 and 1832.[371] Specifically, the court decided that a violation of sections 1831(a)(3) requires that "defendant 'knowingly . . . receives, buys, or possesses a trade secret, knowing the same to have been stolen, appropriated, obtained or converted without authorization" should be construed to mean that "'knowingly' modifies 'trade secret'" and not only "'receives, buys, or possesses.'" Thus, a defendant must knowingly understand "as a factual matter, that information she possessed had the general attributes of a trade secret." The court noted that section 1832(a)(3) contains slightly different language, but did not resolve whether that language would make a difference. The court determined that there was adequate evidence that defendant knew she possessed a trade secret under section 1831(a)(3) because she: knew the information was not readily accessible; knew of Motorola's attempts to keep the information secret; knew the documents were marked confidential; knew of Motorola's efforts to develop the technology; and engaged in a "ruse of returning to work in order to obtain the information."

The court also determined that the government proved that the defendant misappropriated trade secrets under 18 U.S.C.

---

[371] *U.S. v. Hanjuan Jin*, 833 F.Supp.3d 977 (N.D. Ill. 2012).

sections 1831(a)(3) and 1832(a)(3) because the trade secrets "were actually 'stolen, appropriated, or converted without authorization'" and that defendant knew that. In contravention of Motorola's policies, Jin downloaded documents and lied about the documents to the FBI and CBP. The court concluded that Jin knew she took the documents without authorization.

The court found that section 1832(a)(3)'s requirement that "the defendant intended for the offense to economically benefit anyone other than the owner" is satisfied by evidence that the defendant "took the trade secrets to help her prepare for her future employment" even though there was not evidence that her future employer requested the documents or she planned to give them to her future employer. Moreover, she purchased a one-way ticket to China. The court also determined that the government proved that she "knew or was aware to a practical certainty that [her] conduct would cause some disadvantage to the rightful owner" essentially based on the facts that she understood the documents were trade secrets and how much Motorola worked to develop those trade secrets.

Finally, for section 1831(a)(3), the court found that the government failed to prove the economic espionage requirement: that the defendant "knew or intended that her conduct would benefit a foreign Government or a foreign instrumentality." The court stated there were two parts to this requirement: "the intended beneficiary and the intended benefit." The alleged intended beneficiary was the PRC, a foreign government. However, the court did not find that the government proved beyond a reasonable doubt that the defendant intended or knew her conduct would benefit the foreign government even though a "benefit means not only an economic benefit but also reputational, strategic, or tactical benefit." The government failed to provide proof that defendant "was asked or directed to take the trade secrets" or "planned to give the trade secrets to [her new employer], let alone the PRC." Moreover, the evidence was essentially speculative that the PRC may benefit from the technology and there was evidence that there was superior technology already publicly available. The court concluded "this was not cutting-edge technology that would necessarily give the PRC any tactical, reputational, or other benefit."

11.5 Stored Communications Act

The Stored Communications Act [SCA] generally addresses voluntary and compelled disclosure of stored wire and electronic communications. The SCA was enacted to fill gaps in privacy protection for unauthorized access to stored communications such as emails.

The SCA contains numerous provisions. This section addresses unlawful access to stored communications under 18 U.S.C. section 2701. A violation of the SCA occurs if one intentionally accesses without authorization a facility that provides electronic communication service, intentionally exceeds authorization to access these facilities, and obtains, alters, or prevents authorized access to a wire or electronic communication while it is in storage. A violation results in criminal penalties.

11.5[A] Selected Provisions of the Stored Communications Act and Discussion

The SCA creates criminal and civil liability. Section 2701 provides for criminal liability and section 2707 provides for a civil action. Section 2701 of Title 18, provides two separate provisions creating criminal liability. First, subsection (a)(1) provides that a person who "intentionally accesses without authorization a facility through which an electronic communication service is provided" "and thereby obtains, alters, or prevents authorized access to a wire or electronic communication while it is in electronic storage in such system" violates this section. Second, subsection (a)(2) provides that a person who "intentionally exceeds an authorization to access that facility" "and thereby obtains, alters, or prevents authorized access to a wire or electronic communication while it is in electronic storage in such system" violates this section. There is an exception to subsections (a)(1) and (2) if "conduct [is] authorized (1) by the person or entity providing a wire or electronic communications service; or (2) by a user of that service with respect to a communication of or intended for that user.[372] There are harsher penalties for a violation of (a)(1) and (2) if "the offense is committed for purposes of commercial advantage, malicious destruction or

[372] There is an additional exception for conduct authorized in sections 2703, 27704 or 2518 under Title 18.

damage, or private commercial gain, or in furtherance of any criminal or tortious act in violation of the Constitution or laws of the United States or any State . . .." The harsher penalties include a fine or "imprisonment for not more than 5 years, or both" for the first offense and a fine or "imprisonment for not more than 10 years, or both" for the second offense. If the harsher penalties do not apply, then the punishment is a fine or "imprisonment for not more than 1 year or both" for the first offense, and a fine or "imprisonment for not more than 5 years or both" for the second offense."

Section 2707 creates a civil action. Essentially, section 2707 creates a civil action for the violation of any provision in the chapter if the "conduct constituting the violation is engaged in with a knowing or intentional state of mind may, in a civil action, recover from the person or entity . . . which engaged in that violation." Relief includes injunctions, damages and a reasonable attorney fees and costs. The damages may include actual damages and profits with a floor of $1,000. In cases of willful or intentional violations, the court may award punitive damages. A successful action may result in costs and attorney fees. Notably, a remedy is not available against the U.S. government except that disciplinary action may be available against an officer or employee of the United States involved in a violation that was willful or intentional. Section 2707 provides for a defense for good faith reliance in certain circumstances on, for example, "a court warrant or order, a grand jury subpoena, a legislative authorization or a statutory authorization." There is also a two-year statute of limitations measured from "the date upon which claimant first discovered or had a reasonable opportunity to discover the violation."

The following two decisions explore the scope of section 2701. In *Hately v. Watts*, the Fourth Circuit reversed a district court's determination that a violation of 2701(a)(1) did not occur. Section 2701(a)(1) provides: whoever "'intentionally accesses without authorization a facility through which an electronic communication is provided . . . and thereby obtains, alters, or prevents authorized access to a wire or electronic communication while it is in electronic storage in such system.'" "Electronic storage" is defined as: "(A) any temporary, intermediate storage of a wire or electronic communication incidental to the electronic transmission thereof; and (B) any storage of such communication by an electronic communication service for purposes of backup protection of such communication." The district court determined that plaintiff delivered and opened emails that defendant allegedly accessed were not in electronic storage under (A) because they "'are no longer in 'temporary, intermediate storage . . . incidental to the[ir] electronic transmission.'" The Fourth Circuit agreed with the district court because "previously opened and delivered emails" in "a web-based email service" have been "transmitted" and are not "in the middle" of transmission. According to the court, failure to delete means that the emails are not in temporary storage. However, the Fourth Circuit held that the previously opened and delivered emails did fail within subsection (B) as "any [1] storage of [2] such communication [3] by an electronic communication service [4] for purpose of back up protection of such communication." The Fourth Circuit decided that "electronic storage" included emails that were previously opened and accessed because they were "reserved for future use" and that the emails were "wire or electronic communication," and thus fell within the meaning of "such communication." Additionally, the Fourth Circuit decided that "electronic communications service" includes sending and receiving emails, and that a service can be both an electronic communications service and a remote computing service at the same time. Thus, the Fourth Circuit rejected the district court's interpretation of the SCA that an entity had to be one or the other. Finally, the Fourth Circuit determined that the plaintiff's emails were in electronic storage—back up protection—and that is what users desire from web-based email services.

In *Garcia v. City of Laredo, Texas,* the Fifth Circuit determined that the Stored Communications Act does not apply to data stored in a personal cell phone.[373] Section 2701(a)(1) provides: whoever "'intentionally accesses without authorization a facility through which an electronic communication is provided . . . and thereby obtains, alters, or prevents authorized access to a wire or electronic communication while it is in electronic storage in such system.'" The plaintiff argues that a cell phone is a "facility" "in which electronic communication is kept in electronic storage in the form of text messages and pictures stored on the cell phone." The Fifth Circuit rejected the plaintiff's argument and noted that cases have found the SCA covers "'information stored with a phone

---

[373] *Garcia v. City of Laredo, Texas*, 702 F.3d 788 (5th Cir. 2012).

company, Internet Service Provider (ISP), or [an] electronic bulletin board system.'" However, the Fifth Circuit distinguished those cases from situations involving "an individual's computer, laptop, or mobile devices." The Fifth Circuit noted that district courts considering the issue reasoned that, "'the relevant 'facilities" that the SCA is designed to protect are not computers that *enable* the use of an electronic communication service, but instead are facilities that are *operated by* electronic communication service providers and used to store and maintain electronic storage.'"[374] Moreover, the court rejected the plaintiff's argument that text messages and photos constitute "electronic storage." The Fifth Circuit decided that "electronic storage" means "information that has been stored by an electronic computer service provider," such as "information that an Internet provider stores to its servers or information stored with a telephone company."

11.6 Digital Millennium Copyright Act

Section 1201 of the Digital Millennium Copyright Act [DMCA] prohibits the circumvention of "technological measures that effectively control access to a [copyrighted work.]" The DMCA also restricts trafficking or importing circumvention technology in some cases. There are numerous exceptions, including security testing, encryption research and reverse engineering.

11.6[A] Selected Provisions of the Digital Millennium Copyright Act

Section 1201(a) and (b) create numerous potential violations concerning circumvention of technological measures. Section 1201(a)(1)(A) focuses on a violation based on a person's "circumvention [of] a technological measure that effectively controls access to a work protected under this title." Section 1201(a)(2)(A)-(C) and 1201(b)(1)(A)-(C) concern prohibitions on "the manufacture, import, offer to the public, provid[ing] or traffic[king] in any technology, product, service, device, component, or part thereof . . .", which generally concerns circumvention of a technological measure. Section 1201(a)(2)(A) states that "the manufacture, import, offer to the public, providing[ing] or traffic[king] in any technology . . ., that (A) is primarily designed or produced for the

[374] *Id.* (emphasis in original).

purpose of circumventing a technological measure that effectively controls access to a work protected under this title[.]" Section 1201(a)(2)(B) applies when "the manufacture, import, offer to the public, providing[ing] or traffic[king] in any technology . . ., that (B) has only limited commercially significant purpose or use other than to circumvent a technological measure that effectively controls access to a work protected under this title[.]" Section 1201(a)(2)(C) prohibits "the manufacture, import, offer to the public, providing[ing] or traffic[king] in any technology . . ., that (C) is marketed by that person or another acting in concert with that person with that person's knowledge for use in circumventing a technological measure that effectively controls access to a work protected under this title."

Section 1201(a) has specific definitions which apply to "circumvent a technological measure" and "effectively controls access to a work." "Circumvent a technological measure" "means to descramble a scrambled work, to decrypt an encrypted work, or otherwise to avoid, bypass, remove, deactivate, or impair a technological measure, without the authority of the copyright owner". "Effectively controls access to a work" is "if the [technological] measure, in the ordinary course of its operation, requires the application of information, or a process or a treatment, with the authority of the copyright owner, to gain access to the work."

Section 1201(b)(1) provides: "No person shall manufacture, import, offer to the public, provide, or otherwise traffic in any technology, product, service, device, component, or part thereof, that" is utilized in one of three ways set forth in (A)-(C). Subsection (A) states: "is primarily designed or produced for the purpose of circumventing protection afforded by a technological measure that effectively protects a right of a copyright owner under this title in a work or a portion thereof." Subsection (B) provides: "has only limited commercially significant purpose or use other than to circumvent protection afforded by a technological measure that effectively protects a right of a copyright owner under this title in a work or a portion thereof[.]" Subsection (C) states: "is marketed by that person or another acting in concert with that person with that person's knowledge for use in circumventing protection afforded by a technological measure that effectively protects a right of a copyright owner under this title in a work or a portion thereof."

Section 1201(b)(2) contains two specific definitions for "circumvent protection afforded by a technological measure" and "effectively protects a right of the copyright owner under this title." "Circumvent protection afforded by a technological measure" "means avoiding, bypassing, removing, deactivating, or otherwise impairing a technological measure". "Effectively protects a right of the copyright owner under this title" means "if the measure, in the ordinary course of its operation, prevents, restricts, or otherwise limits the exercise of a right of a copyright owner under this title.

There are numerous important differences between the causes of action provided between subsection 1201(a) and 1201(b). First, 1201(a) has a provision directly prohibiting the actual circumvention of a technological measure protecting a "work protected under this title" by a person. 1201(b) does not have a similar provision concerning a "right of a copyright owner under this title in a work or a portion thereof." 1201(b) is focused on prohibiting manufacturing, importing, offering to the public, providing or otherwise trafficking in technology that violates (A)-(C). Second, 1201(a) is directed to protecting "a work protected under this title." Section 1201(b) is focused on protecting "a right of a copyright owner under this title in a work or portion thereof." Third, and relatedly, the definitions between 1201(a) and 1201(b) are different even though they cover somewhat similar terms. Under 1201(a), the definition is for "circumvent a technological measure" and the 1201(b) corresponding definition is for "circumvent protection afforded by a technological measure." Under 1201(a), the definition for "effectively controls access to a work" and the 1201(b) corresponding definition is for "effectively protects a right of a copyright owner under this title." Section 1201(a)'s definition of "circumvent a technological measure" specifically mentions descrambling a scrambled work or decrypting an encrypted work, and thus is directed to the work in general. Section 1201(b)'s definition of "circumvent protection afforded by a technological measure" does not contain similar language, but includes the more general language concerning "avoiding, bypassing, removing, deactivating, or otherwise impairing a technological measure" that is also in 1201(a). Section 1201(a)'s definition of "effectively controls access to a work" is directed towards gaining access to the general work with authority of the copyright owner. Section 1201(b)'s definition of "effectively protects a right of a copyright owner under this title" is directed to a technological measure that "limits the exercise of a right of a copyright owner under this title."

Subsection 1201(c) importantly states that: "Nothing in this section shall affect rights, remedies, limitations, or defenses to copyright infringement, including fair use, under this title." Furthermore, 1201(c) preserves vicarious and contributory liability as well as "free speech or the press for activities using consumer electronics, telecommunications, or computing products." Moreover, subsection 1201(a) is limited by subsection (a)(1)(a) that allows the Librarian of Congress to issue exemptions consistent with that provision. Some of the exemptions include: "Computer programs that operate [Cellphones, Tablets, Mobile Hotspots, and Wearable devices] to allow connection of a new or used device to an alternative wireless network ("unlocking")" and "Computer programs that operate [Smartphones, Tablets and other all-purpose mobile computing devices, Smart TVs and Voice Assistant Devices] to allow the device to interoperate with or to remove software applications ("jailbreaking."). The exemptions also include: "Computer programs that control smartphones, home appliances, or home systems, for diagnosis, maintenance, or repair of the device or system" and "Computer programs for purposes of good-faith security research."

11.6[B] DMCA Cases

This section reviews a series of cases interpreting and applying the DMCA. In *Philips North America v. Summit Imaging*, the district court found that Philips adequately pled violations of apparently sections 1201(a)(1) and (a)(2) based on defendant Summit's alleged hacking of Philips' ultrasound systems.[375] The district court decided that Philips demonstrated that their ultrasound systems were "protected by 'a technological measure that effectively controls access to a work' under [sections] 1201(a)(1) and (a)(2). The district court stated:

> The complaint identifies 'multiple layers of technological controls' that Philips employs on their Ultrasound Systems 'to protect Philips' copyright-

---

[375] *Phillips North America v. Summit Imaging*, 2020 WL 1515624 (W.D. Wash. 2020).

> protected works from unauthorized access.' Specifically, the complaint identifies the following technological measures: (1) user-specific codes; (2) user-specific hardware keys; (3) machine-specific codes and hardware keys; (4) software files with licensed features and optional add-on controls; (5) machine-specific configuration codes that control compatibility between the systems and software and/or the systems and replacement parts; and (6) software disabling if a user attempts to make use of an unlicensed feature.
>
> The complaint also explains how these technological measures work. . . . User-specific access codes and hardware keys 'enable the software access and control features for a particular registered user' by permitting 'access to enabled Philips tools and features based on a user's registered access authorization level.' Machine-specific controls 'only permit user access to the features and tools that have been enabled on a specific machine. Licensed feature controls limit what features users can access on a specific machine, control access to protected software, and limit the options available for use on a specific machine.

The district court further found that Philips adequately pled that Summit "circumvented" Philips technological measures to control access by "remov[ing] the hard drive from [Philips' ultrasound systems] and run[ing] the Adepto program on the hard drive," which "changes configuration files and software files in order to enable unlicensed options on the hard drive." Moreover, "Philips . . . allege[d] that [Summit uses] Adepto to hack onboard tools to force compatibility with otherwise incompatible transducer parts."

The second case is the Ninth Circuit decision in *MDY Industries v. Blizzard Entertainment*.[376] The Ninth Circuit reversed the district court's decision that 1201(b)(1) was violated, but upheld the district court's decision that 1201(a)(2) was violated.

---

[376] *MDY Industries v. Blizzard Entertainment*, 629 F.3d 928 (9th Cir. 2010).

Defendant MDY essentially modified and distributed a program called "Glider" that was designed, in part, to avoid Blizzard's program Warden. Plaintiff Blizzard designed Warden to prohibit programs like Glider from operating. Glider was initially designed to allow automated play of the video game World of Warcraft.

Importantly, the Ninth Circuit explained the differences between subsections (a) and (b)(1). The Ninth Circuit contrasted the two sections by noting that (a) "prohibits the circumvention of any technological measure that effectively controls access to a protected work and grants copyright owners the right to enforce that prohibition" while (b)(1) "is aimed at circumventions of measures that protect the copyright itself: it entitles copyright owners to protect their existing exclusive rights under the Copyright Act." The Ninth Circuit further noted that "preventing 'access' to a protected work in itself has not been a right of a copyright owner arising from the Copyright Act." Essentially, the Ninth Circuit decided that 1201(a) does not require facilitation of an infringement of copyright—just prevention of access to a work--whereas 1201(b)(1) does require "trafficking in devices that facilitate circumvention of measures that protect against copyright infringement." The Ninth Circuit rejected the Federal Circuit's 1201(a) requirement set forth in *Chamberlain Group, Inc. v. Skylink Techs., Inc.*, 381 F.3d 1178 (Fed. Cir. 2004), of an "infringement nexus"—that "the defendant trafficked in a device that . . . facilitate[s] copyright infringement" for reasons regarding statutory interpretation.

The Ninth Circuit analyzed whether 1201(a)(2) was violated by dividing World of Warcraft's attributes between "literal elements and individual non-literal elements" and "dynamic non-literal elements." First, the Ninth Circuit decided that Warden does not effectively control access to "literal elements and individual non-literal elements" because the literal elements—"the game client's software code"—"are available on a player's hard drive once the game client software is installed" and the "individual non-literal elements" are available through third party computer programs. However, the Ninth Circuit decided that 1201(a)(2) was violated relating to the "dynamic non-literal elements." The Ninth Circuit determined that Warden is an effective access control measure with respect to those elements:

> To "effectively control access to a work," a technological measure must "in the ordinary course of its operation, require[] the application of information, or a process or a treatment, with the authority of the copyright owner, to gain access to the work." . . . Both of Warden's two components [the scan.dll and resident component] "require[] the application of information, or a process or a treatment . . . to gain access to the work." For a player to connect to Blizzard's servers which provide access to WoW's dynamic non-literal elements, [Warden's] scan.dll must scan the player's computer RAM and confirm the absence of bots or cheats. The resident component [which operates during game play] also requires a 'process' in order for the user to continue accessing the work: the user's computer must report portions of WoW code running in RAM to the server [which indicate bots or cheats]. Moreover, Warden's provisions were put into place by Blizzard, and thus, function "with the authority of the copyright owner." Accordingly Warden effectively controls access to WoW's dynamic non-literal elements.

The Ninth Circuit additionally determined that subsection 1201(b)(1) was not violated because Warden did not "'effectively protect[the reproduction] right' [against unauthorized copying] of Blizzard under the Copyright Act." The Ninth Circuit noted that Blizzard's End User License Agreement and Terms of Use allow users during game play to copy Blizzard's software code in RAM and violation of the prohibition on using bots does not result in infringement by "continuing to copy code into RAM" because that is a violation of a license covenant and not a condition. Additionally, Warden does not operate to prevent taking screen shots of the World of Warcraft and thus, does not effectively protect non-literal elements from copying.

Finally, in *Davidson & Associates v. Jung*, the Eighth Circuit reviewed the applicability of the reverse engineering exception, which applies to "individuals using circumvention technology 'for the sole purpose' of trying to achieve 'interoperability' of computer programs through reverse engineering."[377] The defendants created an online platform for people to play Blizzard games, such as World of Warcraft and Starcraft, which competes with Blizzard's platform. In designing their online platform, defendants accessed Blizzard's platform to learn Blizzard's code to ensure operability with Blizzard's games, among other things. Defendants' platform allowed unauthorized Blizzard games—without valid CD codes--to be played on their platform. The Eight Circuit further stated that:

> To successfully prove the interoperability defense . . ., Appellants must show: (1) they lawfully obtained the right to use a copy of a computer program; (2) the information gathered as a result of the reverse engineering was not previously readily available to the person engaging in the circumvention; (3) the sole purpose of the reverse engineering was to identify and analyze those elements of the program that were necessary to achieve interoperability of an independently created computer program with other programs; and (4) the alleged circumvention did not constitute infringement.

The Eight Circuit determined that the reverse engineering exception did not apply because the defendants' conduct resulted in numerous unauthorized copies of Blizzard games utilized on defendants' servers and, thus, the alleged circumvention was infringing.

---

[377] *Davidson & Associates v. Jung*, 422 F.3d 630 (8th Cir. 2005).

CHAPTER TWELVE. Internet of Things

12.1 Introduction

This chapter reviews cybersecurity issues related to the Internet of Things (IoT). In prior chapters, we have reviewed cases involving internet connected devices such as WiFi routers. Indeed, with the advent of the ubiquitous home WiFi router, "things" have been connected to the internet for a long time in the form of laptops, pads, and smart phones. Today, those "things" have exponentially increased with the continuous rising adoption of smart home devices. Newsweek published an article titled, "China's Plan to Rule the World's Smart Devices, FCC Urged to Act" on August 8, 2023.[378] The article asserts that commonly used Chinese-made cellular connectivity modules in IOT devices, such as police bodycams and other ubiquitous items that connect to the Internet, can be used to send information back to China and may not be secure.[379] As previously discussed, the Federal Communications Commission is responsible for developing a consumer labeling program for cybersecurity for IOT devices.[380] Moreover, the United States is now engaged in Secure Software Development attestation requirements for software developed by the government.[381] In this chapter, we review materials specifically directed to the IoT such as NIST documents and the Complaint filed against Ring concerning cybersecurity deficiencies.

12.2 IoT Background Information

A major concern of security departments is Denial of Service (DOS) attacks on a company's infrastructure. Basically, a DOS is caused by overloading a service or device with so much network traffic that the service or device becomes unavailable. Distributed Denial of Service (DDOS) attacks are similar and are caused by traffic from a distribution of sources.

---

[378] Shaun Waterman and Didi Kirsten Tatlow, China's Plan to Rule the World's Smart Devices, FCC Urged to Act, Newsweek (August 8, 2023), available at https://www.newsweek.com/chinas-plan-rule-world-iot-smart-devices-fcc-urged-act-1817682.

[379] *Id.*

[380] *See infra*, Chapter 7.

[381] *Id.*

It is a common goal of many hackers to take control of computing resources in order to harness as much computing power as possible. This could come in very handy if a hacker wanted expanded computer power for searching for bitcoins or other efforts that become easier with enhanced computing power. Thus, the hacker forms a network of time-slices of computing power from many computing sources without the individual computer owner even knowing their computer is being used by someone else. These are known as botnets. With the miniaturization of the components of a laptop computer, powerful miniaturized computing power has moved into a smart phone, and from the smart phone into other miniaturized devices that can also contain sensors and Wi-Fi connection capability. In short it has become technologically easy to put a microprocessor with Wi-Fi capability into almost any device, such as:

- TVs
- thermostats
- wireless cameras
- doorbells with cameras
- ovens
- refrigerators
- cars
- printers
- alarm sensors
- watches
- light bulbs
- light switches
- smart meters for water
- lawn sprinkler system controller
- door locks
- washer/dryer
- garage door openers
- connected robotic floor vacuums
- electric toothbrushes
- water leak detection and shut-off devices

And the above are smart devices used mainly for the home. Outside of the home, cities are also adding smart device technologies that may include:

- various meters (water, electrical, parking)
- signaling for traffic and train control
- various sensors that feed into apps such as bus arrival time apps

"The IoT is experiencing what some might describe as hypergrowth. Gartner forecasts that the number of IoT devices will reach 25 billion by 2021, while Forbes forecast that the market will exceed $457 billion before 2021."[382]

The National Institute of Science and Technology (NIST) provides the following take that focuses on IoT devices throughout the business enterprise in addition to the home:

> "The Internet of Things (IoT) is a rapidly evolving and expanding collection of diverse technologies that interact with the physical world. IoT devices are an outcome of combining the worlds of information technology (IT) and operational technology (OT). Many IoT devices are the result of the convergence of cloud computing, mobile computing, embedded systems, big data, low-price hardware, and other technological advances. IoT devices can provide computing functionality, data storage, and network connectivity for equipment that previously lacked them, enabling new efficiencies and technological capabilities for the equipment, such as remote access for monitoring, configuration, and troubleshooting. IoT can also add the abilities to analyze data about the physical world and use the results to better inform decision making, alter the physical environment, and anticipate future events.
>
> While the full scope of IoT is not precisely defined, it is clearly vast. Every sector has its own types of IoT devices, such as specialized hospital equipment in the healthcare sector and smart road technologies in the transportation sector, and there is a large number of enterprise IoT devices that every sector can use. Versions of nearly every consumer electronics device, many of which are also present in organizations' facilities, have become connected IoT devices—kitchen appliances,

---

382 SECURING SMALL-BUSINESS AND HOME INTERNET OF THINGS (IOT) DEVICES: MITIGATING NETWORK-BASED ATTACKS USING MANUFACTURER USAGE DESCRIPTION (MUD), NAT'L INST. OF STANDARDS AND TECH. & NAT'L CYBERSECURITY CTR. OF EXCELLENCE 2 (2020), *available at* https://www.nccoe.nist.gov/sites/default/files/library/sp1800/iot-ddos-nist-sp1800-15-draft.pdf.

> thermostats, home security cameras, door locks, light bulbs, and TVs."[383]

Imagine a commuter train that is approaching a busy crossroad that requires the gates to come down and block the road. This requires sensors communicating with sensors. A mistake here could mean the loss of life. Or imagine a power grid that feeds a manufacturing plant that contains machinery sensitive to voltage. Sensors within the power grid talk to other sensors that control the grid voltage to that particular plant. An uncontrolled spike in voltage could cause damage to expensive manufacturing equipment. Security of these sensors also known as things is obviously important.

The NIST identifies three IoT risk areas for business entities:

"Cybersecurity and privacy risks for IoT devices can be thought of in terms of three high-level risk mitigation goals:

> 1. **Protect device security**. In other words, prevent a device from being used to conduct attacks, including participating in distributed denial of service (DDoS) attacks against other organizations, and eavesdropping on network traffic or compromising other devices on the same network segment. This goal applies to all IoT devices.
>
> 2. **Protect data security.** Protect the confidentiality, integrity, and/or availability of data (including personally identifiable information [PII]) collected by, stored on, processed by, or transmitted to or from the IoT device. This goal applies to each IoT device except those without any data that needs protection.
>
> 3. **Protect individuals' privacy.** Protect individuals' privacy impacted by PII processing beyond risks managed through device and data security protection. This goal applies to all

[383] CONSIDERATIONS FOR MANAGING INTERNET OF THINGS (IOT) CYBERSECURITY AND PRIVACY RISKS, NAT'L INST. OF STANDARDS AND TECH. iv (2019), *available at* https://nvlpubs.nist.gov/nistpubs/ir/2019/NIST.IR.8228.pdf.

IoT devices that process PII or that directly or indirectly impact individuals."[384]

Per a recent NIST study:

"Gartner predicts there will be 25 billion Internet of Things (IoT) devices by 2021. While such rapid growth has the potential to provide many benefits, it is also a cause for concern because IoT devices are tempting targets for attackers. State-of-the-art security software protects full-featured devices, such as laptops and phones, from most known threats, but many IoT devices, such as connected thermostats, security cameras, and lighting control systems, have minimal security or are unprotected. Because they are designed to be inexpensive and limited purpose, IoT devices may have unpatched software flaws. They also often have processing, timing, memory, and power constraints that make them challenging to secure. Users often do not know what IoT devices are on their networks and lack means for controlling access to them over their life cycles. However, the consequences of not addressing the security of IoT devices can be catastrophic. For instance, in typical networking environments, malicious actors can detect and attack an IoT device within minutes of it connecting to the internet. If it has a known vulnerability, this weakness can be exploited at scale, enabling an attacker to commandeer sets of compromised devices, called *botnets*, to launch large-scale distributed denial of service (DDoS) attacks, such as Mirai, as well as other network-based attacks. DDoS attacks can significantly harm an organization, rendering it impossible for the organization's customers to reach it and thereby resulting in revenue loss, potential liability exposure, reputation damage, and eroded customer trust."[385]

"The Mirai malware, which launched a large DDoS attack on the internet infrastructure firm Dyn that took down many of the internet's top destinations offline for much of a day, relied heavily on hard-coded administrative access to assemble botnets consisting of more than 100,000 devices."[386]

---

[384] *Id.* at v.

[385] SECURING SMALL-BUSINESS AND HOME INTERNET OF THINGS (IOT) DEVICES: MITIGATING NETWORK-BASED ATTACKS USING MANUFACTURER USAGE DESCRIPTION (MUD), NAT'L INST. OF STANDARDS AND TECH. & NAT'L CYBERSECURITY CTR. OF EXCELLENCE 1 (2020), *available at* https://www.nccoe.nist.gov/sites/default/files/library/sp1800/iot-ddos-nist-sp1800-15-draft.pdf.

[386] *Id.* at 11.

But an increase in DDoS attacks and size of the attacks are only two of the cybersecurity threats caused by the proliferation of the IoT. Most of these smart devices for the home come with a free app with which to access and configure the smart device. But traffic to the user is not all that goes across the internet. Data can also be pulled down and logged to the manufacturer's server. The manufacturer can then send monthly usage data back to the owner as a service. Accordingly, this creates a data source at the manufacturer or seller of the device that must be protected by reasonable security measures.

Another aspect of IoT devices that can make it difficult to secure IoT devices is that some devices such as security cameras and security sensors do not communicate directly with the Wi-Fi hub but instead with its own aggregator. And then the aggregator communicates with the Wi-Fi hub. Compounding the aggregator issue is that the communication protocol between the devices and the aggregator may not be a single standard communication protocol. Thus, it is possible to have multiple aggregators in one home and each communicating over a different protocol. This presents a challenge for cybersecurity professionals.

Another issue with smart devices is that some of the built-in security features are lacking. For example, some smart devices have been sold, all with the same password, and the user is not required to change the password after startup. Some smart devices are sold with different passwords, but there is no requirement to change the password after startup. Thus, these devices have been an easy target for hackers to take over and then point at a particular IP address to cause a DDoS.

Many devices require an app for control of the device and the user is instructed to download a particular app during the installation of the device. After the app is downloaded, normally to a smart phone or tablet, an account must be opened through the app for control. Normally, the account requires, at minimum, a username and a password with setup options after the initial login for more robust security in the way of two-step verification security. Two-step verification, also known as multi-factor authorization, is normally not mandatory, and many users choose to not implement the two-step verification. Some device manufacturers have started to mandate two-step verification.

Unfortunately, the same poor password creation and management techniques that a user can apply to a laptop password can be applied to device app accounts. Indeed, the human behavior in setting up an app password may be worse because the user may be more focused on getting the device to work and not on good password management.

Another aspect that may affect device security is the security setup of the Wi-Fi router, with which the device or device aggregator communicates. Has the Wi-Fi been placed into a secure mode or is it open to the driving by public? How many people have been given the password to the Wi-Fi? If a guest network feature exists on the Wi-Fi, has it been set up for visitors? Has the original Wi-Fi password been changed? If a hacker can access the Wi-Fi traffic, then the hacker can sniff (monitor) the IoT traffic.

12.3 NIST Guidance Document: Foundational Cybersecurity Activities for IOT Device Manufacturers

The NIST released a guidance document titled, "Foundational Cybersecurity Activities for IOT Device Manufacturers," in May 2020. The document provides cybersecurity counseling for IOT device manufacturers concerning the development of devices to be sold to consumers. The Executive Summary provides, in relevant part:

"The purpose of this publication is to give manufacturers recommendations for improving how securable the IoT devices they make are. This means the IoT devices offer device cybersecurity capabilities—cybersecurity features or functions the devices provide through their own technical means (i.e., device hardware and software)—that customers, both organizations and individuals, need to secure the devices when used within their systems and environments. IoT device manufacturers will also often need to perform actions or provide services that their customers expect and/or need to plan for and maintain the cybersecurity of the device within their systems and environments. From this publication, IoT device manufacturers will learn how they can help to create a baseline of cybersecurity capabilities for IoT devices, and to publish cybersecurity practices for IoT device manufacturers. IoT device customers by carefully considering which device cybersecurity capabilities to design into their devices for customers to use in managing their cybersecurity risks."[387]

12.4 California's Internet of Things Legislation

California has passed legislation concerning cybersecurity and the Internet of Things.[388] The title of the legislation is "Security of Controlled Devices. The main thrust of the California Civil Code 1798.91.04 is to ensure that manufacturers of connected devices have reasonable security features.[389] The reasonable security features must be: "(1) Appropriate to the nature and function of the device[;] (2) Appropriate to the information it may collect, contain, or transmit[;] and (3) Designed to protect the device and any information contained therein from unauthorized access, destruction, use, modification, or disclosure."[390] The law further requires that, "if a connected device is equipped with a means for authentication outside a local area network," it complies with the reasonable security feature requirement if "(1) The preprogrammed password is unique to each device manufactured [and] (2) The device contains a security feature that requires a user to generate a new means of authentication before access is granted to the device for the first time."[391]

The law includes several important definitions including "Connected device," "Manufacturer," and "Unauthorized access, destruction, use, modification, or disclosure."[392] The definition of "Connected device" is very broad: "Connected device" means any device, or other physical object that is capable of connecting to the Internet, directly or indirectly, and that is assigned an Internet Protocol address or Bluetooth address."[393] "Manufacturer" is similarly relatively broad: "Manufacturer" means the person who manufactures, or contracts with another person to manufacture on the person's behalf, connected devices that are sold or offered for sale in California."[394] There is a limitation on the definition: "For the purposes of this subdivision, a contract with another person to

[387] FOUNDATIONAL CYBERSECURITY ACTIVITIES FOR IOT DEVICE MANUFACTURERS, NAT'L INST. OF STANDARDS AND TECH. 4 (2020), *available at* https://nvlpubs.nist.gov/nistpubs/ir/2020/NIST.IR.8259.pdf.

[388] Cal. Civ. Code §§ 1798.91.04–1798.91.06 (West 2018).

[389] *Id.*

[390] *Id.*

[391] *Id.*

[392] *Id.*

[393] *Id.*

[394] *Id.*

manufacture on the person's behalf does not include a contract only to purchase a connected device, or only to purchase and brand a connected device."[395] "Unauthorized access, destruction, use, modification, or disclosure" is defined to mean "access, destruction, use, modification, or disclosure that is not authorized by the consumer."[396]

Importantly, in section 1798.91.06, there are numerous exemptions from the law. The exemptions are so expansive that they arguably render the law ineffective in covering some circumstances. For example, subsection (a) removes the manufacturer from liability the situation where a user adds a unaffiliated third-party's software or applications to the device.[397] Subsection (b) removes from liability "a provider of an electronic store, gateway, marketplace, or other means of purchasing or downloading software or applications, to review or enforce compliance."[398] Subsection (c) ensures essentially that manufacturers do not have to prohibit users from modifying the software or firmware on the connected device.[399] This appears to provide the manufacturer with an argument against liability where the user has modified the device in such a way to make the reasonable security measure ineffective or less effective. Subsection (d) exempts all devices which are regulated by a federal agency.[400] This would seem to exempt medical devices regulated by the FDA as well as a host of other devices. Subsection (e) expressly prohibits a private right of action and places enforcement authority with the "Attorney General, a city attorney, a county counsel, or a district attorney."[401] Additionally, "[a] covered entity, provider of health care, business associate, health care service plan, contractor, employer, or any other person subject to the federal Health Insurance Portability and Accountability Act of 1996 (HIPAA) (Public Law 104-191) or the Confidentiality of Medical Information Act (Part 2.6 (commencing with Section 56) of Division 1) shall not be subject to this title with respect to any activity regulated by those acts.[402]

---

395 *Id.*

396 *Id.*

397 *Id.*

398 *Id.*

399 *Id.*

400 *Id.*

401 *Id.*

402 *Id.*

This law goes a long way in requiring manufacturers to provide reasonable security features with the device. It actually spells out how to meet the "reasonable security feature or features." But the law does not require the homeowner to take action on the devices it already owns. And the law does not appear to require any retroactive actions by the owner. Also, the potential problem of poor password selection still exists.

Also, it is worth noting that this law applies to devices that would enter California. Thus, even if a device is made in Texas but enters California for use, the Texas manufacturer is subject to the laws of California.

12.5 Complaint Concerning Internet of Things and Cybersecurity

There has been an emphasis on securing internet devices so that they cannot be used as botnets in a DDOS. But if the device can be hacked, the functionality of the device can be controlled by an outside threat in the form of an unknown person. This is particularly concerning when the device contains a camera or listening device that can be hijacked. Cameras today are ubiquitous, even smart TVs contain cameras. And listening devices include Siri and Alexa among others.

A complaint was filed against Ring concerning cybersecurity deficiencies in its IoT camera product. The complaint was filed by attorneys Francis J. "Casey" Flynn, Jr. of the Law Office of Francis J. Flynn, Jr. and John A. Yanchunis of Morgan and Morgan. Please note that this complaint was filed in 2019 before the California IoT law went into effect on January 1, 2020.

12.6 NIST SPECIAL PUBLICATION 1800-15 Securing Small-Business and Home Internet of Things (IoT) Devices: Mitigating Network-Based Attacks Using Manufacturer Usage Description (MUD)

Protecting the Network in Lieu of Adding Complex Security to IoT Devices

There are often many technical solutions available for a technical issue. The technical issue of concern with the Internet of Things (IoT) is how to keep billions of smart internet devices from becoming used for a distributed denial of service attack. These smart devices are normally small without complex operating systems. The devices are made from a multitude of manufacturers, the devices are normally not expensive to stay market competitive and adding complex security measures to these devices could add cost that makes the devices unattractive in the marketplace. So perhaps, focusing on implementing robust security in these smart devices is not cost effective. Instead of looking at the devices that can be overtaken for a DDOS, perhaps there is a better defense for consideration. The components of the DDOS attack are the smart devices (assumed overtaken), the network (i.e. the internet) and the target (a server or other large and valuable computing device).

Would it be possible for the Network to stop or control the attack? Actually, industry is already working towards that goal and as expected the National Institute of Standards and Technology (NIST) and the National Cybersecurity Center of Excellence (NCCOE) is also taking an active role.

Because IoT devices are designed to be low cost and for limited purposes, it is not realistic to try to solve the problem of IoT device vulnerability by requiring that all IoT devices be equipped with robust, state-of-the-art security mechanisms. Instead, we are challenged to develop ways to improve IoT device security without requiring costly or complicated improvements to the devices themselves.

A second challenge lies in the need to develop security mechanisms that will be effective even though IoT devices will, by their very nature, remain vulnerable to attack, and some will inevitably be compromised. These security mechanisms should protect the rest of the network from any devices that become compromised.

Given the widespread use of IoT devices by consumers who may not even be aware that the devices are accessing their network, a third challenge is the practical need for IoT security mechanisms to be easy to use. Ideally, security features should be so transparent that a user need not even be aware of their operation.

To address these challenges, the National Cybersecurity Center of Excellence (NCCoE) and its collaborators have demonstrated the practicality and effectiveness of using the Internet Engineering Task Force's Manufacturer Usage Description (MUD) standard to reduce both the vulnerability of IoT devices to network-based attacks and the potential for harm from any IoT devices that become compromised.[403]

MUD is an interesting approach, but will it be universally adopted to a point where it can be effective? Unfortunately, the technical landscape is littered with useful inventions that did not go mainstream. The adoption will likely come down to a cost/benefit analysis.

Regardless of which security measures are adopted to control IoT risk, IoT is here to stay and growing exponentially. As of today, the benefits outweigh the risks. The current adoption rate of IoT would indicate that there will continue to be a place in society for IoT devices and that security efforts to control IoT shortcomings will be a profitable endeavor.

[403] SECURING SMALL-BUSINESS AND HOME INTERNET OF THINGS (IOT) DEVICES: MITIGATING NETWORK-BASED ATTACKS USING MANUFACTURER USAGE DESCRIPTION (MUD), NAT'L INST. OF STANDARDS AND TECH. & NAT'L CYBERSECURITY CTR. OF EXCELLENCE 1 (2020), *available at* https://www.nccoe.nist.gov/sites/default/files/library/sp1800/iot-ddos-nist-sp1800-15-draft.pdf.

CHAPTER THIRTEEN. RANSOMWARE

13.1 Overview

Normally, the authors would not single out ransomware from the myriad of cybersecurity threats and give ransomware a dedicated chapter, but recent events have directed the spotlight on ransomware, and it now deserves its own dedicated chapter.

Ransomware and ransomware attacks are not new. Ransomware attacks have been around for a long time. What is new is the visibility of ransomware and the effect of successful ransomware attacks on a broad swath of society. The Colonial Pipeline ransomware attack caused long gas lines in certain states that affected all who used gasoline and lived in those states. Ransomware attacks that had been previously localized to smaller targets, such as city governments, hospitals, schools, and law firms could no longer be ignored by politicians and the federal government, and of course, the general public. The danger of ransomware was made all too clear. Ransomware can no longer be pushed to the back burner to be dealt with at a later time.

The application of ransomware is quite simplistic. After obtaining access to a data source, ransomware encrypts that data with an encryption key. Without the key, the data is unreadable and thus, unavailable. Encryption is not the issue. Most of us safely use encryption every day without even knowing it. Many systems already encrypt data, cell phone, laptops, to name a few. But the user (or more likely the software that did the encryption for the user) retains the encryption key, which allows the user to use the data. The data is only locked out from those that don't have access to the key. Encryption is good. Encryption provides a safe harbor against many data protection laws for dealing with breached data. The hacker accesses the data, but cannot read the data because the hacker does not have the encryption key. We can also use encryption to destroy data in the cloud at the end of its life cycle. The process is known as crypto-shredding. The data is encrypted, then encrypted again and then the key is destroyed so the data is effectively destroyed. Physically, the data is still available but without the key it cannot be read. Normally, with the word ransom, we think of a person or asset being withheld from the owner or family. But with ransomware, the data is not being withheld, the data is still in the same location it was in before the attack. The encryption key is being withheld.[404]

An encryption key is normally a string of numbers and letters that are required to unlock the encryption coded data. It may look something like: AXXA-UQYD-YERF-7DF6-XBMH-GWDS. This key is what the perpetrators are holding for the ransom payment. And the perpetrators are only willing to provide the key for the payment of the ransom amount. The popularity of crypto currency such as bitcoin has made it easy for the bad guys to receive payment without getting caught.

It was not that long ago that the common criminal was restricted to more traditional methods of ransom, people and assets. The creation of ransomware required a skilled programmer to design, write, and implement the software for ransomware. That is no longer the case. Today, ransomware is available as Ransomware-as-a-Service (RaaS) in the same manner that that word processor software is available as Software-as-a-Service (SaaS). Thus, just as a lay person can use a word processer, a lay criminal can now subscribe to and use ransomware.

The operation of ransomware is fairly straightforward, gain access to data, encrypt the data and return the encryption key to the user of the ransomware. The owner of the data is then notified of the ransom demand. Of course, as soon as the data is encrypted, the user knows that the data is unavailable because every system trying to access the data is not successful in gaining access to readable data. In addition, ransomware attacks have included the exfiltration of intellectual property, such as trade secrets. Gaining access to the data is accomplished through penetrating vulnerabilities, either human or system. A common vulnerability is a human who has authorized access to a system clicking a link that gives the ransomware access to the system's data.

Not having access to its data is devastating for most entities. Without data, hospitals cannot serve its patients. Not only is the hospital not collecting fees for its service, but patients may suffer without access to their records that now are mostly all online. As a society we have moved most of our data online. HIPAA, as discussed in a later chapter, encouraged the moving of records online for the medical profession to be able to better serve patients. Without data, law firms cannot serve their clients. All of the

[404] Critical information may also be exfiltrated.

documents and court management data is online. Attorneys cannot work if they cannot access their documents and court dates could be missed if the court docket system data is not available. For a large firm, millions of dollars in billables can be lost in a single day without access to data. Both of these examples are quite painful to those involved with those entities. But the major risk is critical infrastructure. What if a nuclear power plant operations center cannot access its data? What if an electrical grid cannot access its data to manage power flows to areas needed because it cannot access its data? What if a gasoline pipeline that supplies the East Coast of America cannot access the data its need to operate its pipeline? We know the answer to this last question.

In an effort to inform the nation on ransomware, CISA and the Multi-State Information Sharing & Analysis Center (MS-ISAC) released the "Ransomware Guide" in September 2020 that "includes industry best practices and a response checklist that can serve as a ransomware-specific addendum to organization response plans."[405] The Secret Service[406] and NIST[407] have also released helpful information.

The U.S. Treasury Department Financial Crimes Enforcement Network released a report on October 15, 2021, concerning Bank Secrecy Act Suspicious Activity Reports from financial institutions which may indicate the scope and depth of ransomware attacks and payments made by victim entities.[408] The Executive Summary states, in relevant part:

> FinCEN analysis of ransomware-related SARs filed during the first half of 2021 indicates that ransomware is an increasing threat to the U.S. financial sector, businesses, and the public. The number of ransomware-related SARs filed monthly has grown rapidly, with 635 SARs filed and 458 transactions reported between 1 January 2021 and 30 June 2021 ("the review period"), up 30 percent from the total of 487 SARs filed for the entire 2020 calendar year.3 The total value of suspicious activity

---

[405] https://www.cisa.gov/stopransomware/ransomware-101

[406] https://www.secretservice.gov/investigation/Preparing-for-a-Cyber-Incident

[407] https://csrc.nist.gov/publications/detail/nistir/8374/draft

[408] FINANCIAL TREND ANALYSIS: RANSOMWARE TRENDS IN BANK SECRECY ACT DATA BETWEEN JANUARY 2021 AND JUNE 2021, U.S. DEP'T OF TREASURY FINANCIAL CRIMES ENFORCEMENT NETWORK, available at Financial Trend Analysis (fincen.gov).

reported in ransomware-related SARs during the first six months of 2021 was $590 million, which exceeds the value reported for the entirety of 2020 ($416 million). Trends represented in this report illustrate financial institutions' identification and reporting of ransomware events and may not reflect the actual dates associated with ransomware incidents. FinCEN's analysis of ransomware-related SARs highlights average ransomware payment amounts, top ransomware variants, and insights from FinCEN's blockchain analysis:

Average Monthly Suspicious Amount of Ransomware Transactions: According to data generated from ransomware-related SARs, the mean average total monthly suspicious amount of ransomware transactions was $66.4 million and the median average was $45 million. FinCEN identified bitcoin (BTC) as the most common ransomware-related payment method in reported transactions. Top Ransomware Variants: Ransomware actors develop their own versions of ransomware, known as "variants," and these versions are given new names based on a change to software or to denote a particular threat actor behind the malware. FinCEN identified 68 ransomware variants reported in SAR data for transactions during the review period. The most commonly reported variants were REvil/Sodinokibi, Conti, DarkSide, Avaddon, and Phobos. Insights from Blockchain Analysis: FinCEN identified and analyzed 177 unique convertible virtual currency (CVC) wallet addresses used for ransomware-related payments associated with the 10 most commonly reported ransomware variants in SARs during the review period.4 Based on blockchain analysis of identifiable transactions with the 177 CVC wallet addresses, FinCEN identified approximately $5.2 billion in outgoing BTC transactions potentially tied to ransomware payments. FinCEN Identified Ransomware Money Laundering Typologies: FinCEN identified several money laundering typologies common among ransomware variants in 2021 including threat actors increasingly requesting payments in Anonymity-enhanced Cryptocurrencies (AECs) and avoiding reusing wallet addresses, "chain hopping" and cashing out at centralized exchanges, and using mixing services and decentralized exchanges to convert proceeds. . . .

Attacks on small municipalities and healthcare organizations have also increased, typically due to perceived weaker security controls and higher propensity of these victims to pay the ransom because of the criticality of their services, particularly during a global health pandemic. Additionally, since at least late 2019, ransomware groups have adopted new extortion tactics to maximize revenue and create an additional incentive for victims to pay. In one such tactic, known as "double extortion," ransomware operators exfiltrate massive amounts of a victim's data encrypting it and then threaten to publish the stolen data if ransom demands are not met.7 Lastly, ransomware attackers are finding new ways to obfuscate their identities by requesting payment in AECs.

Ransomware Variants: FinCEN identified 68 ransomware variants reported in SAR data for transactions during the review period. Ransomware variant analysis can help determine potential threat actors behind an attack. Ninety SARs did not name the ransomware variant used in the attack, and some SARs reported multiple incidents involving more than one variant. . . . The top 10 variants with the highest cumulative payment amounts identified in SARs during the review period accounted for \$217.56 million in suspicious activity. The highest total suspicious payment amounts for individual variants reported in SARs range from \$30 to \$76 million. Monthly suspicious payment amounts reported in SARs for the top 10 variants range from \$3,095 to \$43.06 million with a median average of \$27 million and mean average of \$36.26 million. In June 2021, the highest cumulative suspicious payment amounts were associated with Variant 1

> ($11.78 million) and Variant 2 ($8.53 million), according to SAR data.[409]

As mentioned *supra*, relatively small city governments have been the subject of ransomware attacks by hackers. In 2020, the city of Lafayette in Colorado had to deal with a ransomware attack. The city released the following statement, in part:

> The ransomware that invaded the City's system was used by criminals to block access to the City's computer data until a sum of money is paid. The City was coerced into paying a $45,000 ransom to retrieve a "key" to unlock encrypted data. Ransom payment was not the direction the City wanted to go, and pursued all avenues to find alternative solutions. In a cost/benefit scenario of rebuilding the City's data versus paying the ransom, the ransom option far outweighed attempting to rebuild. The inconvenience of a lengthy service outage for residents was also taken into consideration. While there is no way to eliminate the risk of these types of attacks, the City is taking steps to install crypto-safe backups, deploy additional cybersecurity systems, and implement regular vulnerability assessments to prevent future data threats.[410]

On October 1, 2020, the U.S. Department of Treasury released a document titled, "Advisory on Potential Sanctions Risks for Facilitating Ransomware Payments," which warns that ransomware payments to certain individuals or entities may run afoul of laws and regulations concerning, for example, transactions with certain blocked entities and individuals, or countries with sanctions against them.[411] The ransomware space will continue to

---

[409] *Id.*

[410] City of Lafayette, *Cyberattack Causes City Computer Outage* (August 4, 2020), https://cityoflafayette.com/civicalerts.aspx?AID=5729 (last updated October 9, 2020). For additional information concerning the Lafayette ransomware attack, please read: Tamara Cheung, *After a Small Colorado City Paid Cyber Attackers a Ransom, There's Concern About the Rest of the State*, COLORADO SUN (Aug. 10, 2020), https://coloradosun.com/2020/08/10/cyber-attack-ransomware-small-towns-data-breach-malware-lafayette/ (last updated October 9, 2020).

[411] U.S. DEP'T OF TREASURY, *Advisory on Potential Sanctions Risks for Facilitating Ransomware Payments* (Oct. 1, 2020),

develop. The U.S. Department of Justice has announced a new task force addressing ransomware[412] and the U.S. government co-hosted a counter-ransomware initiative with many countries.[413]

13.2 Ransomware Prevention

The best prevention against ransomware is to take your laptop, unplug the laptop from any ethernet cables and turn off the Wi-Fi connection, and then place the laptop in a locked drawer. Obviously, this is not a viable solution. Likely just as hard is to keep employees from visiting dangerous websites and from not clicking on unknown links that are links to malware such as ransomware.

Training can go a long way in addressing ransomware attacks. But even with adequate training there might be that one back hyperlink that looks official, and an employee clicks on the link considering it a valid link. Thus, training can only go so far as protection against ransomware attacks. There are also technical solutions available for minimizing ransomware attacks such firewalls that do not permit traffic from black-listed IP address; segmenting the network to protect at least parts of a network from attack; and the best solution, create a backup that is protected from the ransomware attack and that can be used in place of the encrypted data. This requires a well thought-out backup solution because attackers have started using the tactic of "deleting system backups, that make restoration and recovery more difficult or infeasible for impacted organizations."[414]

13.2[A] Awareness and Communication

Awareness and communication are also helpful in combating ransomware. CISA recommends that organizations join and information sharing group such as one of the following:

---

https://home.treasury.gov/system/files/126/ofac_ransomware_advisory_10012020_1.pdf.

[412] Dustin Volz, *Ransomware Targeted by New Justice Department Task Force*, WALL STREET JOURNAL (April 21, 2021).

[413] David E. Sanger, *U.S. Holds Global Meeting to Fight Ransomware, Minus the World's No. 1 Culprit*, N.Y. TIMES (October 14, 2021).

[414] https://www.cisa.gov/sites/default/files/publications/CISA_MS-ISAC_Ransomware%20Guide_S508C_.pdf at page 2.

- Multi-State Information Sharing and Analysis Center (MS-ISAC)[415]
- Election Infrastructure Information Sharing and Analysis Center (EI-ISAC)[416]
- Sector-based ISACs – National Council of ISACs[417]
- Information Sharing and Analysis Organization (ISAO) Standards Organization[418]

CISA also invites building "a lasting partnership and collaborat[ion] on information sharing, best practices, assessments, exercises, and more" through CyberLiaison_SLTT@cisa.dhs.gov for SLTT organizations and CyberLiaison_Industry@cisa.dhs.gov for private sector organizations.[419]

CISA advises that "[i]t is critical to maintain offline, encrypted backups of data and to regularly test your backups. Backup procedures should be conducted on a regular basis. It is important that backups be maintained offline as many ransomware variants attempt to find and delete any accessible backups. Maintaining offline, current backups is most critical because there is no need to pay a ransom for data that is readily accessible to your organization."[420] A risk analysis should be performed to determine how often data should be backed up. In other words, how many minutes / hours of data can an organization afford to give up to restore service from backups, one hour, two hours, three hours? It depends on the business model. Some organizations run hot backup, which means backing up each record to a fully functional offsite system so that the organization can fail over to that system without losing any data. For organizations that run hot backups, care should be taken to secure that system from ransomware attacks from the operational system. For entities that backup data in the cloud, the entities should understand the protection provided by the cloud provider for maintaining backups.

Organizations should also maintain base-line configurations for systems and hardware should hackers also affect those areas. This would apply to organizations' legacy systems that are maintained on company premises. In the event that the company uses cloud-based infrastructure and services, the

---

415 https://learn.cisecurity.org/ms-isac-registration

416 https://learn.cisecurity.org/ei-isac-registration

417 https://www.nationalisacs.org

418 https://www.isao.org/information-sharing-groups/

419 https://www.cisa.gov/sites/default/files/publications/CISA_MS-ISAC_Ransomware%20Guide_S508C_.pdf at page 2.

420 *Id.* at 3.

company should review its cloud-based contracts to verify the cloud providers are taking the appropriate measure to ensure recovery from attack.

13.2[B] Address Ransomware Infection Vectors

Infection vectors are basically the paths that ransomware uses to infiltrate a system and encrypt the data. Without getting into the weeds of the technical applications, here are the infection vectors identified by CISA.[421]

- Identify and fix internet-facing vulnerabilities and misconfigurations of software and hardware. This can often be accomplished with available cybersecurity tools to discover the vulnerabilities and then applying software and operating system patches to fix the vulnerability

- Implement a training and awareness program, and technical controls to combat phishing

- Look for precursor malware infections

- Determine the risk of using third parties and managed service providers

13.3[C] Create and Maintain an Incident Response Plan

Assume that the ransomware attack will occur on a Friday evening after a majority of the work force has left for a long weekend. The attacker has the benefit of choosing the time of the attack. An incident response plan will provide the guidance needed at this moment and can be followed by those trained to use. An often-exercised incident response plan is even better. The exercise can be a tabletop exercise carried out by the designed participants. A tabletop exercise is just a made-up scenario that is war gamed at a conference table by those designated as incident response plan team members. All teams perform better if they practice.

13.3 Post-Ransomware Attack

[421] *Id.* at 4-6.

A good incident response plan always include a checklist of tasks and actions to perform. A good starting place for checklist content is provided by CISA.[422] The checklist should be modified to fit the particular entity. Also, the checklist as well as any IRP should always be evaluated after an incident and modified with lessons learned.

The incident response team should understand its legal obligations after an attack. On June 3, 2021, the Department of Justice (DOJ), in the wake of the Colonial Pipeline attack, issued the following memo: "Guidance Regarding Investigations and Cases Related to Ransomware and Digital Extortion"[423] The memo establishes new requirements "relating to ransomware or digital extortion attacks and investigations and cases with a nexus to ransomware and digital extortion."[424] The memo requires additional notifications and coordination within the Justice Department.

It is important to understand whether a payment to retrieve the encryption key after an attack is illegal. Currently, the FBI provides the following guidance: "The FBI does not support paying a ransom in response to a ransomware attack. Paying a ransom doesn't guarantee you or your organization will get any data back. It also encourages perpetrators to target more victims and offers an incentive for others to get involved in this type of illegal activity."[425] And the FBI has recommended to Congress on July 27 that the United States should not forbid payment of ransom after a ransomware attack.[426]

13.4 Ransomware Related Laws and Lawsuits

As discussed *infra*, a ransomware attack may indicate that cybersecurity related laws have been violated. Depending on the business model of the victim as well as the federal regulator, a specific federal regulation may have been violated which may lead to an enforcement action. In some cases, a state agency may be able to enforce a federal regulation such as HIPAA. Notably, the federal

---

[422] *Id.* at 11-5.

[423] https://www.justice.gov/dag/page/file/1401231/download

[424] *Id.*

[425] https://www.fbi.gov/scams-and-safety/common-scams-and-crimes/ransomware

[426] https://www.cnn.com/2021/07/27/politics/senate-judiciary-ransomware-hearing/index.html.

Computer Fraud and Abuse Act likely will apply to a ransomware situation as well. Additionally, many states have enacted laws similar to the federal Computer Fraud and Abuse Act which may also apply. Importantly, several states have enacted laws specifically dealing with extortion and the access to computers without authorization. These laws are discussed, *infra*.

A ransomware attack may also give rise to a data breach. As discussed *supra,* there are numerous potential causes of action that arise out of data breaches. The requirements for these lawsuits, such as standing and class action prerequisites, as well causes of action such as negligence are discussed *supra*. There have been several cases involving data breaches and ransomware.[427]

---

[427] *See, e.g.*, *Graham v. Universal Health Service, Inc.*, __ F.3d __, 2021 WL 1962865 (E.D. Penn. May 17, 2021); *Blahous v. Sarrell Reg. Dental Ctr. For Public Health, Inc.*, 2020 WL 4016246 (M.D. Ala. July 16, 2020).

CHAPTER FOURTEEN. An International Perspective

14.1 Introduction

Cybersecurity law and policy has significant international competition, relations and economic impact. Countries have moved toward adopting cybersecurity provisions in treaties as well as attempting to address cybersecurity issues through applying traditional legal concepts to cybersecurity problems. This Chapter reviews some international issues concerning cybersecurity and privacy. However, it is not a comprehensive examination of all related issues. This Chapter provides a general overview of the following subjects: 1) the European Union's General Data Protection Regulation (GDPR); 2) the European Convention on Cybercrime;[428] 3) the Tallinn Manual (2.0) concerning cyberwar; 4) U.S. Cyberspace Solarium Commission Report; 5) Regional Free Trade Agreements; and 6) Movement Toward a Comprehensive Cybersecurity Treaty.

14.2 GDPR

The GDPR is fundamentally a privacy rights regulation as demonstrated by the beginning of the first two recitals of the regulation:

"The protection of natural persons in relation to the processing of personal data is a fundamental right."[429]

---

[428] The United Nations is working on a Cybercrime Treaty. *See* United Nations, Ad Hoc Committee to Elaborate a Comprehensive International Convention on Countering the Use of Information and Communications Technologies for Criminal Purposes, available at https://www.unodc.org/unodc/en/cybercrime/ad_hoc_committee/home. The draft treaty has been criticized. *See* Katitza Rodriguez, First Draft of UN Cybercrime Convention Drops Troubling Provisions, But Dangerous And Open-Ended Cross Border Surveillance Powers Are Still on the Table, Electronic Frontier Foundation (July 20, 2023), available at https://www.eff.org/deeplinks/2023/07/first-draft-un-cybercrime-treaty-drops-troubling-provisions-dangerous-and-open.

[429] Regulation (EU) 2016/679, 2016 O.J. (L 119) 1.

"The principals of, and rules on the protection of natural persons with regard to the processing of their personal data should, whatever their nationality or residence, respect their fundamental rights and freedoms, in particular their right to the protection of personal data."[430]

But with that said, the GDPR does provide a cybersecurity enforcement mechanism that we will explore further in a few paragraphs. But first a little background.

As per Article 2 of the GDPR, the GDPR covers processing "by automated means" and "personal data which form part of a filing system."[431]

For purposes of the GDPR, "'personal data' means any information relating to an identified or identifiable natural person ('data subject'); an identifiable natural person is one who can be identified, directly or indirectly, in particular by reference to an identifier such as a name, an identification number, location data, an online identifier or to one or more factors specific to the physical, physiological, genetic, mental, economic, cultural or social identity of that natural person[.]"[432]

Article 9 of the GDPR further addresses personal data by enumerating special categories of personal data: "Processing of personal data revealing racial or ethnic origin, political opinions, religious or philosophical beliefs, or trade union membership, and the processing of genetic data, biometric data for the purpose of uniquely identifying a natural person, data concerning health or data concerning a natural person's sex life or sexual orientation shall be prohibited."[433]

The GDPR first touches on security of data in Article 5: "Personal data shall be: f. processed in a manner that ensures appropriate security of the personal data, including protection against unauthorized or unlawful processing and against accidental loss, destruction or damage, using appropriate technical or organizational measures ('integrity and confidentiality')."[434]

---

[430] *Id.*
[431] *Id.* at 32.
[432] *Id.* at 33.
[433] *Id.* at 38.
[434] *Id.* at 35–36.

It is interesting that Article 5 mentions two parts of CIA (confidentiality and integrity) but does not refer to "Availability." Availability remains important in the goals of the GDPR because a natural person needs to be able to review its data and to review its data, it must be available.

There are two concepts that are key to understanding the GDPR, the 'controller' and the 'processor'.

"'[C]ontroller' means the natural or legal person, public authority, agency or other body which, alone or jointly with others, determines the purposes and means of the processing of personal data; where the purposes and means of such processing are determined by Union or Member State law, the controller or the specific criteria for its nomination may be provided by Union or Member State law;"[435]

"'[P]rocessor' means a natural or legal person, public authority, agency or other body which processes personal data on behalf of the controller;"[436]

Both the controller and processor "shall implement appropriate technical and organizational measures . . .."[437]

The GDPR outlines the security required in processing personal data in Article 32:

Article 32 Security of processing

1. Taking into account the state of the art, the costs of implementation and the nature, scope, context and purposes of processing as well as the risk of varying likelihood and severity for the rights and freedoms of natural persons, the controller and the processor shall implement appropriate technical and organisational measures to ensure a level of security appropriate to the risk, including inter alia as appropriate:

(a) the pseudonymisation and encryption of personal data;

(b) the ability to ensure the ongoing confidentiality, integrity, availability and resilience of processing systems and services;

---

[435] *Id.* at 33.
[436] *Id.*
[437] *Id.* at 47.

(c) the ability to restore the availability and access to personal data in a timely manner in the event of a physical or technical incident;

(d) a process for regularly testing, assessing and evaluating the effectiveness of technical and organisational measures for ensuring the security of the processing.

2. In assessing the appropriate level of security account shall be taken in particular of the risks that are presented by processing, in particular from accidental or unlawful destruction, loss, alteration, unauthorised disclosure of, or access to personal data transmitted, stored or otherwise processed.

3. Adherence to an approved code of conduct as referred to in Article 40 or an approved certification mechanism as referred to in Article 42 may be used as an element by which to demonstrate compliance with the requirements set out in paragraph 1 of this Article.

4. The controller and processor shall take steps to ensure that any natural person acting under the authority of the controller or the processor who has access to personal data does not process them except on instructions from the controller, unless he or she is required to do so by Union or Member State law.438

Article 32 is where resilience is added to CIA. It is interesting that this is the only mention of resilience.

As with many U.S. state breach notification laws, encryption can be a silver bullet:

"The communication to the data subject [of a breach] shall not be required if any of the following conditions are met:

a. the controller has implemented appropriate technical and organizational protection measures, and those measures were applied to the personal data affected by the personal data breach, in particular those that render the personal data unintelligible to any person who is not authorised to access it, such as encryption."[439]

14.3 European Convention on Cybercrime

[438] *Id.* at 51–52.

[439] *Id.* at 53.

The European Convention on Cybercrime (also known as the Budapest Convention on Cybercrime) is a treaty (November 23, 2001) that provides provisions concerning cybercrime. It also contains provisions concerning discovery of electronic data and systems, extradition and mutual assistance. The goal is to "deter action directed against the confidentiality, integrity and availability of computer systems, networks and computer data as well as the misuse of such systems, networks and data by providing for the criminalisation of such conduct, as described in this Convention, and the adoption of powers sufficient for effectively combating such criminal offences, by facilitating their detection, investigation and prosecution at both the domestic and international levels and by providing arrangements for fast and reliable international co-operation . . ." Convention Preamble. Measures to be taken at the national level include:

- adoption of substantive criminal law for "*Offences against the confidentiality, integrity and availability of computer data and systems*"
- *adoption of* "legislative and other measures as may be necessary to establish as criminal offences under its domestic law, when committed intentionally, the access to the whole or any part of a computer system without right. A Party may require that the offence be committed by infringing security measures, with the intent of obtaining computer data or other dishonest intent, or in relation to a computer system that is connected to another computer system."
- adoption of "legislative and other measures as may be necessary to establish as criminal offences under its domestic law, when committed intentionally, the interception without right, made by technical means, of non-public transmissions of computer data to, from or within a computer system, including electromagnetic emissions from a computer system carrying such computer data. A Party may require that the offence be committed with dishonest intent, or in relation to a computer system that is connected to another computer system."
- adoption of "legislative and other measures as may be necessary to establish as criminal offences under its domestic law, when committed intentionally, the damaging,

deletion, deterioration, alteration or suppression of computer data without right."

- adoption of "legislative and other measures as may be necessary to establish as criminal offences under its domestic law, when committed intentionally, the serious hindering without right of the functioning of a computer system by inputting, transmitting, damaging, deleting, deteriorating, altering or suppressing computer data."
- adoption of "legislative and other measures as may be necessary to establish as criminal offences under its domestic law, when committed intentionally and without right:

  a) the production, sale, procurement for use, import, distribution or otherwise making available of:

  i) a device, including a computer program, designed or adapted primarily for the purpose of committing any of the offences established in accordance with Articles 2 through 5;"

- adoption of "legislative and other measures as may be necessary to establish as criminal offences under its domestic law, when committed intentionally and without right, the input, alteration, deletion, or suppression of computer data, resulting in inauthentic data with the intent that it be considered or acted upon for legal purposes as if it were authentic, regardless whether or not the data is directly readable and intelligible. A Party may require an intent to defraud, or similar dishonest intent, before criminal liability attaches."
- adoption of "legislative and other measures as may be necessary to establish as criminal offences under its domestic law, when committed intentionally and without right, the causing of a loss of property to another person by:

  a) any input, alteration, deletion or suppression of computer data,

  b) any interference with the functioning of a computer system, with fraudulent or dishonest intent of procuring, without right, an economic benefit for oneself or for another person."

- adoption of "legislative and other measures as may be necessary to establish as criminal offences under its domestic law, when committed intentionally, aiding or abetting the commission of any of the offences established in accordance with Articles 2 through 10 of the present Convention with intent that such offence be committed."

14.4 Tallinn Manual

The Tallinn Manual essentially restates the international law as applied to cyberwarfare. There are two Tallinn Manuals. An article by Eric Talbot Jensen, *Tallinn Manual 2.0: Highlights and Insights*, 48 Geo. J. Int'l L. 735 (2017),[440] discusses some of the issues addressed in Tallinn Manual 2.0 such as:

- Part I covering general international law and cyberspace;
- Part II covers specialized regimes of international law and cyberspace;
- Part III concerns international peace and security and cyber activities, which is drawn mostly from Tallinn 1.0; and
- Part IV is the rest of Tallinn1.0 and applies to the law of cyber armed conflict. As Tallinn 1.0 has already been extensively commented on, this Article will draw exclusively on Parts I and II and a small portion of Part III.

Professor Jensen notes that there is significant disagreement among experts concerning the Tallinn Manual's substance and that the second Tallinn Manual sets the stage for further discussions.

14.5 U.S. Cyberspace Solarium Commission Report

The U.S. Cyberspace Solarium Commission Report issued in March of 2020. The US Cyberspace Solarium Commission was formed by Congress to develop a strategy for confronting cyberattacks. The Report includes over 80 recommendations for

[440] This article was partially presented at a symposium on International Justice in the US Context: Where We Stand, Where We Fall, and Where We Need To Be.

action. A good number of the recommendations have been adopted by the U.S. government. The notes following the Executive Summary discuss some challenged facing the United States concerning cybersecurity and warfare.

Higher Level Sections from the U.S. Cyberspace Solarium Commission Report

AN URGENT CALL TO ACTION

For over 20 years, nation-states and non-state actors have used cyberspace to subvert American power, American security, and the American way of life. Despite numerous criminal indictments, economic sanctions, and the development of robust cyber and non-cyber military capabilities, the attacks against the United States have continued. The perpetrators saw that their onslaught damaged the United States without triggering a significant retaliation. Chinese cyber operators stole hundreds of billions of dollars in intellectual property to accelerate China's military and economic rise and undermine U.S. military dominance. Russian operators and their proxies damaged public trust in the integrity of American elections and democratic institutions. China, Russia, Iran, and North Korea all probed U.S. critical infrastructure with impunity.

Criminals leveraged globally connected networks to steal assets from individuals, companies, and governments. Extremist groups used these networks to raise funds and recruit followers, increasing transnational threats and insecurity. American restraint was met with unchecked predation.

The digital connectivity that has brought economic growth, technological dominance, and an improved quality of life to nearly every American has also created a strategic dilemma. The more digital connections people make and data they exchange, the more opportunities adversaries have to destroy private lives, disrupt critical infrastructure, and damage our economic and democratic institutions. The United States now operates in a cyber landscape that requires a level of data security, resilience, and trustworthiness that neither the U.S. government nor the private sector alone is currently equipped to provide. Moreover, shortfalls in agility, technical expertise, and unity of effort, both within the U.S. government and between the public and private sectors, are growing.

The 2019 National Defense Authorization Act chartered the U.S. Cyberspace Solarium Commission to address this challenge. The President and Congress tasked the Commission to answer two fundamental questions:

What strategic approach will defend the United States against cyberattacks of significant consequences? And what policies and legislation are required to implement that strategy?

THE STRATEGY

After conducting an extensive study including over 300 interviews, a competitive strategy event modeled after the original Project Solarium in the Eisenhower administration, and stress tests by external red teams, the Commission advocates a new strategic approach to cybersecurity: layered cyber deterrence. The desired end state of layered cyber deterrence is a reduced probability and impact of cyberattacks of significant consequence. The strategy outlines three ways to achieve this end state:

EXECUTIVE SUMMARY

1. Shape behavior. The United States must work with allies and partners to promote responsible behavior in cyberspace.

2. Deny benefits. The United States must deny benefits to adversaries who have long exploited cyberspace to their advantage, to American disadvantage, and at little cost to themselves. This new approach requires securing critical networks in collaboration with the private sector to promote

national resilience and increase the security of the cyber ecosystem.

3. Impose costs. The United States must maintain the capability, capacity, and credibility needed to retaliate against actors who target America in and through cyberspace.

Each of the three ways described above involves a deterrent layer that increases American public- and private-sector security by altering how adversaries perceive the costs and benefits of using cyberspace to attack American interests. These three deterrent layers are supported by six policy pillars that organize more than 75 recommendations. These pillars represent the means to implement layered cyber deterrence.

While deterrence is an enduring American strategy, there are two factors that make layered cyber deterrence bold and distinct. First, the approach prioritizes deterrence by denial, specifically by increasing the defense and security of cyberspace through resilience and public- and private-sector collaboration. Reducing the vulnerabilities adversaries can target denies them opportunities to attack American interests through cyberspace.

Second, the strategy incorporates the concept of "defend forward" to reduce the frequency and severity of attacks in cyberspace that do not rise to a level that would warrant the full spectrum of retaliatory responses, including military responses. Though the concept originated in the Department of Defense, the Commission integrates defend forward into a national strategy for securing cyberspace using all the instruments of power.

Defend forward posits that to disrupt and defeat ongoing adversary campaigns, the United States must proactively observe, pursue, and counter adversaries' operations and impose costs short of armed conflict. This posture signals to adversaries that the U.S. government will respond to

> cyberattacks, even those below the level of armed conflict that do not cause physical destruction or death, with all the tools at its disposal and consistent with international law.[441]

14.6 Overview of Trade and Cybersecurity

For an overview of trade and cybersecurity, the reader is directed to the Joshua P. Meltzer and Cameron F. Kerry article, Cybersecurity and Digital Trade: Getting it right, The Brookings Institution Report (September 18, 2019).[442]

14.7 Asia-Pacific Economic Cooperation Cross-Border Privacy Rules System

The Asia-Pacific Economic Cooperation Cross-Border Privacy Rules system contains numerous relevant parts including the Promotion of technical measures to protect privacy and Providing for appropriate remedies in situations where privacy protections are violated.

Section IV titled, "Promotion of technical measures to protect privacy" includes two relevant provisions. The first provision preferences the use of technical measures to protect privacy alongside the use of legal protection. The provisions encourage their use amongst information controllers. The second provision further notes that use of "readily available technical safeguards and measures . . . may promote research and development, encourage further privacy innovation and support the

---

[441] The US Cyberspace Solarium Commission has continued to issue reports addressing cybersecurity issues, including "Countering Disinformation in the United States," "2021 Annual Report on Implementation," "Transition Book for the Incoming Biden Administration," "Building a Trusted ICT Supply Chain," "Growing a Stronger Federal Cyber Workforce," and "Cybersecurity Lessons from the Pandemic," See United States Cyberspace Solarium Commission, available at https://www.solarium.gov/home (last visited, August, 9 2023).

[442] Joshua P. Meltzer & Cameron F. Kerry, *Cybersecurity and Digital Trade: Getting It Right*, BROOKINGS (Sept. 18, 2019), https://www.brookings.edu/research/cybersecurity-and-digital-trade-getting-it-right/. This article originally was published by the Brookings Institution.

development of technical standards that embed best privacy practice into systems engineering."

Part IV concerning Implementation provides guidance including section VII which allows for remedies for the breach of privacy protections. Under section 53, the remedies can include damages as well as prospective relief and other remedies. Notably, member nations can consider the following factors in setting remedies, such as: "a) the particular system in that member economy for providing privacy protections (e.g., legislative enforcement powers, which may include rights of individuals to pursue legal action, industry self-regulation, or a combination of systems); and b) the importance of having a range of remedies commensurate with the extent of the actual or potential harm to individuals resulting from such violations." Under section 54, member nations should either require or encourage notice of a "significant security breach affecting personal information under its control" by the relevant Privacy Enforcement Authorities. Moreover, timely notice to individuals should be encouraged as well if "feasible and reasonable."

14.8 Comprehensive and Progressive Agreement for Trans-Pacific Partnership

Chapter 14 of the Comprehensive and Progressive Agreement for Trans-Pacific Partnership contains a section on Electronic Commerce. The relevant articles related to cybersecurity and privacy follow:

Article 14.1 Definitions

. . .

electronic authentication means the process or act of verifying the identity of a party to an electronic communication or transaction and ensuring the integrity of an electronic communication;

electronic transmission or transmitted electronically means a transmission made using any electromagnetic means, including by photonic means;

personal information means any information, including data, about an identified or identifiable natural person;

. . .

Article 14.6: Electronic Authentication and Electronic Signatures

1. Except in circumstances otherwise provided for under its law, a Party shall not deny the legal validity of a signature solely on the basis that the signature is in electronic form.

2. No Party shall adopt or maintain measures for electronic authentication that would: (a) prohibit parties to an electronic transaction from mutually determining the appropriate authentication methods for that transaction; or (b) prevent parties to an electronic transaction from having the opportunity to establish before judicial or administrative authorities that their transaction complies with any legal requirements with respect to authentication.

3. Notwithstanding paragraph 2, a Party may require that, for a particular category of transactions, the method of authentication meets certain performance standards or is certified by an authority accredited in accordance with its law.

4. The Parties shall encourage the use of interoperable electronic authentication.

Article 14.8: Personal Information Protection

1. The Parties recognise the economic and social benefits of protecting the personal information of users of electronic commerce and the contribution that this makes to enhancing consumer confidence in electronic commerce.

2. To this end, each Party shall adopt or maintain a legal framework that provides for the protection of the personal information of the users of electronic commerce. In the development of its legal framework for the protection of personal information, each Party should take into account principles and guidelines of relevant international bodies.6

3. Each Party shall endeavour to adopt non-discriminatory practices in protecting users of electronic commerce from personal information protection violations occurring within its jurisdiction.

4. Each Party should publish information on the personal information protections it provides to users of electronic commerce, including how: (a) individuals can pursue remedies; and (b) business can comply with any legal requirements.

5. Recognising that the Parties may take different legal approaches to protecting personal information, each Party should encourage the development of mechanisms to promote compatibility between these different regimes. These mechanisms may include the recognition of regulatory outcomes, whether accorded autonomously or by mutual arrangement, or broader international frameworks. To this end, the Parties shall endeavour to exchange information on any such mechanisms applied in their jurisdictions and explore ways to extend these or other suitable arrangements to promote compatibility between them.

Footnote 6 For greater certainty, a Party may comply with the obligation in this paragraph by adopting or maintaining measures such as a comprehensive privacy, personal information or personal data protection laws, sector-specific laws covering privacy, or laws that provide for the enforcement of voluntary undertakings by enterprises relating to privacy

Article 14.16: Cooperation on Cybersecurity Matters

The Parties recognise the importance of: (a) building the capabilities of their national entities responsible for computer security incident response; and (b) using existing collaboration mechanisms to cooperate to identify and mitigate malicious intrusions or dissemination of malicious code that affect the electronic networks of the Parties.

Article 14.17: Source Code

1. No Party shall require the transfer of, or access to, source code of software owned by a person of another Party, as a condition for the import, distribution, sale or use of such software, or of products containing such software, in its territory.

2. For the purposes of this Article, software subject to paragraph 1 is limited to mass-market software or products containing such software and does not include software used for critical infrastructure.

3. Nothing in this Article shall preclude: (a) the inclusion or implementation of terms and conditions related to the provision of source code in commercially negotiated contracts; or (b) a Party from requiring the modification of source code of software necessary for that software to comply with laws or regulations which are not inconsistent with this Agreement.

4. This Article shall not be construed to affect requirements that relate to patent applications or granted patents, including any orders made by a judicial authority in relation to patent disputes, subject to safeguards against unauthorised disclosure under the law or practice of a Party.

14.9 United States-Mexico-Canada Agreement (Article 19 et seq.)

The United States-Mexico-Canada Agreement has numerous provisions related to privacy and cybersecurity. Article 19.16 concerns source code and prohibits a requirement for the disclosure of source code as a condition for import of software or products containing that software. There is an exception for regulatory or judicial authorities with appropriate protections of the code. Article 19.8 recognizes the importance of establishing a legal framework for the protection of personal information privacy to digital trade. Importantly, "[i]n the development of this legal framework, each Party should take into account principles and guidelines of relevant international 19-5 bodies, such as the APEC Privacy Framework and the OECD Recommendation of the Council concerning Guidelines governing the Protection of Privacy and Transborder Flows of Personal Data (2013)." Subsection 3 sets forth important principles to be considered in the legal framework: "limitation on collection; choice; data quality; purpose specification; use limitation; security safeguards; transparency; individual participation; and accountability." The legal framework's personal information protections are also balanced against "ensuring that any restrictions on cross-border flows of personal information are necessary and proportionate to the risks presented." Moreover, that the domestic legal frameworks should be compatible through the adoption of mechanisms to promote that interoperability. The parties "shall endeavor to adopt non-discriminatory practices in protecting users of digital trade from personal information protection violations occurring within its jurisdiction." "Each Party shall publish information on the personal information protections it provides to users of digital trade, including how: (a) a natural person can pursue a remedy; and (b) an enterprise can comply with legal requirements." Finally, "[t]he Parties recognize that the APEC CrossBorder Privacy Rules system is a valid mechanism to facilitate cross-border information transfers while protecting personal information.

Article 19.15 directly addresses cybersecurity concerns. That section provides:

Article 19.15: Cybersecurity

> 1. The Parties recognize that threats to cybersecurity undermine confidence in digital trade. Accordingly, the Parties shall endeavor to: (a) build the capabilities of their respective national entities responsible for cybersecurity incident response; and (b) strengthen existing collaboration mechanisms for cooperating to identify and mitigate malicious intrusions or dissemination of malicious code that affect electronic networks, and use those mechanisms to swiftly address cybersecurity incidents, as well as for the sharing of information for awareness and best practices.
>
> 2. Given the evolving nature of cybersecurity threats, the Parties recognize that risk-based approaches may be more effective than prescriptive regulation in addressing those threats. Accordingly, each Party shall endeavor to employ, and encourage enterprises within its jurisdiction to use, risk-based approaches that rely on consensus-based standards and risk management best practices to identify and protect against cybersecurity risks and to detect, respond to, and recover from cybersecurity events.

14.10 U.S. and Japan Agreement on Digital Trade

The U.S. and Japan entered an agreement on digital trade.[443] The agreement has provisions directed to privacy and cybersecurity. For example, a privacy directed provision is Article 15 that provides that both parties will provide a legal framework to protect personal information used in digital trade which includes remedies for natural persons. Article 17 provides that access to source code or an algorithm cannot be required as a condition to import, sell or use products or software in that country. However,

---

[443] Office of the U.S. Trade Representative, U.S. and Japan Agreement on Digital Trade Text, available at https://ustr.gov/sites/default/files/files/agreements/japan/Agreement_between_the_United_States_and_Japan_concerning_Digital_Trade.pdf.

under some circumstances, a regulatory or judicial body may inspect that source code or algorithm. Article 19 is titled, "Cybersecurity." This Article has two main parts. First, the parties agree to build the competencies of their respective authorities designated to respond to cybersecurity incidents and strengthen collaboration to work together to mitigate and respond to problems such as malicious code, including sharing information concerning incidents and best practices. Second, the parties agree that a risk based approach to cybersecurity is better than a prescriptive approach to address cybersecurity incidents and detect, respond and recover from those incidents. The agreement also addresses encryption.

14.11 The U.K. and Singapore Digital Economy Agreement

The U.K. and Singapore have entered a Digital Economy Agreement.[444] The Agreement includes privacy and cybersecurity provisions. A privacy provision, includes Article 8.61E which obligates both parties to establish a legal framework for protecting individual privacy. The legal framework shall "shall include: limitation on collection; data quality; purpose specification; use limitation; security safeguards; transparency; individual participation; and accountability." The parties also agree to ensure interoperability between legal frameworks. Additionally, the parties agree to collaborate concerning innovating in data sharing practices, including data portability and trusts. On cybersecurity, the parties agree to work to build competencies on cybersecurity and collaborate concerning addressing cybersecurity incidents. The parties further agree to favor a risk based approach to detect, respond and recover from cybersecurity issues instead of a prescriptive approach. Moreover, the parties will move toward an understanding of a certain level of protection for IOT devices and collaborate on cybersecurity research including in the academic sector. The agreement also addresses digital identities and the regulation of new technology such as artificial intelligence.

---

[444] U.K., UK/Singapore Digital Economy Agreement, available at https://www.gov.uk/government/publications/uksingapore-digital-economy-agreement-cs-singapore-no12022.
[https://www.nationalarchives.gov.uk/doc/open-government-licence/version/3/]

14.12 The Future of a Multi-lateral Comprehensive Treaty on Cybersecurity

It is unclear whether a multi-lateral comprehensive treaty on cybersecurity will be adopted. The United Nations recently released a report that is designed to start the discussion concerning such a treaty. An issue concerning the treaty includes the responsibility of state actors for cybersecurity breaches. It is common knowledge that governments, including the United States, engage in the collection of cybersecurity vulnerabilities and cybersecurity espionage. This may result in serious reluctance on behalf of governments to handicap their own ability to engage in cybersecurity espionage to address issues such as terrorism. Any adopted treaty would likely include broad exemptions for certain types of conduct and, thus, may minimize any true effectiveness of the treaty to address some cybersecurity-related issues. Additionally, doctrines concerning foreign sovereign immunity as well as immunity extending to agents and contractors of foreign governments may be addressed.

INDEX